THIRD WORLD
WARRIORS
...terrorists talk

This is a true story of the journey one needs to understand Terrorists...
More importantly, why we need Third World Warriors

A.J. Toro

Third World Warriors
© A.J. Toro 2014

All rights reserved. No part of this publication may be reproduced, stored in a retrieval system, or transmitted in any form or by any means electronic, mechanical, photocopying, recording, or otherwise, without the prior written permission of the author.

National Library of Australia Cataloguing-in-Publication entry (pbk)

Author:	Toro, A. J., author
Title:	Third world warriors : terrorists talk / A.J. Toro
ISBN:	9780994304179 (paperback)
Subjects:	Government accountability Sustainable living Global environmental change World politics--21st century
Dewey Number:	320.1

Published by A.J. Toro and InHouse Publishing
www.inhousepublishing.com.au

Printed using Envirocare paper

Dedication

I'm dedicating this book to those that cannot or will not read this book. In particular, the victims of war, domestic violence, legal injustices, and terminal illness, as well as the ignorant: the men, women, and children condemned to poverty and third world lives without an education.

God forbid they should ever know the true nature of our creed.

Cover photo was taken by the journalist Mr Musa Al- Shaer and printed with his permission to show the modern David-Goliath war of those in the third world.

Acknowledgements

It's not until we finish a journey, a job, or complete a mission that we realise we could never have done it alone. Our families are always the first people we recognise as being the pillars of our strength. In particular our parents. I was fortunate to thank my parents for the love, the unconditional support, and the courage they showed me before they departed our earth to be united in the Kingdom of Heaven with our universal God.

Then we remember the many people that contributed directly and indirectly to make the impossible become a reality. These are the people that helped, that taught us, that supported our weaknesses, and encouraged us with their inspiration like friends, companions, and peers, or the many people we crossed paths with along the way; too many to thank as individuals, but they all know how they contributed to this book and with these written words I honor their help and say thank you.

However, there are some distinguished and remarkable people that we may never see again, and it is they who contribute the most selflessly to ensure our work is completed to the very best standard, with the very least doubt or mistakes. For me, those people are:

Rema Albess, a Palestinian writer/journalist from Amman, Jordan.
Ghassan Khalid Ali, English/French graduate, Baghdad University.
Yakiko Muragishi, ballerina from Inunkamigun Shinga, Japan.

Dr Huda Salih Mahdi Ammash, Ba'ath party deputy, Baghdad, Iraq.

Prof. Jose Bell and Dr Luisa Lopez from Havana University, Cuba.

Judith Karpova, human rights and environmental activist, USA.

Steven Hawke, Don Hawkins, and Darrell Runyan, USA.

Rosemary 'Waratah' Gillespie, human rights lawyer, Australia.

George Gittoes, Australian war artist.

Usma Bashir, humanitarian activist, United Kingdom.

Ken O'Keefe, founder of the Human Shields.

George W. Bush, for showing us the danger of ignorance and nepotism.

Tony Blair, for teaching us the cost of subservience.

John Howard, for teaching Australians the need to break the chains of colonial domination with his submissive servitude to the Queen of England rather than serving the Australian people as he was entrusted to do.

Jose Maria Aznar, for the lesson in cowardice and not standing up to those who are clearly and criminally wrong.

And then there are those who motivate us to write so that we may correct their mistakes or prejudices, such as The United Nations; Australian Federal Police; FBI; Mossad; CNI; ASIO; CIA; MI5; and all the Western intelligence-gathering agencies who failed to act, without prejudice, on the starving needs of the third world when the clarity and transparencies between right and wrong beg us to believe that these agencies represent us, the people who work to pay their salaries.

A very special thank you to the wizardry of Ocean and all who work at InHouse Publishing, with a distinguished recognition to the amazing editorial skills of Kaya. Her touch is what this book needed before it could be shared with you and those aspiring to become third world warriors.

And finally I thank God for giving me the strength, courage, and wisdom to undermine all authorities and talk to the terrorists so that we may achieve peace among ourselves, as we declare war against global warming and begin the restoration of our natural environment before the consequences of our ignorance threaten us all.

Contents

Dedication	iii
Acknowledgements	v
Chapter 1 The Need to Know	1
Chapter 2 Our Warrior Instinct	11
Chapter 3 The Will to Fight	21
Chapter 4 Yin and Yang: The Universal Law of Opposites ☯	33
Chapter 5 The Third World	45
Chapter 6 Family Traditions	55
Chapter 7 The Cradle of Civilisation	65
Chapter 8 NASYO	79
Chapter 9 Saddam's Children's Hospital	89
Chapter 10 The Australian Spirit	97
Chapter 11 Eleventh Commandment	107
Chapter 12 God's Will	119
Chapter 13 Democracy with Prejudice	127
Chapter 14 Anything but the Truth	135
Chapter 15 Angels in Baghdad	147
Chapter 16 Human Shields	157
Chapter 17 Israeli Justice	173
Chapter 18 Talking Terrorists	183
Chapter 19 Jerusalem, the World's Capital	199

Chapter 20 Third World War-riors — 209
Chapter 21 The Balance of Power — 223
Chapter 22 Military Diplomacy — 239
Chapter 23 Economic Hitman — 255
Chapter 24 Man-made Hell — 265
Chapter 25 Saddam's Message — 275
Chapter 26 Natural Laws — 285
Chapter 27 David and Goliath — 295

Bibliography — 307

Chapter 1
The Need to Know

G. W. Bush threatens to use nuclear against Iraq.
Sydney Morning Herald
December 11, 2002

"I hate the truth!" my mate Greg screamed across the roof of a sports car. "You know why?" he asked, screaming, before answering his own revelation. "Because it's true ... the truth hurts!"

He paused momentarily to gasp in some polluted air from a passing car that left a trail of white smoke lingering in its wake; a white cloud, like a smoke signal of the looming natural and man-made catastrophes to come. However, everyone was asleep, drunk, or sedated with meaningless entertainment and exhausted from the lifetime sentence to hard labour: all were oblivious to the truths that unravelled around their lives.

Whilst the smoke signal faded Greg coughed as if clearing his throat from some internal pain causing phlegm: perhaps the first symptom of cancer caused by his habituous smoking. Or perhaps it was the realisation that I would not change my mind, as he hoped, about going to Iraq and facing the evil regime of Saddam Hussein.

Greg was amongst my most trusted friends. He stood tall at over six feet in height and had developed a broad, rock-solid muscular frame from surfing at South Sydney's Maroubra Beach ever since his infancy. He was also a history teacher at Pendle Hill High School in Sydney's western suburbs, which was perhaps the most disadvantaged school he could work in. It had been his choice to teach those kids that needed the education the most. "They are the most disadvantaged kids in Sydney, with many parents having grown up in the cycle of ignorance that is passed down to their own children," Greg once said. Education could help them break that cycle, was one of many things he taught me.

That night, we were arguing about my decision to go to Baghdad before the 2003 war. This was the premise of our violent argument and Greg's midnight lecture parroted what our Western media alleged as a crime for the Iraqi people to possess weapons of mass destruction (WMD). He echoed our Western party line about the need to get rid of the terrorists who now threatened life on earth like a plague—and more disastrous than the impact of overpopulation within the limits of our confined lands. Why we were not arguing how to prevent a catastrophic modern war that will simply contribute to global warming, or about the abusive powers that condemn our lives to labour while these powers misappropriate our taxes was beyond words.

He knew too well the evil nature of Saddam's regime in contrast to the goodness of the George W. Bush's policy to make the world a better place. This was irrespective of the fact that Saddam Hussein was never given a chance to speak on Western television while the big brother image of a well-spoken gentleman and leader of the most powerful nation on earth, repeatedly argued for the need to depose this evil dictator.

"That's why nobody likes to know the truth! And that's why we are happy! Because we don't know the bloody truth! Most people don't want to know the truth ..."

Greg paused again to catch his breath and it seemed like the prophecy of George Orwell continued to whisper the wisdom that only a few would understand: 'Ignorance is strength!'

Sadly, my mate Greg O'Shea and George Orwell were right. The truth does hurt, and ignorance really was blissful to us; we were the modern-day slaves to ignorance.

"Okay," I agreed with him.

However, my addiction to knowledge would not allow me to sit idle or remain apathetic.

"But we are not ignorant," I assured him. "We have gone to university and we are blessed to have an education so don't we have an obligation to continue learning so that we may reveal truths that can make our world a better place for all life?" I asked him desperately, as he walked around the sports car with his fists clenched and ready to hurt me.

"So how are you going to make this world a better place by getting killed in Iraq?" he asked, yelling across the roof of the car.

He was determined to stop me from going to Iraq, knowing the war was inevitable. History had taught Greg that control of the Middle East's oil fields was the essence of world domination. The British had relinquished that power in 1949 to the Americans who in turn used the Israelis to keep the Islamic world divided, impoverished, and ready to be conquered. Meanwhile the British took a backseat, pulling the strings of Saudi sultans, the North American presidents, and the Jewish governments, for the benefit of the ruling class kingdom rather than the people they needed to defend their luxurious lifestyles.

"I'm not going to get killed!" I yelled back at Greg. "I'm going there to learn!" I assured him.

My parents had planted the seed for knowledge in our family since my memory sprouted. They were both well-educated and understood why knowledge empowers us as individuals to accomplish great things with our lives. This concept that knowledge was power did not become clear to me until much later, when as an adult I was promptly promoted to supervise fifty hard-working men in London's West Ferry newspaper printers. It was there, as I read *The Evening Standard, The Guardian, The Daily Telegraph* and *The Star* every night whilst the United Kingdom slept, that I developed a deeper understanding of the forces that govern and decide how we live in this brave new world.

"You don't have to go to Iraq to learn how to die," Greg advised me, almost whimpering.

Then suddenly, he jumped on the bonnet of the car and then chased me down the road, yelling, "I can show you that right here, right now." He yelled in rage behind me until I found refuge behind another parked car where he couldn't reach me.

As we both paused to catch our breath, I recalled reading how George W. Bush had used his father's name to boost his own position of power. This was a common practice amongst those with successful parents. It is called nepotism, and history had taught us the deficiencies of this unjust phenomenon. This was one of my reasons for wanting to go to Iraq, where I knew Saddam Hussein's sons were abusing the power they had inherited rather than earned.

"So what do you know about the Iraqis?" I asked Greg, between hard breaths full of air that tasted of burnt diesel oil.

"I know they've got stockpiles of chemical weapons and they are hiding them from the inspectors." He paused to catch his breath. "Besides, I don't have to know anything about them to know that they are terrorists," Greg shouted back angrily. "Just like Al Qaida and all those bloody Muslims."

He echoed the same concerns; the same main stream Western beliefs about the terrorist Muslim world that we had all heard again and again. This naïve understanding of Muslims surprised me from Greg, who as a history teacher should have known better. I had already learned that the first act of terrorism was committed by a Jewish-Zionist group called 'The Stern Gang' on 27 February, 1939.[1] They killed thirty-eight innocent Muslims as several explosions were detonated across Palestine. This terrorist group was responsible for other crimes like the murder of Lord Moyne, The English Minister for the Middle East based in Cairo, 1949, which prompted Winston Churchill to acknowledge in the British House of Commons the similarity between the Zionist Jew and a Nazi German[2].

So at that moment I realised how little we in the Western world actually knew about both terrorism and Islam. How we were led to believe with prejudice that Muslims were our greatest enemies, or that all terrorists were Muslims. Even though Greg was a well-educated high school history teacher, he too shared the same belief that Iraqis and Al Qaida were going to kill me, invade the Western world, and become the greatest threat to world peace.

But now was not the time to lecture an angry Celt that threatened to cripple me like my mate Greg.

"Well that's your opinion," I puffed out at him. "But I need to go to see for myself, to understand how we can justify another war when we already know that modern warfare is futile," I said between heavy breaths. "Only a handful of weapon dealers and criminal megalomaniacs win!"

I justified my decision to go to Iraq before what I already knew was an inevitable war.

"You don't have to go there to know that, Al!" he yelled back at me.

---

1 The Origins of the Arab Israeli Wars, 2nd edition by Ritchy Ovendale p.77
2 United Kingdom Parliamentary Debates House of Commons, 404, col. 2242 17 Nov.1944Cab 66, 65, ff 272–3, wp (45)306 Memorandum by Stanley, 16 May 1945.

"No, Maybe not, but there is a piece of the puzzle that I just don't get," I replied, trying to explain why I had this innate feeling that I needed to go.

"So who do you think you are? Do you think you going there will make any difference to the war? Do you think anyone will care when you go missing?" he asked, with seeming certainty about my imminent death. "That's not your job! It's not up to you, it is up to our leaders and they know what is best because they already have intelligence and great minds advising them on what to do." Greg shouted this information at me.

"Do you think any great mind would declare a modern war?" I challenged him, only to aggravate him further as he leapt forward and chased me around the parked car, first to the right and then to the left until we stood facing each other from polar perspectives over the roof of a BMW.

When I looked at his enraged face sucking in deep breaths of air, it dawned on me that perhaps that was what a megalomaniac looked like if they didn't get things their way. A megalomaniac was a person obsessed with his or her own power to dominate others. Having defined it as such, a megalomaniac did not care for the good will of others as much as they cared to satisfy their own whims. A megalomaniac would not go to fight in the frontlines or work laboriously as most of us had to do. Megalomaniacs believed they had been chosen by God to rule, to dictate, and in some cases to invent new laws that suited their regimes. The fact was that megalomaniacs belonged to an exclusive club that any logical thinking person would label as true terrorism. Yet our media seemed to protect or praise such megalomaniacs, if they favoured oil rich Sultans, banking dynasties, and royal interests. Such was the alliance between media moguls and the powers that be, that we, the people, would learn only what the megalomaniac that governed us would want us to believe: hence the universal right to freedom of the press, speech and thoughts.

"So what or who are these terrorists?" I asked Greg as he leaned on the bonnet of the car that divided us.

He was catching his breath and continued threatening to hurt me if he caught me so that I would remain in Australia rather than to go and be killed in Iraq.

"Terrorists are crazy, mad people that don't care about anyone!" Greg answered, drawing the same conclusion that a terrorist was a megalomaniac.

"But I want to know the truth," I said to Greg, whose face now shone on the polished roof of the expensive parked car.

As he sucked hard for breath I recalled the extent of Greg's academic training and realised that if he, with all of his education, was unable to comprehend the origins of terrorism, then how could the rest of us understand or accept the nature of a Zionist terrorist? Did anyone even know what a Zionist was?

"What good is it to be educated if we don't use that education to continue learning perpetually…" I added.

Fortunately, one thing we learned at university was that the truth was relative. However, justice must always prevail. Many great men and women had risked their lives and in most cases died so that we could live in a free and prosperous world. So to risk my life by going to Iraq seemed justifiable in my mind.

"That's because we were lucky to have free education here." He acknowledged the greatest achievement of Gough Whitlam, a previous Australian prime minister that stood up against his peers but gave the Australian youth an equal chance to be educated without the prejudices or barriers that wealth could create. "That's what is so good about living in Australia. We have freedom to study and learn and say whatever we want. But to go to Iraq and get killed just because you want to know the truth? That's suicidal madness and selfish Al, don't you understand? It's going against popular belief."

"Popular belief is to not attack Iraq," I attempted to justify my decision yet again.

"No, that's not right! Saddam Hussein is killing hundreds of thousands of innocent people, he has weapons of mass destruction, he is a ruthless dictator, and they will kill you after they torture you there because those people are primitive! They are not civilised. What do you think a totalitarian dictatorship is?" He was reiterating an echo of the popular news stories covered in our mainstream media. It was the early hours of the morning and we were waking up some neighbours, as I saw lights being turned on in a nearby house.

"Don't yell! Or we will get arrested and charged for disturbing the peace," I said to him with a contained voice, realising that our freedom came at a price policed by the state and paid by our taxes.

"I'll scream and I'll shout if I bloody well want to!" he screamed and shouted in a brave act of rebellion against the English man-made laws created to keep the peace and quiet. "Because I'm free!" he yelled, defying our Australian made-laws, seeking a fight.

"Not if the police arrest you for disorderly behaviour," I assured him with the reminder that the free world slaves like us were chained to the laws of our lords and their law-makers.

Regrettably, we were drunk on the cheap alcohol on offer at our local club. It was little wonder that the Muslims had learned a long time ago to accept that alcohol makes a demon of a saint. On that night, alcohol had made a demon of Greg who now terrorised me while a handful of dynasties made colossal profits from this legalised drug. In fact, Western law administrators like lawyers, judges, and corrupt police made grand incomes from the stupid acts perpetrated by drunks; hence the legalisation of alcohol. In particular, modern slaves were easier to chain with alcohol and entertainment than steel cuffs. And there was money to be made from administering the law.

In preparing to travel to Muslim lands, I began studying the Quran and Islam. What I learned is that Islam is more than just a religion. It is a philosophical devotion to living in harmony with our society and our natural environment. In fact, the English translation of 'Islam' was 'knowledge'.

Perhaps that was my way of compensating for the ignorant fool I had become. Muslims had learned that alcohol only benefitted the producers and the legal industry, as it made the drunks aggressive, violent, and immoral, causing untold damage to individuals and families, while lawyers pounced to profit from alcohol induced domestic violence and an array of drunken misdemeanours.

"Come here so I can break your legs," he threatened again. "You're not going to Iraq!" he yelled, and ran around the car.

Physically, Greg was like a giant with a rock-solid body. He was also a state kick-boxing champion, and as a resident of Sydney's South Maroubra

Beach, there was no-one in the infamous BRA boys gang that he feared. Greg was the most realistic embodiment of a modern warrior I knew, as he feared no-one. Yet, he understood the need for ethical reasons to fight or go to war. In fact, Greg O'Shea was perhaps the best-read person I knew. His idea of a good time was to read a good book in a single sitting. His warrior instinct as a man was unquestionable.

However, when he was drunk, he became a menacing monster that threatened anyone in his path. I had seen him fight men larger than him both in the boxing ring and on the street. He was truly capable of killing or maiming me with his hands, and I knew I had to run away from this crazed terrorist whose threats were real.

"I have to go—my tickets are already paid for," I reasoned, knowing that Greg could be reasonable.

"You're not going anywhere!" he said, charging at me again.

As he charged I ran away, thinking, why Greg? With his profound knowledge of history and awareness of his Celtic roots, why couldn't he understand my determination to go and see for myself what our media was not telling us?

As an Irish descendent, he understood the process of colonisation and believed that Iraq would simply become the next nation to be colonised by the Anglo-Saxon warmongers who thrived on absolute power and possession of lands and its minerals by force. He seemed the ideal candidate to teach the strife-hardened kids from the working class suburbs of Sydney—or anywhere in the world for that matter—the values of culture and the needs for education to resolve any problem under the sun.

"Mate, if I don't break your legs now the terrorists will kill you after they torture you. Is that what you want?" he asked between breaths.

He was certain that I was going to be killed by the Iraqis. But now I felt death at the hand of the Iraqis terrorists would be more merciful than death by Greg. I was truly scared for my life in the southern suburbs of Sydney and fearful of the grim reaper in the shape of a charging Celtic warrior—nay, a demonic madman. I bravely ran for my life, petrified with genuine fear.

Like so many others I had spoken to, Greg simply did not want to know the painful truth that terrorists had their own reasons to kill and destroy.

But none of us knew those reasons, and all we knew was that Allah would ensure their safe passage to heaven, as martyrs.

Greg was drunk and tired and I knew it, and my saving grace was that I was sober, fitter, and had higher stamina. So I bravely sucked in my breath and puffed out my chest in a victorious stance and asked, "Have you had enough?"

He looked at me sympathetically, nodding his head in disbelief, and began to weep. His love for me was without doubt. This was the first and only time I had ever seen tears running down my mate's cheeks.

"Okay. Go! You selfish bastard. But think about the anxiety and grief you're going to cause your family when you go missing … think of your mum and think about your father when they get told you've gone missing."

He knew exactly what to say to rub acidic vinegar into my raw, open wounds. That hurt more than a blow to my nose or a kick in the guts. I swallowed hard, knowing he was right. Yes, the truth hurt me more than a physical blow. I breathed out, deflating my puffed-up lungs, and whimpered again. He was right, yet again. I hated him more than before for telling me the truth. He knew it. So he calmly gathered himself and staggered away into the night in search of a taxi.

The fact was, there came a time when we all needed to know the truth to our lives. A time when we needed to know that we worked to feed, clothe, and care for our families for a good and meaningful reason other than instinct. We watched television to learn or be entertained, not to be misled and hoodwinked. We paid education fees to teach our children how to survive in the world we left behind, not to fantasise about having material possessions that offered short-term joy. We needed to know that our taxes were paying for innovative ideas that could benefit all of us, not to funding overpaid and underperforming politicians or bureaucrats. Or worse, destroying our environment or people's lives with bombs and modern warfare.

We needed to know how we were going to survive in a world with limited and diminishing food-producing land with increasing populations demanding more food in conjunction with our limited natural resources. We needed to know how global warming, melting ice caps, extinct animals, or our shrinking oxygen levels would affect all of us. There was simply so much more we needed to know rather than waste our resources on modern warfare that I simply had to go to Iraq to learn why we were going to start another war.

I went to sleep that night oblivious to the fact that we are all living within the Australian Aboriginal philosophy of The Dreamtime as wondering ghosts of our ancestor's beliefs.

Chapter 2
Our Warrior Instinct

Iraq is free of these weapons of mass destruction.
Saddam Hussein
Daily Telegraph
February 6, 2003

When I awoke the following day, I begun to pack my bags and prepare for the long road to Baghdad. It seemed surreal that I would be going to see Saddam Hussein's evil regime and the nerves began to grow like a hunger. However, I found courage by recalling my mentors and those experiences that teach us to stand firm and fight.

One of these mentors was a family friend from South America called Frank Claic. Frank was a Peruvian Indian with a spiritual outlook on life and death that was unknown to me in my young childhood, as I was only nine years old when I met him.

He was a tall, dark-skinned man and his dark brown almond-shaped eyes allowed him to pass as an Indonesian or a Persian, Chinese, or even an African-Arab. He described himself as an 'international man' and claimed to not have a nationality other than being an earthly man. However, to everyone else, he was a South American or a Peruvian or an Inca Indian.

Frank was softly spoken, mild, and always calm. One day shortly after turning ten, I told him about my weakness in school as other kids mocked me and laughed at my inability to speak English as an immigrant to Australia. He calmly suggested I join him to train at a local YMCA gym where I could develop my warrior spirit. Frank was a bodybuilder and health was an integral part to his daily life. As we trained we talked and he was always attentive, explaining correct procedures, techniques, and the use of each muscle that we trained.

"Your body is the vehicle that your spirit and soul use to travel on this Earth," he once said to me as we trained. By then I was eleven years old and we had already covered some ground as my young body began to take a more solid frame. "Always remember, that you need to look after your body as best as you can—don't drink or smoke or take drugs, that way your soul can exist in peace in this life that you have and your spirit may never be broken," he advised between repetitions in the gym.

As a Qantas airline flight attendant, Frank had visited just about every country in the world. He spoke Spanish, English, French, German, and was now learning Mandarin Chinese to match his basic grasp of the Japanese and Arabic languages. To me, he was a giant, and having won prizes for bodybuilding, he was an inspiration and somewhat of an idol; he was a true mentor.

As a truly international man, Frank was also a spiritual master in his own right. He was a dear friend of my parents and whenever he visited Sydney he would stay in our house as a guest. When I told him how I was constantly picked on at school by kids that were bigger than me, he invited me to learn the martial arts of karate, judo, and kung fu, but he called them self-defence and prohibited me from hitting anyone unless they hit me first.

"If you learn these skills you will become a true warrior." He spurred me on when I was too tired to continue one of his strenuous exercise sessions.

I also recalled the many times he spoke to me about the South American Inca Indians and the nature of their fighting spirit. He once explained how the Spanish conquistadors were the equivalent of the European crusaders that were sent in to destroy the rising Islamic world. According to Frank, these were the fighters who justified the rape, pillage, and plundering of non-Christians and were sponsored by royal monarchs and blessed by the Christian church to destroy the Inca people and culture.

"These were the mad men that almost annihilated my people," Frank said with a hint of sorrow in his eyes.

"But they were warriors," I said to him, hoping he would understand my childish understanding of the Spanish Anglo-Saxon definition of a warrior.

"No, they were not warriors, they were terrorists," he said adamantly.

"But terrorists kill innocent people," I said to him with my media-influenced young mind.

"Yes, that is true," he agreed, making me feel smart, and then added, "but an army that kills and maims civilians like the Inca Indians or the Aboriginal or the Vietnamese or any innocent people, are also terrorists." He said this with aggravated voice.

"Oh—um, I suppose," I stuttered.

I was beginning to understand why, as a South American Indian, Frank should be so angry with the Spanish Christian crusaders that invaded, colonised, and imposed their way of life upon his people. It was then as a young boy that I first began to understand the concept of a warrior. And to me, Frank was undoubtedly a warrior.

One day after training we walked for almost an hour to our house. My young legs were pained from the long walk after training them, but he was convinced that I would learn to push myself and not quit.

It was along that walk that Frank discussed the concept of a warrior as opposed to a terrorist. It seemed that Frank was well aware of the man I was to become, as he had nurtured and trained me for several years and knew perfectly well my inner feelings and thoughts as a child.

By this stage the television, the cinemas, and the newspapers were making me more interested in the warrior spirit than the madness of terrorists. After all, I was a white-skinned Jewish-descended Spaniard that had migrated against my will to this foreign land called Australia.

My initiation into manhood was a series of events that my father deemed necessary, for I was the eldest son of the family and had to care for and protect my siblings and our way of life. Shortly after turning nine years of age, I was taken hunting by my father and his mates and left alone on the top of a hill to guard the dead rabbits as the hunters went to kill some more. The memory of protecting dead rabbits on that hill was forever empowering. It was the first time in my life that I looked at death in the opened black eyes of those rabbits and the whistling wind that howled like ghosts alerted me to the fact that men must kill to survive.

However, the fear of abandonment or that something sinister was taking place from the distant gun shots made me cry like the scared child I was. But later, when my father retuned to see the tear stained cheeks he calmly taught me saying, "Men don't have time to cry. We have to be strong and learn to be sad. There is nothing wrong to feel sad or scared, it's just a part of life…"

Later, before turning thirteen, I was given a baby pig and told to nurse him and make sure he was always fed and well cared for. A task any child would embrace given the joy one got from a defenceless animal that was happy every time it saw you with bread, water, and other food scraps, or the occasional hidden bowl of fresh milk. And then, the first Christmas after turning thirteen, when my little pig had grown to become a larger friend, I was given a heavy mallet and had to prove my manhood by killing him using my hands and the mallet, as the men-only gathering cheered against the background noise of the squealing pig.

When I struck, the first blow was the softest, as I tried in vain to not hurt him too much, but that made it worse as he squealed and struggled to break free from the hands that held him down. The second was hammered down harder, and it silenced the squeals, but his struggles continued until the third and final blow was struck with all my might to ensure any suffering was minimised.

It took three blows and all the cold blood I could muster to comply with the peer pressure to kill my first pet. And in the following silence I felt that senseless emotion of perpetual loss, and a void in which to step forward and accept that we live to survive. It was a brutal reality that at times we must kill to stay alive.

"Now you're a man," I was told by one of my father's bearded Swedish friends as the pig lay dying from its crushed skull, and I held back the tears that were bursting to explode.

***

Frank was more refined, and as an educated man he would speak to me always like a teacher keen to see his student progress and develop his intellectual or physical skills.

"Warriors fight only when they need to defend themselves," the Inca Indian taught me. "Terrorists are those that attack, invade, and occupy lands against the will of the local inhabitants, like the Spanish conquistadors were terrorists to the South American Indians; or the English that terrorised our brothers in the North Americas; the red Indians; or the European colonising armies that terrorised the African people. You see Al ... you cannot label a warrior a terrorist if the warrior is acting in self-defence," he said as we walked.

To me, Frank Claic was not an ordinary person, and in some ways he was more of a guru than a mentor. He was the first man I knew that practiced complete control of his body and mind in a bizarre practice he called yoga. He liked to pray, or 'meditate' as he called it. One time I walked into his room and saw him seated like a Buddha, meditating so intensely that he didn't recognise I was in the room. I just looked at him deeply engrossed in meditation, wondering where his mind was or if he even knew I was in the room. If it wasn't for the haunting silence in the room as I stared at him I would have stayed longer, but I was more frustrated by the fact that he didn't answer my nagging questions and remained in the trance-like state until I left the room.

Sometimes when he visited our home he would spend hours talking about the human spirit; South American magic; the Inca Indians; the Peruvian Highlanders; the metaphysical spirit; and the physical world of our body. He spoke about the magic of fire, the mystery of wind molecules, or the life contained in the sun's rays: in particular he prophesised how the tropical rainforests were the lungs of our planet and our industrial pursuits were the cancers that would eventually kill us all. As far back as the 1970s, Frank was one of what today we call greenies or environmentalists. I remember throwing a chocolate plastic wrapper on the ground and Frank made me chase it and pick it up as it floated with the wind.

"If you pollute our world you are guilty of a crime," he accused.

Sometimes he would return from an Asian country like Indonesia or Malaysia inspired by a new ideology, or with a story that he would share with us. It was Frank who taught me to control and regulate my heartbeats by controlling my breathing. To this date I practice the breathing exercises Frank taught me, and regulate my beating heart. I credit Frank as one of my most important teachers other than my parents.

"Breathe in slowly and count to four … one … two … three … and four … now hold your breath for ten seconds … and slowly count to four as you release the toxins in your blood," he instructed me. "Now repeat that two more times and do that every day that you feel stressed or ill," he concluded.

Later, in 1985 when I was shot in the chest and the bullet punctured my lungs, it was the breathing exercises that Frank taught me that I credit for saving my life, as I had learned to sink into my thoughts and remain calm to avoid the state of shock, which was often the cause of death to those in an accident.

It was Frank who made me understand that a warrior was not just a soldier. A warrior defends, while soldiers take orders and attack.

"Any criminal could become a soldier. But to be a warrior, you need to learn and understand the reason for your war," he told me.

***

As fate and destiny were the paths that God opened for us in the journey of our lives, it was shortly before my twelfth birthday when I saw my two elder sisters in a street-fight outside the local high school and the time I would learn the importance to fighting with physical aggression.

J. J. Cahill High School was in that time an infamous school, renowned for drugs, ethnic gangs, and violent fighting. The fights were mostly between the wogs; Aussies; Abbos; Chinks; poofs; Lebs; nerds; Pakis; Indians; gooks; chooks; rag-heads; niggers; or sluts—make up any name you wanted for anyone you didn't like. Hatred was encouraged and sides had to be taken to blend amongst the television-brainwashed youth.

Marilyn, my elder middle sister, was a strikingly beautiful Spanish girl with long dark hair, olive skin, Persian green eyes, and a petite ballerina's body. So when she arrived at the new high school, it didn't take long for her to become the most admired girl in the school by her male companions.

Unfortunately for Marilyn, the other girls felt threatened as their boyfriends also started to talk about the new beauty queen of the school. This was enough reason for two bigger girls to gang up and start hurling abuse at my frightened small big sister.

"Go back home to wog land!" I heard a girl's voice scream at my sister.

When I turned to look, I saw a large girl with the body of a man screaming at my sister. So I just stood and stared like a frightened child.

"Fuck you!" my sister screamed back.

"You're a dirty wog! You don't belong here," shouted the second girl, whose face was covered in acne.

By this time a crowd was gathering and everyone seemed to know what was going to happen. I looked around, but as the new kids on the block, we were outnumbered. I looked for my brothers and other sisters but couldn't see them. *Maybe they're already running for their lives*, I thought, getting ready to run and join them.

I heard a glass bottle break as the pimply girl cracked a near-empty green glass coke bottle on the ground and now threatened to cut my sister open.

"I'm going to kill you, slut," she warned Marilyn, who now took refuge behind another of her teenage male admirers.

I stood and stared, looking for my escape route, getting ready to run home crying to my mom and screaming that a man dressed like a woman had killed my sister.

Unexpectedly, I saw the man wearing a skirt throw a roundhouse swing at my sister, who ducked gingerly and cracked back with a beautiful uppercut that I was certain would knock that she-devil out. But her head sprang back as if spring-loaded, and the two entangled each other in a hair-pulling, eye-scratching, clothes-tearing spectacle while the pimple faced girl stood ready to finish killing my sister with a broken bottle.

I was about ready to run home crying and turned to run, when all of a sudden, I saw a mess of blonde hair from the corner of my eye in the distance. I looked again and it was my youngest sister Nenni.

Nenni had two older sisters to compete against and three younger brothers to use as sparring partners or whimpering punching bags. She was only thirteen at the time, but had developed a strong, athletic body that made her captain of her softball team and a state sporting champion. But more importantly she had a stubborn approach to life that made all of us run from her when she was in a foul mood. Indeed, when she was in a rage, she was a menacing figure that was clearly worth running away from.

Pimples was about to begin the open-heart surgery on my sister Marilyn when Nenni reached her with a perfectly executed and faultlessly timed full roundhouse punch to the jaw. That was the end of splattering Pimples as she collapsed, unconscious, after flying through the air, eyes facing the heavens and wondering where that truck came from.

Nenni then focused on her next victim: the man dressed in a girl's outfit who was now on top of Marilyn, pulling her hair out for what I thought was to make more wigs for her she-devil outfits. But Nenni grabbed her hair and proceeded to pump a relentless volley of face re-arranging punches.

By this time, the elder boys that goggled at my sisters' fighting had seen enough, and stepped in to stop the little blond surgeon from doing any more damage. They pulled Nenni away screaming, biting, scratching, and kicking anyone in her reach.

The fight was now over, so I bravely puffed up my chest and walked over to where my sisters now stood surrounded by drooling teenage boys.

"Gee, I'm glad you girls didn't need me."

"Where were you?!" Marilyn screamed at me.

"You're going to cop it when we get home," Nenni threatened.

That's when I knew I had done something wrong. I had stood and watched my sisters get attacked and rightfully defend themselves, and I did nothing about it. I was the ultimate coward.

When we arrived home, my sisters, still charged with the adrenaline of their encounter, retold the story to my parents in detail. My mother was sympathetic and looked at the scratches on Marilyn's face and arms whilst Nenni polished her fingernails like a cunning feline leopard after a successful hunt. Everything was going well until my father asked the dreaded question.

"Where was your brother Al, when this was taking place?" he asked, and all eyes turned to me. I could feel the sudden change in the weather as my face reddened and sweat glands opened to let out the steam.

"I don't know," Marilyn said genuinely.

"He was just watching!" Nenni confessed.

"Um. But. I was busy," I think I may have said.

Whatever I said, however, was not enough, as my father again reached for his belt and kicked and belted me from one side of the house to the other, and back straight to the safe refuge under my bed. There he was able to sit on top and give me another one of those after-beatings father-to-son explanations.

"Consider yourself lucky that I can't get you under there," he warned, sitting on the bed to catch his breath. I had already learned the first rule to fighting. Rule One: always be sure you can run faster than any enemy that wants to kill you. Rule Two: look for an alternative plan of escape in case Rule One fails. So from under the bed, I could see the opened window inviting me to jump out to safety and never return.

"You know you're going to be a man soon. And by God, I will teach you to be a man!" he said between breaths. "A man doesn't sit and watch his brothers or sisters get hit or humiliated. A man doesn't hide when he sees an injustice or a crime against an innocent person. A real man will fight if he has to. In particular, if he has to defend his family or honour those that can't fight back," he said between hard breaths as I huddled under the bed, whimpering and sniffing back my tears whilst looking at the red welts on my legs and arms. "Next time I hear you stood by and did nothing to help your family, I will beat you twice as bad! Understand?"

"Ye-es," I managed to say between sobs.

In retrospect, this was among the more important lessons my father had taught me, as later in life I would learn that crime and violence was a way of life for many people in the world who had little, if anything, to lose. I would later learn that not fighting back could result in worse outcomes.

It was thus that I learned how the warrior instinct was both innate and learned. Perhaps we should understand the difference between an aggressive force and those who defend their families, lives, or lands before invading others, citing the misguided use of the term 'defence'.

Chapter 3
The Will to Fight

What you will see is an accumulation of facts and patterns of behaviour ... that Saddam Hussein made no effort, no effort! To disarm as required by the international community ...
Secretary of State Colin Powell
to the United Nations Security Council
February 5, 2003

The following week, my sister Nenni was being harassed by Jim, a tall lanky Greek boy who we all knew as a troublemaker. Nenni had already earned herself a reputation as the most feared and best fighter in the school after she took out the kingpin singlehandedly with an all-out assault after he naively mistook her for a typical girl that cowers and cries when humiliated.

Now, we were in the school bus and Jim wanted to claim the school title that Nenni rightfully had as the best fighter in the school. Jim was also among the most feared in the school, because he always fought with his brother Angelo close by and always ready to pounce on the unsuspecting victim. But I was well aware of their tactics, and fearing my father's wrath or the humiliation of hiding under the bed again, I went to her rescue.

"You're a wog! Dirty wog! Go home wog!" His schoolboy chant echoed over the constant murmur and humdrum of the school bus. Angelo, the executioner, waited, ready to attack Nenni from behind.

"Why don't you pick on a boy?" I challenged the big-mouth calling my sister names.

Jim stood up and I was instantly overshadowed by his size. I knew instantly that I had made a mistake. This was the first time in my life I faced the grim reaper and death was imminent.

"What did you say?" Big Jim challenged back.

"Agh. I ... um ... I said, um," I stuttered.

"Are you picking a fight?" I heard his brother Angelo courageously asking me.

"No I just said—" smack! Smack! I was hit twice on the face before I could finish my answer. The blows sent me reeling back and collapsing on a cushioned bus seat. The stars in my watery eyes were still too distant to make out my navigational tracks back to reality.

Smack! Whack! The assault continued and instinctively I raised my hands to protect my already battered face. It seemed like I was doomed to die in the back of the school bus.

Unexpectedly, I heard a loud piercing scream that shook my yielding mind back to consciousness. I looked up from my grave and saw that Angelo was being pulled off me from the front of his hair, back toward the unyielding grip of my little sister's direction.

Thump! And Angelo was on his back next to the whimpering Big Jim who held his bloody nose, crouched on the floor and crying. It didn't take long to analyse the situation as I saw Nenni, unfazed and standing over the two of them, screaming at them.

"Next time you call me wog? I'll kill you," she threatened.

But I don't think they realised how lucky they were to still be alive. Once again, I puffed my chest and for the rest of the journey I stood victorious next to my secret biological weapon of mass destruction as my big sister sat by my side and attended to her fingernails once more. She now seemed oblivious to the two brothers who started to abuse and blame each other for their wounds.

"You see. I told yah!"

"It's your fault!"

"No it's your fault!"

"But you told me to do it."

"But I didn't think you would!"

Their arguing continued until the bus pulled up at their stop and they both got out, fighting each other. We were never picked on for the rest of the year by anyone else. But above all, I had learned from my sister the importance for a family to help each other and defend themselves from a terrorising aggressor's attack.

More important was my sister's natural instinct to save and protect me from the terrorism of childhood bullying and the stupidity of physical aggression.

***

The following year, however, my sister Nenni would graduate and go to high school, and I would be left alone to look after my two smaller brothers without my secret biological weapon. With this insight, I ventured to learn more about war, fighting, and assault weapons. So I started from the top.

"Why are kids so aggressive?" I asked my peace-loving mother as she laboured over the hot stove to feed the troops.

"Because some kids don't learn to love or to talk and discuss differences like we do in our family," she said, stirring lentil stew.

"But I want to learn how to fight," I confided.

"Well then, you better do what those stupid kids do to learn how to fight," she said, "as a matter of fact."

"What?" I asked, surprised that a peace activist and loving mother would have inside information on military tactics, war, and fighting techniques.

"Go and watch the idiot box," she said smartly.

"What?"

"You'd better go watch television." I wasn't sure if she was serious or telling me to get out of the kitchen. So I stared at her quizzically.

"Huh?" I grunted.

"You heard me. Go watch television."

"Television?"

"Do those English have a different word than us Spaniards for a television?" my mum asked, genuinely curious to learn more English.

"No," I said, realising the universal power of having telescopic vision at the push of a button to learn how to fight. Wow, what a gift, I mused.

"Then go. I have things to do here," she said, dismissing me with the backhand wave like she would wave off a nagging Spanish fly.

I walked away, philosophising on the wisdom of a mother's maternal instinct to detect secret intelligence and strategic military planning that was so obvious that it would pass completely over the heads of the most astute modern-day thinkers. Or so I thought.

I went to the television where my two younger brothers sat watching an American police drama called S.W.A.T. The first thing I saw was a brawl. So I stood, transfixed, as the handsome good guys beat the ugly bad guys to a pulp.

The program was followed by another show with handsome good guys and poor, ugly, bad men. Then, a war film showed the heroic American good guys fighting the ugly bad guys. This was before the feature movie presentation that was a screening of *The Dirty Dozen* on one channel, *Anything But Lose* with Clint Eastwood on another channel, or *The Guns of Navarone*. All movies seemed to show violence, fighting, war heroes, and good-looking good guys fighting and killing lots of ugly, bad men.

Over the years, I would always watch television wondering why there was such an obsession with war and violent films. In the first instance, I concluded that I was going to be a warrior like a man should be according to the television. An American marine or a Green Beret or a commando or a fearless war hero whose gun never runs out of bullets to kill as many bad people as possible. Then there was an abundance of police shows and I switched roles to want to become a policeman. When I saw the English-produced James Bond movies I wanted to be a suave, cool secret agent. But then, I saw kung fu, and I wanted to be a martial artist fighting ugly men and gangs of criminals. By the time Rocky hit the screens I wanted to be a boxer. I saw a film called *Cannon Ball Run* and I wanted to be an idiot or a funny fellow. Bruce Lee films made me do karate on my two younger brothers, and after watching the world wrestling I would throw them around, wanting to hurt them for no apparent reason. So finally I wanted to be a heavyweight wrestler, but I had to eat lots more to make my small, fragile body take on those hulks. I would eat twice as much and asked Frank to train me to grow muscles. Such was the power of television over the developing mind of a young child.

The violent drama was as appealing as candy was to any child. But then again, musicals, art house films, and artistic performances were equally dramatic. It wouldn't be until much later when I sat talking to American soldiers in Iraq, that I realised the political advantages of bombarding an influential youth with brave, handsome, heroic warriors and weak, ugly, violent criminals mostly in the shape of Middle Eastern men from either Arab or Persian origins.

The following year, my father managed to buy a working class terrace house in the South Sydney industrial ghetto of Zetland. It was here that I would learn the shame of poverty, the pains of hard labour, and the brutal violence of street-fighting.

One day, I met a Turkish Muslim boy who I had seen walking the streets alone mostly dressed in dirty rag-like clothes. His dark, curly hair matted as if he had just woken up and there were food stains down the front of his holey T-shirt. He didn't seem to have any friends and he looked to be a few years older than I was. Yet he was always friendly and respectful. As I didn't know anyone in this small forgotten industrial suburb on the city fringe, I approached him and introduced myself. He replied but his name seemed strange and I never remembered it, so I called him Ticker. A name that made him smile, as I called him Ticker the great Turk.

One day, late that same year, Ticker and I talked in the back lane about boy things like our favourite war films, favourite wrestlers, action heroes, and who was the greatest boxer in the world.

"Muhammad Ali," we both agreed simultaneously.

"He is a Muslim you know," Ticker said with a proud tone to his voice.

"A what?"

"A Muslim, just like me," he said, glowing with pride.

"So?" I asked, not knowing what the big deal was as I had never even heard the word 'Muslim' until this time nearing my thirteenth birthday.

"So that's why he is the best boxer and street-fighter in the world," Ticker said, sounding more proud than before.

"Street-fighter?" I asked, confused by another expression I had never heard before.

I imagined that gangs were claiming streets, and now the streets where owned by the local emerging gangs. Or was that just an American way of life that I had seen in movies? In any case, it made sense to me now why I was sometimes chased by gangs of kids on the streets as I collected precious aluminium cans to recycle for spare change. I often surrendered my hard-earned bag of squashed cans to their demands or faced the consequences of a thrashing.

"Yeah, fighting in the streets," he said, as if I was supposed to know all about street-fighting at this stage of my life.

"Oh. I see."

But he obviously detected my ignorance on the subject, as he continued to give me a lecture that was followed by a quick training session in his small garden shed makeshift gym.

"The first thing you have to know is the golden rule," he said, pointing at my chest as he stopped me from walking along the garbage-littered back lane.

"What's that?"

"You never, ever and I mean in no way do you ever start a fight," he said, almost threatening me. "Because street-fighters know that we can kill a man with our hands." He retreated, showing me his hands in the shape of menacing claws.

"Oh—um, okay," I said, starting to get a bit scared at this time.

"If you obey the street-fighters' golden rule, you will never lose," he asserted confidently.

"Why not?" I suddenly wanted to know his secret.

"Because if you don't start a war, then you have nothing to lose," he rationalised.

"But what if they're picking on me?" I asked, knowing that my bag of squashed aluminium cans was a bounty worth fighting for.

"Then, you must learn to be a fighter," he added, to my delight.

I could sense that now I was going to be the true tough guy: a real warrior! A street-fighter!

"But how do you know I won't lose?" I asked to make sure I heard him right.

"Because if you don't start the fight, then it means that someone else has started the fight; right?"

"Right," I answered smartly.

"Then you have the right to finish it," he said as we walked along the back alley to where he shared one of those run-down workman's terraces with his parents.

"But I like the idea of walking away from trouble," I said, remembering my mother's advice and thinking maybe he was going to use me as a punching bag. I was searching for a reason to go home.

"Yeah, me too. But trust me, the future is going to get worse than the past and one day you may not be able to run away and you're going to need to learn to fight back," he corrected me.

"But I don't know how to fight," I said, realising that television only taught me how to become aggressive and mad with rage at the stupidity that kids were watching on the screen.

"I know," he smiled. "But you will after today."

"In one day, you're going to teach me?" I asked, thinking this guy was a wizard.

"If you listen to me carefully, I promise you will never lose a fight in your life," he said confidently as we entered through an old termite-eaten wooden gate hanging on one rusty hinge.

His gym was a marvel of ingenuity. He had a variety of steel cans that ranged in size from small 250-gram baked bean cans to large five-litre cans of Danté olive oil. They were all filled with concrete and some were united with a matching can by a heavy metal pipe.

"These are weights," he said, pointing at cans on the mud-covered ground. "That's the punching bag," he said, throwing a straight jab at a stuffed old green army-issued kit bag. "There is the shadow you must protect." He pointed at a body-sized mirror leaning on the fence. "And that's the bench," he pointed at a raw plank leaning on an angle against a plastic milk crate.

"But what do I need these things for?" I inquired.

"These are the only tools you need to sharpen your weapons," he said, clenching both fists and shaping up for the first time.

"But I get scared." I admitted my cowardice.

"So do I," he said. "But that's Allah's way of preparing men to defend the good from evil."

"Allah?" I asked, wondering what he was talking about.

"Yeah, Allah! God, Jehovah! Dios! The creator, anything you want to call Allah—it's all the same, just a different language," he said.

"Oh, I see," I said, accepting his logical explanation.

"You see, good men don't like evil. And evil men like evil—that's why they start fights and go to war. But now I have to teach you the silver rule of fighting."

"Silver rule?"

"Yes: that is that you have a duty and responsibility to warn the other man that you will hurt him if he continues to threaten you," he said as if I should have known that.

"Oh yeah," I said, as if I knew.

"So you always give them three warnings. First one you must be humble and polite so that he has a chance to correct himself," he said, unbuttoning his shirt. "Second time you make it clear that you have the ability and faith in Allah—or in your case God—to kill him," he threatened, removing his shirt and tossing it aside and exposing his sculpted, tanned body. "By the third time you can smile because Allah is with you and you make it perfectly clear that that is the third and final warning. After that—"

Snap! Bang! Kick! Crack! Smash! Whack! And he continued to pulverise the unsuspecting green army-issued kit bag for what seemed to be an eternity in the life of that punching bag. Then he grabbed a steel pipe from the ground and proceeded to strike the bag from the top, the bottom, and all sides. The bag thumped every time he struck with a full swing from different angles. Finally he took two small cans filled with concrete and did a round of sit-ups whilst lying feet-up and body-down on the plank, holding the cans on his chest. When he stopped to catch his breath, he was sweating, and his knuckles were reddened with hints of blood.

"You see Al," he said, between sit-ups, "on the streets … there is no law … no rules … no refs … and no second prizes … It's just Allah and you … to fight the stupidity … the ignorance … and the ugly face … of evil," he managed to say, breathing heavily, before standing up.

I looked in horrific awe at the violent display I had just witnessed against the innocence of the docile army punching bag as it swayed to and fro in a dizzy circle.

"Now it's your turn. Have a go," he said, inviting me to do the same as he had done. He stood away and his muscle-ripped body shone in the midday sun.

"Okay," I said, accepting the invitation. I stepped up to the docile green army victim and started my first assault against the evil of war. After about a minute, I was ready to collapse, and so I skipped the steel pole and just sat on the sit-up bench.

"That wasn't bad for your first time," he said, looking at my bleeding knuckles. "But you could do with some training to toughen you up."

During that summer, after selling newspapers around the neighbourhood, pulling at my cart as part of my training, I would visit Ticker's gym and trained almost ritualistically. Here he showed me the basics like jabs; hooks; combinations; kicks; grabs; dumps; gouges; knifes; bottles; poles; and the lawless nature of street-fighting survival tactics. It was nearly the end of summer and the start of the school season when one of the local hoods and a confirmed troublemaker approached me as I rode my bike around the back lane.

As a local thug, Johnny was the equivalent of a local Aussie terrorist. All the neighbours knew him as a hood. He was with another friend and his twin sister, Shirley. I feared Shirley even more than my small big sister Nenni, simply because she had broader shoulders and stood more like a wrestler than a girl. Johnny was wielding a long branch that he used as a whip, and as I passed him he whipped me square across the face for no logical reason.

I considered that to be the first warning as I casually got off my bike and confronted him, with my face still stinging as a welt flared up.

"If you do that again, I'm going to hurt you," I warned him, thinking about the golden and silver rules of street-fighting and believing that my confronting him would be enough.

Swoosh.

"Argh!" I screamed, feeling the sting across my face where he had just whipped me again. I immediately abandoned the rules of street-fighting and instinctively swung and hit poor Johnny cleanly on the nose, relocating it from the centre of his face to his right side. Naturally, this caused him to collapse in shock while reaching for his broken nose, blood instantly pouring out, making him stand before running off crying. Shirley and the other boy looked at me, horrified, and ran after Johnny.

My immediate reaction was to gloat with pride. I had claimed my street and my first victory. I thought and continued to ride my bike. But shortly after, I saw the grossly overgrown figure of Big Brett who is Johnny's big brother come marching down the street accompanied by Shirley and the other boy. I sensed trouble, but didn't expect Big Brett's reaction after he spoke in a hoarse, angry voice.

"What did you do to my little brother?"

"I—"

Smack!

I went down and stayed down, crying, with the hope that my streaming tears would save me from the next encounter with death.

"You ever do that to my little brother again, and I'll kill you!" he shouted, showing mercy.

Then he turned and left me to think that if someone ever did that to a brother of mine, I'd have to do the same. Exactly as my father had taught me earlier. This seemed to be a natural law. Was Big Brett a terrorist also? Perhaps he too had learned the importance of defending his family.

When I conveyed to Ticker the Turk my first street-fight, he laughed and said that I partially deserved it but it was partly his fault for not having taught me the last rules of street-fighting.

"Bronze rule: you never invite your opposition to a fight or to hit you, that's just playing dumb. And you don't stay around waiting for others to glorify you, because there is no glory in street-fighting. So you have to get away from the fight scene. But above all," he said sternly. "You must have a heart, and self-discipline, to know when to strike and when to stop." He added after a deep breath, "Because if you don't stop, then you become lower than a criminal: you become a murderer! A killer that is willing to take a life for no reason other than self-interest."

I was forever grateful that my father, Ticker the Turk, Frank Claic, and my sister Nenni had taught me about the fighting spirit we all have within. It saddened me to know there was always going to be some fool that would want to show off his or her superior strength over a weaker person, nation, or entity.

As I recalled those who inspired me to stand up and fight for what was right, I wondered if the son of a wealthy man like G. W. Bush; Uday Hussein; Omar Gadafy; Prince Charles; or Jim Jon-ung from North Korea and those who inherited power would lead an army from the front or send others to kill on their behalf. I knew that nepotism was filled with flaws, prejudices, and megalomaniac disorders.

We, the people of Earth, should never forget the idiom that's said to remind us of our united responsibility: 'evil triumphs when good people do nothing'. We had to be ready and willing to fight against those who told us to sacrifice our lives on their behalf; in particular if we went to war to fight for those greedy people with more money than sense.

The question on our minds was, "How do we stop the senseless leadership that misleads us and lies to us with the premise of fighting a modern war that ultimately will have a negative impact on all our lives?"

Chapter 4
Yin and Yang: The Universal Law of Opposites ☯

Cost of Iraq and other wars since 2003 war as of June 2015:
US$4,400,000,000,000 and increasing ...

Cost of labour in third world:
$2.00 per day and decreasing ...

It was truly senseless. I woke up in a hospital from the coma of a clinical death, the result of a twenty-two millimetre bullet that punctured both lungs and tore the two arteries at the top of my heart. I was oblivious to the daily concerns of the world; both body and mind were linked by the same nerve that defined euphoria. Pain and joy collided until a heavenly nurse injected more morphine into my blood stream to take me higher into the realm of heavenly bliss.

Here was the perfect balance we would all experience as we died, waiting to transcend that celestial border that separated life from death.

And if we continued living, we were reminded in perpetuity that our lives were fragile, precious moments filled with experiences and events during the short span of a measured lifetime. We all shared the same sun, moon, stars, and the air we breathed, like the water we drank. We were all in the same spaceship called Earth and we were all destined to live and then die.

Many of us who return from death may understand the Australian Aboriginal people who live in The Dreamtime. This is a simple way of life, as we live in tune with the environment, oblivious to the lies of advertising campaigns or propaganda machines.

I awoke every morning into the bliss of life after death. Only one day, after lazily getting out of bed, I strolled to the abode of my spacious bathroom and let the warm clean drinking water cleanse my body and run down the sink. I had already completed my cleaning duties the previous day, and everything seemed to be perfectly in place. Yes, it was good to live in the developed first world that could bring you back to life from the dead.

Opening my front door, I let the magic of a new day enter my house as I stepped into the sunlight. It was a glorious summer day with that crisp, clean, blue summer sky to remind us that heaven could be on Earth for our children to inherit. *What more could any person want?* I thought as I collected the newspaper delivered to my front door still warm off the press—or was it the mid-morning sun?

My front garden had blossomed and the spectacle of birds twittering, bees buzzing, and the distant humdrum of traffic murmured with contentment. The wheels of time forever turning as the lonely planet Earth tirelessly spun around our exhausted, burning sun, the same sun that fed the plants we ate and gave life to our ancestors, our enemies, and our animal kingdom. We had all seen this sun rise and fall without missing a beat. The blooming roses, lavenders, and wild flowers that now adorned my front garden simply added colour and a sweet scent to this paradise I called heaven.

I inhaled a full breath of perfumed oxygen into my lungs, performed a long, reaching stretch, and I walked back inside to the comforts of my humble suburban home. I poured a gigantic bowl of my favourite cereal and mixed it with rich pasteurized milk. The habitually strong brewed coffee and the bees' honey smeared across raisin toast. There was a relaxing outlook on the Sydney Olympic Park from the rear of my house where nature sang and danced in the shape of free-flying birds of varying species that never seemed to argue. My dog named Sultan was ever ready to play, chase balls, or add to his collection of fetched sticks now lying sprawled, basking, or admiring our sun.

Ah, yes! Another day alive to enjoy life in perfect harmony with our natural environment; another day to read and learn about our world and how mankind was unifying to research stem cells and cures against AIDS, cancer, and the long list of terminal diseases. How wonderful life was when mankind united to resolve issues and find solutions to complex problems diplomatically or scientifically; the world's academic environment had great thinkers determined to research and find new sustainable energies and less polluting by-products. Perhaps our scientists were nearer to finding that illusive cure to cancer, or the many infectious diseases torturing us to death, or any other global problem.

Yes, with an educated mind, anything really was possible under the sun. Stem cell research; nuclear fusion; the colonisation of Mars; underwater residencies. A great myriad of scientific studies continued to provide an infinite number of challenges, an endless number of possibilities for the human race to create new green industries, new avenues for the human race and the animal kingdom to live in the same harmony that my dog Sultan and I now shared. Yes, anything was possible under the sun. Carbon credits; desalination plants large enough to irrigate deserts; floating homes or towns; green industries—all these were great employment opportunities awaiting all across the world.

It made me feel good that world peace was a reality and not a dream. With the internet, we now had global communications systems in place that united the human race as one. We had the resources and combined wealth to ensure slavery was completely abolished and all humanity would finally be working together in endless roles to ensure life in our star planet, our vehicle to eternity, would be sustained and immortal. The natural beauty of this great spaceship called planet Earth always made me marvel as we were all in it together meandering through the galaxy in search of a higher kingdom and other intelligent life between infinity and this hard rock with only the will of God to guide our great global thinkers.

"What on Earth!" I gasped aloud, in disbelief when I read that G. W. Bush was intent on attacking Iraq without the United Nations Security Council's mandate. I had already been petrified when he threatened to use nuclear bombs against Iraqi civilians that same early December 2002, but to go to war against Iraq? Was he mad? That was simply wrong.

Having lived a privileged life with a second chance to live, it would have been wrong for me to remain apathetic to the injustice that was about to take place. I felt it would make me an accomplice to murder, or far worse, like an apathetic witness to the Jewish Holocaust, who just watched the genocide from the side-lines and justified my apathy with the most basic and simplistic statements: "There was nothing I could do about it." Or worse still, "It was my job to kill them Jews."

The truth was, there was something that we could all do when a crime was about to be committed. We screamed, we yelled, and collectively we all saw to it that the criminal did not get away with that crime. Or if a crime was committed, we reported it and testified so that justice may prevail, or forever hold your peace.

Thus it was that on the 14th of February I found myself in the Mascot International Airport going to Baghdad.

Amidst the global fashion parade one saw in any international airport, I noticed a sea of white robe-wearing Muslims going on their individual 'hajj'.

As I learned, the hajj was a compulsory pilgrimage that should be taken by all Muslims at least once in a lifetime if possible. This journey of self-discovery was a spiritual journey, where the individual was encouraged to learn about his or her own inner self and our relationship with our surrounding environments so that we might understand our own personal strengths and weaknesses as an individual, and above all to strengthen our relationship with Allah, God, Jehovah, Fate, destiny, or whatever you might call Dios in your own language. As Ticker the Muslim Turk had made me understand—our future.

With the annual hajj soon to start, there were many Muslim men and women congregating to board my flight. I was flying with the Emirate Airlines, so there seemed to be more people dressed in all-white turbans and shawls than in fashionable and colourful Western designer attire. I had always been amazed that these Muslim people had no sense of fashion. Rather they always seemed to wear the same things. Not surprisingly, we were never taught in our Western education why the Muslim people wore the same—all white or black gowns.

The only way I was going to learn was by asking questions. So I asked an elderly man who sat facing me, reading a Qur'an.

"Excuse me Sir, but why do Muslims wear the same white gown?" I asked, interrupting his concentration.

When he looked up his long, untrimmed white beard hid a pleasant and humble smile. He had striking blue eyes and white skin. It seemed like he was overjoyed to be asked this question and his reply in perfect Australian-English would preoccupy my mind for the rest of my journey to Baghdad.

"Mate," he said, looking proud, "because we are Muslims and as Muslims we are all the same people, no better, no worse, no richer, no poorer and we should not show off or pretend to be better than others simply by wearing expensively tailored suits or designer dresses—that is why!"

"Oh—um, thank you," I replied and sat in silence thinking about his encompassing answer. I felt like a young school child that had just come to understand that he was capable of learning new things. But above all, I was perplexed by this white Australian man that defied my naïve perception of Muslims.

It seemed amazing that the vast majority of people I knew stopped learning when they reached their teens. However, this old man going on his hajj continued to read and study the Qur'an like that school child seeking to learn about our purpose in life.

"I'm Al, what's your name?" I asked, extending my hand in friendship and not satisfied with my ignorance.

"Good day mate, I'm Abdullah," he replied with a strong native Australian accent as he shook my hand.

"You sound Australian," I said, surprised to hear a Muslim speaking with such a distinctive Australian accent.

"That's because I am." He smiled as he answered. "I know, we are a rare kind. But I used to be a surfer before I converted, if that makes you feel any better," he added.

"You mean you stopped surfing after you converted?"

"No man, I still surf. But I stopped drinking booze, eating pork, and smoking pot so I can have a better control of my life," he replied.

"So why did you convert to Islam?" I asked him.

"Because Islam means knowledge, and if you ask any Muslim, none of them know everything about our lives—that's why we become Muslims. So that we can continue to learn and never stop learning about such things like the many meanings in the Qur'an or science or space or whatever we can learn about ourselves." He answered, almost excited, with a warm, soft smile.

"I see," I said as our boarding call was announced through the loud speakers.

"Where are you going to?" he asked me.

"Jordan," I replied, not wanting to disclose my true destination of Baghdad.

"Ah, great place. Be sure to visit Aqabar, on the red sea, the diving there is second to the Barrier Reef," he advised as he collected his luggage to board the plane.

This brief encounter gave me some comfort. I was relieved to know that in Australia there were Muslims that enjoyed surfing, diving, and I would later learn, football, rugby, and everything that represented Australia.

What we already knew was that education was a slow process. That is why it took up to ten years of university for students to become surgeons. Or four years to be a licensed tradesperson, or one year to be a soldier, or five for a doctorate. Time was the blackboard of our learning process, and unfortunately it took a lifetime to learn the purpose of our lives.

Later, in Jordan, I would learn more about what it meant to be a Muslim. Like Muslims with wealth, they voluntarily rather than legislatively gave away ten percent of their income as a tax called 'zarkat'. This gesture was fundamental to maintaining the circular flow of income. You couldn't call yourself a Muslim if you did not give away ten percent of your income to charity. The onus was on the beholder of wealth to live with a clean conscience that he or she was living a good and pure life according to the principal teachings of Islam. So they gave away that ten percent to whomever they saw being in need of it.

Prophet Muhammad may not have been an economist, but he was absolutely right to make zarkat one of the most significant conditions of Islam. Perhaps we should all understand the importance of job creation and the distribution of income. But surely, there could be more practical and logical measures we could take to distribute wealth and create jobs across the globe fairly while not unjustly over-taxing us in the name of corrupt governments.

Perhaps if world travel was more affordable and travel visas were basic to obtain, or obsolete, then we could all individually participate in the global distribution of income. The fact was, the world economy depended heavily on travel, transport, service providers, and tourism. These were fundamental to keeping the circular flow of income healthy as the average person distributed wealth during their own hajj.

These Muslim pilgrims were doing just that: spending replaceable money on travel operators; hotels; souvenir merchants; restaurants; cafes; and transport providers.

Many cafes; restaurants; museums; galleries; tour guides; and local communities of artists and craftspeople at large would benefit from the influx of traveling tourists on their personal pilgrimages. The funds spent went a long way in allowing those local people to, in turn, travel abroad and thus keep the circular flow of wealth distribution throughout most if not all of our world. I truly did have a lot to learn about the Muslim way of life.

"Salam Alecum," a beautiful airline hostess greeted me as I boarded the plane.

She wore a white almost transparent hijab, which was a simple scarf covering only her hair and worn mostly by single Muslim women, in contrast to the burka that covered the face and was worn by married women who vowed the promise that only their family would see the beauty of their faces in private; a concept many Westerners misunderstood as much as I did. I could just make out that the hostess must have long hair. I found the absence of her exposure more attractive and her feminine nature more seductive to my manly instincts than any scantily dressed vixen.

"Hello," I greeted back.

"You are going to Amman?" she asked me politely.

"Yes," I replied, feeling more relaxed.

"Very good Sir, please be seated and prepare for take-off," she advised in broken English, calming my excited nerves.

Perhaps Greg was right, I may be mad to be going to Iraq now. But I had already travelled and seen the third world, and now I was honouring a promise I made to three Ethiopian children long ago.

As I had stated previously, it was on 22 October 1985 when a drunken local Australian terrorist shot me in the chest mistaking me for someone else, and according to the surgeon Dr Newman who operated on me, I was proclaimed to be clinically dead. However, the blessing of modern medicine revived my heart to beat some more.

The double blessing was my father's education, which provided me with the good fortune to join my parents on board their luxury sailing yacht, which was appropriately named the *Nova Vida* meaning 'the new life'. My parents were circumnavigating our Earth on their very own pilgrimage with my younger brother Jimmy, so when Mum asked my brother Val and I to join them, we knew ourselves to be blessed yet again.

As I recall, travelling with my father, he always paid without ever negotiating or bargaining with prices in any of the poorer countries we visited, and often gave money to beggars and left appropriate tips to those who performed good services.

"You negotiate in business transactions where you know the margins allow for negotiations. But you don't negotiate with small vendors who you know are scraping a living," I remember my father advising me.

"Why not?" I asked, thinking it was customary to trade and negotiate deals. After all, the fun in making deals was the negotiations. Knowing what to ask, how to walk away, or how to settle a deal.

"Because these are the people that keep the economy running," he said sharply.

"I thought it was the banks?" I asked smartly.

"No, the banks are the bastards that we need," he corrected. "But the trick is to never borrow if you can avoid it and if you do then give them their money back as soon as you can."

Perhaps my father was already in tune with the need to be distributing funds along the way as he never hesitated to spend his limited funds to ensure we had everything we needed during the journey.

When I joined them the *Nova Vida* was docked at the port city of Galle in south-western Sri Lanka. This was a city that would be wiped out by the 2004 Boxing Day tsunami claiming over two hundred thousand lives—yes that was over 200,000 dead—and countless crippled, maimed, and tortured from a natural disaster. *Aren't natural disasters more terrifying than a handful of nut-cracking terrorists?* I wondered—as global warming threatened life on Earth.

One day, as we waited for the monsoons to pass and the winds to change so that we may have the best passage to cross the vast Indian Ocean, I decided to visit an old Buddhist temple I had seen near the harbour. There I met a fragile old Asian man who called himself a monk. It was surprising to hear this little man speak English with a strong Asiatic accent. I quickly and excitedly explained to him that I had recently been shot and died and that I was on my pilgrimage in life. But he simply smiled and asked me to follow him to where we sat and drank plain water at the feet of a sitting Buddha. For most of the time he just sat and listened as I pored over my history and talked endlessly of my past, but all he seemed to say was:

"I see ..."

Other times he would nod his head with understanding facial gestures, or at times he would simply murmur a small grunt like a hum from deep within his body. Yet mostly he sat quietly and listened; saying:

"I see ..."

After what seemed like hours, when I finished talking at him, he calmly spoke and asked me, "Do you know of the universal law that unites all things great and small, dead or alive?"

"Huh?" I grunted, like the world's first Neanderthal man.

"Have you not heard of the Universal Law of Polarities?" he asked, slightly surprised by my ignorance.

"What are you talking about?" I asked, completely ignorant.

He looked disappointedly down at the floor as if bowing to His Excellence, the Royal King of Ignorance that I realised I had become at my prime age of twenty-one.

The small Buddhist monk went on to explain the law of opposites that makes up the fabric of our immense universe that sheds light on the goodness of God and the evil darkness in the Satanic. My mind remained centred between my living, conscious spirit and the hollow emptiness I now understood as death.

"Everything in this universe has two sides that oppose each other." He spoke with a gentle tone. "Look around and you will see through the air there are solids that stop the light of vision. Beyond that there will be darkness. Look up, then down. East or west, in or out, and you will always find polarities. These are the opposites that we need to look at when living our lives to reach our journey's end we call death. Women have men, predators have prey, gas has solids, fire has water, knowledge has ignorance, and good has evil," he continued sombrely.

"You are a living creature that has experienced the dead of our cosmos. That is a unique blessing. But now, as you have spoken mostly for over an hour, you need to sit in quiet meditation and reflect on what you have said to me in silence for the same period of time. Look deep within and find the answers to your questions and the solutions to your problems. They are all within you, if you harness all your energies to remain centred and neutral from bias or prejudice, you will find peace of mind and harmony in your spirit. Not happiness or sadness, only contentedness."

I remember a long pause as he stared, studying me.

"Seek now and you will find what it is that the negative forces do not want you to know, and find what the positive forces want you to see."

As I sat there facing him with a numbed expression of disbelief, he stood up and walked away. Leaving me alone at the feet of the gigantic statue of Buddha, sitting cross-legged as I was. My mind drifted and I closed my eyes to block out the light. In the newfound darkness I was surprised to think about the Dreamtime, the Australian Aboriginal belief that I'd heard about from an Aboriginal elder and neighbour called Mr Daily. He had said, "The Dreamtime has no beginning and no end, we are always living in the Dreamtime …"

I focused all my energy to conceptualise the very tip of a peak on a mountain. Here, I sat with my left and my right hands holding decisions to be made. Questions to be asked, dreams to be realised, and fantasies to be forgotten: these were concepts that would influence many decisions in the years to come.

What the Buddhist taught me without so many words was to open my mind and continue learning before making raced decisions. Time seemed to stop as moments passed and the hunger pains awoke me from a deep trance in thoughts that mirrored my life. However, I lacked intellectual academic knowledge and had little understanding of the human spirit or complex systems like governance, international relations, and many other deep philosophical revelations.

The universal law of opposites had never even crossed my mind. I was simply happy to live and let be without complicating my life with knowledge.

The little monk never returned and I finally left the temple feeling empty and rejected. Yet his words still echoed in my head every time there was a moment of crisis or a decision to be made. I continue to look for balance and maintain equilibrium when making decisions or passing judgment. This was the main reason I refused to accept what our media was telling me until I could hear the other side of the story. Why didn't we hear Saddam Hussein speak and give us his account with the opportunity to argue through the world media?

What I learned later in Baghdad, was that Saddam had asked George W. Bush for a peaceful and intelligent debate to be broadcast for the world to understand the Iraqi argument for peace. However, Bush had denied Saddam that peaceful request.

The truth, I would learn, was criminally hurtful.

Chapter 5
The Third World

*I gave my heart and soul to stop you
[the Tony Blair administration] from committing
the disaster that you did commit by invading Iraq.*
George Galloway
British politician

What is the cause for the existing third world nations? I often wondered as I walked the Earth witnessing many man-made tragedies. While I travelled on my journeys, there were moments to reflect on my life. Often we hear our family and friends voices echo and we resolve complex problems with clarity. As we approached Jordan, my nerves seemed to intensify. There was comfort in recalling my own hajj many years before on board the *Nova Vida*. By delving into my past, I recalled the main drive and real reason for going to Iraq.

After a month traveling around Sri Lanka, we sailed across the Indian Ocean into Aden and then up through the Red Sea into Port Sudan. In 1985 and 1986 Sudan was experiencing a severe drought and like many third world nations, was divided by civil war.

When we arrived in Port Sudan a large cargo ship with the word BAND-AID was unloading donated cargo of foods, medicines, and drinking water. It was concerning to know that with so many royal monarchs and sultans, with the vast number of billionaires and millionaires, and the growing need to create new industries in travel, education, research, and exploration, only one English man Sir Bob Geldof was able to unite the world to help the third world.

It was in Sudan that I would confront the poverty, the hardship, and the total desperation of the third world. In Sri Lanka, the crippled children begged to beggars who themselves begged from the poorest people I had ever seen. However, in Sudan, the full horror of the third world existence was about to awaken me to the reality that hell was a man-made destination.

Having spent six weeks at sea, I decided to travel inland to the town of Kassala, where I was told a mass of refugees had come from Ethiopia seeking Sudanese help. The only bus that was scheduled to leave Port Sudan was like an American yellow school bus now painted in a kaleidoscope of bright colours. It was almost symbolic that this old school bus that transported American school children should be transporting Africans who were less privileged than slaves.

It was due to leave early in the morning and to my surprise it was jammed packed full with people riding on the roof and many others sitting in the walking aisles. Shame was cast upon me when the bus operators moved people from the front seat so that I, as the only white man, would be seated in the best spot. This experience was horribly embarrassing as I could see everyone in the bus from the driver's rear vision mirror staring at me with heartrending contempt.

The journey to Kassala would be most memorable not for the beautiful landscapes, the picturesque dry river beds we crossed, the buzz of small towns, or the sense of adventure that kept us alert and sensitive to our surroundings; but for when hell opened the gates and before my eyes Satan's demons greeted me. This was the refugee town of Kassala.

To be the only white man that stepped from the old bus, I was an instant attraction gaining celebrity status, nay, royalty. A sultan among paupers, strong among the weak. Healthy, among lepers, wealthy among beggars, and wise among hawkers. Like a white light of hope, I became a shining star to so many, which resulted in a mini riot as armed militants and police cleared the black sea of pleading hands and whimpering voices so I may walk freely to a nearby hostel with a police escort. Here, I dug my grave, and in the darkness of that flea-infested mud-floored hut, I wept and I wept until sleep overcame the reality that hell was a man-made construct in our very own world.

The following day I awoke before sunrise and was able to walk around the town mostly unnoticed, disguised, the only white man with a tea towel over my head and covering my face like some Arab sultan. I remember the smell of rotting flesh that wormed its way through pockets of rancid air and my recently punctured lungs inflated with hatred, fear, and physical paranoia that I had not yet experienced either death or hell.

I walked through a sea of shanties; temporary shelters made from cardboard boxes and oil drums pressed as cladding and plastic garbage bags as curtains that waved gently like flaps on a tent. I knew there were people inside these shelters. However most slept under the stars; stars that would soon be swallowed by the heat of the rising sun's rays.

Whilst walking amongst the poorest shanty towns on our Earth, I remembered a phrase that inspired some courage to walk further: 'Angels whisper to a person that walks'. Thus I continued to walk until I reached the outskirts of this shanty-town.

There, in the middle of my walk, I noticed a small group of three children huddled together. Their skeletal frames were joined by wrinkled skin that remained motionless, making me believe they were dead. Their wide open protruding eyes stared aimlessly toward the rising morning twilight. It was as if they had died with the disbelief that they had to endure another day of this torturous life with the hunger of hell.

As I stared down in complete disbelief at this abomination, I grasped the horrific understanding that terrorists live amongst us. These deaths were taking place all around me, not in the hundreds, but in the tens of thousands. With tears dropping freely on the powdery Earth, I wept as if my own mother had died.

It was like Satan had successfully consumed their souls, slowly savouring their tormented agony. Across the road, other bodies lay sleeping or dying under the sky. Beyond them, more bodies, and as I looked around I realised I had walked into the valley of death where the fate of all who were brought here was already predetermined. I stared down at these children, fighting the growing pain in my throat that was now aching to explode with more tears.

Suddenly, one of the boys gasped loudly for air and stared right into my eyes, frightening me to my wits. His dark, piercing pupils pleaded with me to help, to rescue, to do something, anything—to prevent him from dying like that. Dying from hunger, from a curable disease. Without his mother, his father! Next to what may have been his brothers or sisters! With no dignity, no crime or reason. God, no, God, have mercy … I wept aloud in fear of this satanic wrath.

Asking for help was meaningless. Yet instinctively I looked around for some help, but there was no one around. The few people that walked nearby were themselves at death's door and there simply was no one to help anyone as this sea of dying and dead bodies slowly perished as statistics rather than the individual lives they all represented. How dare we praise stick-thin fashion models or celebrities when we have children dying of starvation? I would forever ask this question.

I had never felt so powerless in my life. All I could do was crouch down and hold that child's hand. With tears running down my face I stroked his hair and apologised for my ignorance, my selfishness, and my blind stupidity. Again, I looked for someone to help me, but I could only see walking skeletons and dying corpses. There was simply no one that could help these children and all I could think about was the Hollywood obsession with looking glamorous, paying for sex, overpriced fashion accessories, overfilled jewellery boxes, and the self-indulgence of drugs. Anything but to care for third world needs and pleads for help.

The look on that child's face would forever haunt me. I felt the guilt of my sins as I realised my ignorance was very much a part of the problem. I wept till there were no more tears to shed at this injustice, as there was no way of saving this child. I wanted to take them to a hospital but I had already learned that there was no hospital in this shanty-town, only one UNICEF office and an International Red Cross tent, which consisted of a large marquee and a handful of Westerners that would have been overworked, stressed, and under-paid. I handed those children some paper notes, but I doubted they would either live long enough or have strength enough to do anything with that money.

I waited for someone to come and help them, but none arrived. As they lay dying alone at the outskirts, I had the shocking realisation that these children had remained where they dropped, with no more energy to live. Soon their bodies would be picked up by the authorities and dumped in the nearby mass grave like meaningless waste, with no burial ritual, no blessings, and no family to sanctify their existence. *With so much money on Earth, there has to be someone or some people responsible for this holocaust?* I reasoned.

I turned away from those children with the vocational need and desire to learn. To study and to understand more about the world we live in. How could we be so powerless to allow these crimes to happen? On that morning, I vowed my allegiance to the third world.

Walking away was among the hardest things I had ever done in my life. I walked with a heavy burden that weighed me down and a deep, sincere guilt that to this date haunts me. However, I did promise them that I would find the culprits. And if I ever did find who it was that was guilty of this heinous crime, I would expose them to the world and fight relentlessly to ensure they were jailed for life as violators and the most dangerous criminals against humanity.

Now I had a reason to learn and thus continued my pilgrimage by crossing the Sahara Desert, and sailing down the Nile with Sudanese Muslim students where I asked questions and learned that Muslims truly were a spiritual, peace-loving people. When I arrived at Port Suez at the entrance of the Suez Canal, I visited a mosque and met Sheik Ali, a fragile yet wise elderly man that would teach me the strength of the Islamic faith.

Why is our Western media so obsessed with demonising Muslims? I asked myself as I began to learn the contrary. The truth of the matter was that Western and pro-Israel nations used the actions of an extreme few crazed criminals to punish, conquer, and expand the land grabs. So it was paradoxical to hear Sheik Ali teach me about Islam.

"To be a Muslim," Sheik Ali told me, "you must first be Jewish, then you must embrace Christianity, and finally you must learn more. Read, among other writing, the Qur'an," he advised me. "Then if you accept that the teachings of Prophet Mohammed, peace and blessings be upon him, are true, as the last prophet on Earth, then you can call yourself a Muslim," he said in a broken but understandable English.

We sat in the mosque and talked for a long time. I asked him questions, which he answered almost always with another question and without hesitation. We talked about the Jews, Christians, and the uniting father Abraham. We discussed world poverty, hunger, and social diseases. It was interesting to hear him say that mental illness was a worldwide concern and that only through education would we resolve such problems. He taught me the correct process of washing myself before prayer and the importance of praying as often as possible in order to find peace within. He explained the concepts of Eid, Ramadan, hajj, zarkat, and salah. These were the fundamentals of a Muslim way of life. But above all he emphasised several times the need for all humans to exercise self-discipline in both prayer and everyday life.

"A man without spirit can be a dangerous man," he said. "Can you imagine a world without law and order? Or imagine a man without a spiritual conscience?" He answered with questions.

I remained quiet, thinking about some of the people I knew who stopped reading books or learning.

I asked him about female circumcision.

"That is not an Islamic practice," he assured me. "That is tribal, mostly African," he said.

"But why are Muslim women treated like second-class citizens?" I asked him a common question among non-Muslim Westerners.

"Have you spoken to any Muslim women?" He answered again with a question.

"No, not really!"

"Then perhaps you should speak to some and ask them. Don't you think?"

"But am I allowed to speak to Muslim women as a non-Muslim?" I vocalised my ignorance about Islamic women.

"I see that you really do have a long learning path ahead of you. Don't they teach you anything about Islam in the West?' I thought his questions where aimed at challenging me to think on my own accord and inviting my reaction so that he would be able to demonstrate his point.

"No," I lied.

I had learned that Muslims were dirty and not trustworthy as they were all terrorists. Muslims beat their wives, oppressed their women, and circumcised their daughters. Muslims were evil and they would rob you if you turned your back on them. Muslims were barbaric and uncivilised. Muslims were the bad guys in films and books. Muslims stoned prostitutes to death, cut thieves' hands off, and killed murderers. They tortured their prisoners and would be a threat to world peace. But how could I tell him these things? How could I explain the total ignorance of the Western countries that were incapable of reading or understanding books, let alone the complexity of the noble Qur'an?

"Then I will send you an English translation of the Qur'an," he said humbly. "Read and study the contents and you will understand that we are all from the same family as brothers and sisters. Entitled to our own thoughts but committed to the same struggle in unifying humanity in the name of Allah, Allah the almighty and most merciful, this is a way of all humanity standing together as one. You will understand if you study and learn more about the Jewish Torah, the Christian Bible, and the holy Qur'an, that we are all linked with Allah. Is that okay?" he asked again.

"Yes, but how can Allah be merciful when there is so much hunger and poverty around the Islamic world whilst sultans indulge in absurd riches?" I asked him, slightly angry at his blind faith in the book he offered me to read.

"Ah—I see you are angry. And as you are a young man, you have the fighting instinct burning in you for retribution," he said patiently. "You see. Satan works in mysterious ways—"

"Satan?" I interrupted him. My image of Satan was the devil with horns, a long tail, and a pitched fork.

"Satan is the name we give to the evil forces of the universe. Just as we associate the good and positive forces with Allah, we see the negative actions of men and the harmful nature of our ignorance as the stupidity of Satan," he said calmly.

"But what if I don't believe in God or Satan?" I challenged his theological wisdom for my amusement.

"Then you know you are a fool that is happy to remain in the bliss of your own ignorance. You will probably drink alcohol, smoke, take drugs, and live a very sad, lonely, and confused existence. But that is also okay because that is what I mean by satanic forces and the world knows we need fools," he said, adding support and merit to the teachings of that little Buddhist monk in Sri Lanka.

A cold shiver ran up my spine and I began to understand more about the good and evil forces of the universe. At that point, I remembered the three children I killed indirectly with my ignorance near the Ethiopian border in Kassala. How could I have walked away from them so callously when I still had access to over three thousand American dollars in my wallet? Was it the evil forces at work? Or Satan's will? Or my own instinct to survive …?

"How does one become good and avoid evil actions?" I asked, now genuinely interested in wanting to do good things with my life so that the next time I died, I could die without regrets.

Sheik Ali smiled and with a warm tone in his voice he said, "First you must change yourself from the ignorant materialistic man and learn to embrace the spiritual generosity of a believer." He paused to ensure I would digest what he had said. "Do you understand?" he asked.

I wanted to smack him for insulting me, but I realised the hurt was the result of truths in what he had just called me. So I bit my tongue and asked him to explain. "Um no, what do you mean?"

"Well, evil lurks everywhere, and none stronger than where power and ignorance can be found. You see, Islam is more about the self-control and total respect for the goodness in Allah, the merciful and compassionate. Islam is about gaining knowledge, reading and writing poetry rather than consuming drugs or alcohol … this way, we avoid being tempted by evil deeds. Do you know what I mean?" he returned the question.

"I think so," I said, knowing that white-collar criminals; corruption; corporate theft; drug and alcohol sales; prostitution; rape; weapon manufacturing; murder; domestic violence; and slavery were man-made constructs that flourished in the free world of the West. These were negative actions toward humanity and crimes committed by the spiritually poor and materialistically wealthy.

"What is important is that you fight any temptation that gives evil any justification. So if you want to fight for justice, you must first learn to use your spirit with your brains and not your body with the physical violence," he said, pointing to his heart.

"What about terrorists?" I asked him.

"Oh, terrorism is not an Islamic invention. Terrorists are just individuals who lost loved ones to an unjust act, and they exercise their right to avenge their families. Do you think that if every Israeli soldier that killed an innocent Palestinian was charged for murder, do you honestly believe that only a handful of terrorists would exist? Remember that the British have Irish terrorists, the Spanish have Basque terrorists, Africans have white terrorists, in Palestine they have Israeli terrorists and vice versa. You see, Muslims are not terrorists. A terrorist can be any individual. In America the Ku Klux Klan terrorise their own people and drug-crazed individuals terrorise their own neighbourhoods."

Naturally, the way he described terrorists was not exactly as I remember, but it was along those lines, which made more sense than the way our pro-Western and Pro-Israeli propaganda made us believe.

A few years later, a white North American Christian man detonated a massive bomb that killed over one hundred and sixty-eight innocent souls while injuring over six hundred others. This was described as the worst act of terrorism in North America before the Twin Towers of New York were attacked.

In the 1940s, The Stern Gang was a Jewish terrorist organisation who not only killed and threatened Palestinians, they also killed a United Nations convoy. The fact is that terrorism is not a Muslim construct.

"All you need to do is remember, in Islam, we believe that the pen is mightier than the sword. So what you need to do is ask more questions before you pass judgment. Ask yourself, what is it that you haven't read and have yet to read?" he asked, challenging my undeveloped intellect.

"You mean the Qur'an?"

"That's just one of many books you need to read if you want to find answers," he said encouragingly.

"I guess there is much more to learn other than the Qur'an." I acknowledged the tormenting truth to my ignorance.

"Yes we do, you are not alone," he said with a comforting smile.

"What about the differences between Shiite and Sunni? How will I know what I am?" I asked him, curious to know more about the Islamic beliefs.

"Ah, Shiite and Sunni are the same. We are all Muslims, brothers from the same family. You will know what you are when you pray as you will know what feels more comfortable to you … because we are all the same family of Muslims … do you know what I mean?"

"No, because I know that Shiites and Sunnis are killing each other," I challenged him.

"But that is not so," he assured me. "That is just what the Western media wants you to believe. Do you think thugs, hoods, and gangs walk only in the Western nations?" He continued to answer with questions and again I was forced to think.

"No."

"So who says that Shiites and Sunnis are so different that they will kill each other?"

"That is what we are told in our media."

"Ah, it makes sense to me now," he concluded. "That is an old strategy used to divide and conquer a people. You see, like in 1975 the Israelis started the war in Lebanon between the Christians and the Muslims. Or the war between Iraq and Iran, which I believe the Americans started with economic interests of their own. It seems that now the American propaganda machine wants to divide the Shiites and Sunnis when all we have are crooks, thugs, and gangs fighting each other like American gangs. No different than, I believe, in your country. Does that make sense?"

"Yes," I replied, remembering the terrorist that shot me.

"People don't want war. Only those with an interest like weapon manufacturing companies, or those who know they have nothing to lose and everything to gain, like governments, want wars," he concluded.

As I recalled that meeting with Sheik Ali from Suez, I felt a sense of relief. But I was not aware that my going to Baghdad was going to comply with my promise to the three dying children and the growing third world. Or that I may learn to respect and understand Islam as a fundamentally good philosophy that teaches more good than the evils of justifying war.

Chapter 6
Family Traditions

Nepotism. n: Favouritism shown by somebody in power to relatives and friends, especially in appointing them to good positions over better-qualified or more suitable people.

However, the real value of Islam did not become clear to me until I reached my birthplace on the Mediterranean town of Torrox. There I was greeted and welcomed with open arms, warm hugs, and loving kisses. At the time, I didn't know that the visit to my grandparent's house would mark the end of my pilgrimage. These two old and fragile people would finally teach me the most important lessons of my travels, as they placed all values and importance on the roots of the family.

"Are you strong enough to walk with me?" my grandfather asked me one day as we sat facing the sun to the east of the terrace overlooking the Andalusian Highlands to the north and the Mediterranean Sea to the south with our backs to the west.

"I'm strong enough to run!" I challenged this old man, who stood over six feet tall and at ninety-three years of age held an upright posture with broad shoulders that had undoubtedly carried the weight of our entire family.

"Where are you going now?" my petite four-feet-nothing hunchbacked grandmother asked with a whine in her tone and a squint in her eyes.

It always amazed me that this tiny woman had given birth to eight children. All my uncles and aunts where big-boned and heavily built. This tiny woman had given birth to all of them and weathered wars, depressions, famine, and social isolation. Yet all were happy to just live in the most simplistic and carefree lifestyle I ever had the pleasure of learning from.

"For a walk, woman, is that alright with you?" he asked for her approval.

"Where are you going to walk to?" she demanded to know.

"To the plaza," he answered.

"You're not going to take Al to meet those silly mates of yours in the plaza, are you?" her interrogations continued.

"No," he replied, almost apologetic as he gathered his beanie.

"Well don't go too far, you hear? I want you back here in twenty minutes or you aren't eating tonight, hear me?" she threatened this giant man that stood taller than me. I laughed inside as he made a face whilst her back was turned and motioned for us to run away before her demands increased.

"Women, they're never happy if they don't have something to talk about or criticise," he said as we walked outside.

The street was too small for cars but just wide enough for donkeys, mules, horses, and oxen to carry sacks of cargo, comfortably missing the adjacent all-white terraces.

We walked along the narrow lanes and alleys, climbing elongated steps that stopped at the very top of the town where we finally sat in the shadow cast under an old olive tree. It was a perfect spring day complete with a rich marine blue sky, complementing the aqua clear blue sea deep down in the distance. Light seemed brighter, sharper, and clearer than ever I had seen as I looked all around the 360-degree views.

"It looks amazing," I said to him as I looked around the spectacular views with colours that seemed to be alive with celestial richness. But he just looked out toward the sea and remained silent, in a trance. His bright blue eyes now reflected a mix between the marine blue Andalusian sky and the aqua blue Mediterranean Sea.

"We came from there," he said, breaking the eerie silence and pointing to the Mediterranean past the all-white village below us.

"What do you mean we came from there?" I asked him, not sure what he was talking about.

"Our family, your great grandfathers, our ancestors ... we all came from the sea and settled here because there was no one here," he answered.

"You mean we are not Spanish?" I asked him, horrified to think I had been duped for so long.

"Yes, we are all Spanish. In fact, the whole world is Spanish. Spain is a bastard country that belongs to the world and we are all kings," he said, preparing me for a long lecture and perhaps a domestic argument as I recalled my fragile grandmother waiting anxiously for her lifelong companion.

"What do you mean?" I asked him to clarify.

"We came here because we are a royal family," he said, looking at me as if to see my reaction. I dismissed his delusional comment by staying motionless and staring out to the blue Mediterranean Sea. "You will see many in Spain wave the Spanish flag with a bull and we are bulls. That's why we're more Spanish than King Juan Carlos. Because King Juan Carlos is the king of Bon Bon. Not the King of Spain as Franco wanted us to believe," he said with a proud smile. "You see, our ancestors came on ships from the sea and others came on horseback from Leon. They wore horns on their head and covered their bodies in thick furs that made us look like a Minotaur to our enemies. That's why we are called Toro [bull] and our town called Torrox [many bulls]."

As he spoke, I had images of the Scandinavian Vikings arriving on long boats and inhabiting this remote mountainous region.

"And ever since our ancestors have seen the passing armies from the Iberian Indians to the Greeks, the Romans, the Phoenicians, Celts, and the Arabs. That's why this country is the bastard country in the middle of Europe and Africa … that's why we have Celts next to the Gaelic, we have Arabs and Catalans, Africans and Persian Gypsies, or communities that have travelled from China, Iran, and India."

As he continued my family history lesson, it was easy to picture Iberian Indians that had settled in the Nerja caves going out to the coastal rocks and fishing from the rich sea life, Or the Greek, Roman, and Arab armies marching along the lower flats going from Malaga to Almeria.

While my grandfather spoke, I remembered Spain as being the first nation on Earth to unite seven autonomous regions, some with distinct languages under the one banner. In Toledo, Spain, the three faiths Judaism, Christianity, and Islam collaborated and worked together for the first time. It was this unity that later established Spain as the leading empire of the seventeenth century. It was this unity that England later used as a role model to establish the United Kingdom. It was the same unity that united the very different states of America, and now the European Union, the Soviet Union, and the People's Republic of China, that united hundreds of different cities and regions as the one great nation. The fact was obvious that for mankind to co-exist in this limited space we call Earth, we would all need to unite when the natural environment threatened all of us.

Looking around the environment from the top of that hill on the town of Torrox, one could see the damage caused by our ancestors as they cut down the forests to build fishing boats, houses, bridges, and to fuel their burning ovens and open fire stoves. Now the mountains remain treeless and the farms produce avocados, olives, corn, almonds, sugar cane, grapes, and a wide range of vegetable produce that had been grown under the warm Andalusian sun.

"Over the centuries, our ancestors have learned to protect the wealth of this land and to live together with people that are different to us," he continued. "You see, our town has produced great people and outstanding women like your grandmother and your mother," he said, making me feel proud of my mother, "and warriors like Al Mansour[3]," he added abruptly. I was transfixed to hear my grandfather use the word 'warrior'.

I had grown up in the warmongering Hollywood hero era that encouraged young influential men and women to join the armed forces. But my grandfather was a country farmer and a gentleman. At least that's what I thought. From all accounts, he had been described as a passive and humble family man, so to hear my grandfather talk about a warrior like Al Mansour was surprising. Yet proof that the warrior instinct was innate in the most passive one of us.

"But wasn't Al Mansour a Muslim. An Arab Moor?" I asked him, knowing a little about the legacy of the Andalusians that helped make Spain and Portugal a Muslim nation for over 800 years.

"Yes, he was a Muslim Moor, but he was also one of the few educated emperors that knew Torrox has the best climate in Europe. Many of the best-educated families came to live in Torrox, but Al Mansour also learned the skills of war and governance from here," he answered.

"What do you mean?" I asked, fascinated with my brainwashed desire to become a crazed soldier killing hordes of bad ugly terrorists and bad ugly bad guys like a Hollywood warrior one sees in the movies.

---

3   Abu Aamir Muhammad ibn Abdullah ibn Abi Aamir, al-Hajib al-Mansur (Arabic: أبو عامر محمد بن عبد الله بن أبي عامر الحاجب المنصور) (c. 938—August 8, 1002) better known as **Almanzor**, was the *de facto* ruler of Muslim al-Andalus in the late 10th to early 11th centuries. His rule marked the peak of power for Moorish Iberia.

He inhaled slowly, inflating his large ninety-three-year-old chest, and spoke softly. "I mean he was well-educated and had no fear of fighting for what is right—and without the fear of dying!" he added.

"But death doesn't scare me," I admitted, having died and realised the painless ecstasy of death. "It's not dying that scares," I confessed my indifference to death. "It's *not doing something* with my life that scares me," I admitted my fear.

"I know," he conceded.

"So what are you trying to tell me?" I asked, puzzled by his intuitive remarks.

"I'm going to tell you a family secret," he whispered softly, as if someone could hear us on top of the mountain. "But you can do with it as you wish," he continued. "As I said before, our family is very different; here in Torrox we found the best climate in Europe and it's been our home ever since—the best-educated families learned this secret. I have taught all my eight children to be individuals. That's what my grandfather taught me and now I teach you ..." He paused to take in some fresh highland air and then continued. "But more importantly, we don't tolerate greed in our family. I have taught my children to fight for what is right just as my father was taught by his grandfather. Understand?"

I nodded, encouraging him to continue.

"Well, we value our good health, that is what makes us happy with what we have, and not wanting more than we need is how I have raised my eight children. That is how our ancestors have survived in this town for so long."

"Where are you going with this?" I asked, wondering about the great family secret and thinking about the peaceful and articulated life of the Celts, the Saxons, and the Scandinavian Vikings as they had set sail along the Western European coast line to reach Torrox.

"Let me explain," he continued. "By living the simple life and not wanting more than what we already have, we have always assimilated and changed, be it the Greeks, the Romans, or the Arabs—or whoever is infected by that disease called greed. All that is important is that we have control of our own destiny," he explained. "That's what makes us kings," he said proudly.

"Kings?" I asked him, trying to make sense of this hyperbole.

"Yes, kings. As only kings have the control of their own destiny and the interest of others at heart," he answered my curiosity.

It was all making sense to me. The Spanish were the first people on Earth to unite different cultures, languages, and customs under the one flag. This unity was later used by English monarchs to create the United Kingdom, the United States of America, and now the European Union. In effect, it gave the individuals the right to live as free, liberated people. However, there were other external forces with interests in the division to conquer this Spanish sovereignty.

"But how can we control our own destiny if we are not in control of our lands?" I asked, confused by what he was saying to me.

"I'll tell you. That is why I have brought you here," he said, now looking directly into my eyes.

At that instant, I knew there was no doubt that this old man was my grandfather, as the colour of his eyes matched the same shade of blue as mine and his white skin was as white as my own.

"You have moved to a new land that I know is down under," he said, pointing down to the ground.

It amused me to think that if it were possible to dig a hole through the Earth's core from Spain you would discover Australia.

"Australia is your new home now. That's where your father and my daughter have taken you to live." It was odd to hear him call my mother his daughter for the first and only time.

"Yes," I acknowledged humbly.

"There in Australia, is where the ships of our ancestors have taken you. But I understand that Aboriginal people owned that land before the English."

"That's right," I said.

I knew that after many years of Spanish barbarian colonisation and meaningless bloodshed, the Civilian democratically elected government of Spain returned the South American continents to those that inhabited it and many countries were created as a result, like Chile, Argentina, Peru, Bolivia, Mexico, Cuba, Columbia, and Venezuela. I also knew that the

French, Portuguese, Dutch, and more recently the English, were slowly returning the lands to the traditional indigenous people, like those of Hong Kong; Brazil; South Africa; Sri Lanka; Ivory Coast; Ghana; India; and Papua New Guinea.

It seemed that we, the first world, had finally understood that the injustices and pointless exercise of colonisation, along with occupation by force, could be replaced by the advantages of peace and free trade through diplomatic dialogue. World peace was becoming a true possibility. Diversity of cultures, the spice of life on Earth, was a healthy and conceivable reality.

"Well, I am concerned for you because I know that you have the fighting instinct that runs in our blood. I'm worried that you will become like most men that need to be in an army so that you don't need to think and only need to do whatever you are told whether those that control you are right or wrong," he added.

"Why do you say that?" I asked, feeling surprised at the similarity of our thoughts.

"Because you are no longer a child, you are now a man!" he said, casually turning his stare back toward the sea.

At that very moment, I felt a sense of pride that instinctively made me fill my lungs with air. I didn't realise how proud a man could feel to hear those words spoken to you for the first time by your own flesh and blood. My eyes gathered a tear contained only by that cursed male pride.

"But I'm not in the army," I said.

"I know, but in our blood, we have an instinct to fight for what is right so that we don't lose what we have worked for, our destiny or our lands ..." He paused to take in a big breath of this fresh mountaintop air, then continued. "You have a new home. There in Australia you will start your family. There in Australia, you will carry the traditions of the Toro's clan. It is there in Australia that you now call your home that I want you to take care of your mother and your family. You are a man and men sometimes need to fight to protect what they have but not to take away from another man by force, do you understand?" he asked, turning me around and looking straight in my eyes.

"Yes," I replied in earnest.

"Good, you're a bull," he flattered me.

Then he turned to face the Mediterranean again. I was amused by his willpower to walk me up here when I knew it would have been painful for his arthritic joints to cover the distance. I looked at him and as he continued to look toward the blue sea with his matching bright blue eyes, I noticed they were watering. At first I thought he was going to cry from sadness. But then, I realised it was a tear of joy—it was as if he had been waiting all his life for this moment.

"We better go or that woman won't feed us tonight," he said, standing.

As we stood, I gave him a strong bear-hug and as I did that we both burst out in delirious tears of joy, crying and laughing at the same time.

There we stood, two men embracing as the kings of our town Torrox, overtly crying, with tears running down both our faces, and laughing aloud. That day with my grandfather was a celestial moment in my life. It marked the end of my pilgrimage and the start of my life as a man. I would forever remember his words; above all, I would be inspired by the concluding sentence he used to sum up our visit to the mountaintop.

"Don't forget, you are a man, and you must stand up and fight for what is right."

They were almost identical to the words my own father had used after I had seen my sisters brawling. Perhaps the Palestinian men we called terrorists also had similar beliefs and were now defending with their lives. Perhaps the Israelis were now fighting Palestinians for the same reasons.

But what if the Americans invaded Iraq; would Iraqi men defend their land?

Above all, that day with my grandfather enlightened me about the importance for a family to remain together. Too often in the Western world families were getting married for the wrong reasons. The growing number of relationships that enjoyed the ecstasy of great sex before marriage seemed to credit the growing number of divorcing families. Perhaps there was some credence to the religious ideology that true love was worth waiting for, and only then for the great sex to begin.

My personal opinions on this subject were being reinforced as I studied the sexual revolution of the feminist movement as a heterosexual man after graduating from university. The truths I learned were terrorising. For example, it was sad that we were not educating the divorcing families about matrimonial dispute-solving techniques, or the importance for the child to see love as an endless challenge of problem-solving. Domestic violence alone in Australia makes terrorism insignificant. With two women getting killed by enraged men every week and countless numbers of children being abused, ignored, or institutionalized, Australians have too big of a social war within to be concerned about terrorists in foreign lands.

In fact, it was heart-wrenching to know we would be spending trillions of dollars in destroying lives, property, and our environment by bombing Iraq, rather than teaching our children and young families like my Grandfather was able to do in a single sitting against my grandmother's will.

However, as I would later learn, the real problems we faced were not from terrorists or from the divorcing families, but rather the legal regime that benefitted from absurd legal fees generated from the human error of ignorance. An industry that gained unfair advantages from their elite education and the assurance that education remained unaffordable or inaccessible to most of us who would at some stage of our lives require the absurdly expensive service of a western lawyer.

In Australia, England, and many Commonwealth nations, divorcing and separating families by the English law regime was a billion-dollar a year industry. Many lawyers, prosecutors, judges, and legal practitioners would enjoy the benefits of disputing families that went to court from sheer desperation, rather than encouraging our governments to invest in educating our children and young families on the benefits of family dispute resolutions, such as those taught in the holy books. Our law-makers created and invented new complex laws at will. The financial gains to our law industry were absurdly astronomical for a few.

However, the war against poverty and ignorance was yet to come.

Chapter 7
The Cradle of Civilisation

Welcome to Baghdad, city for peace.
The people of Baghdad
(a phrase I heard repeatedly)

When I told my family and friends that I was going to Iraq, it became clear that the anti-Saddam propaganda was working. Everyone seemed to forget that Saddam had once been an American ally, fighting the Iranians. The Americans were as happy to sell Saddam the weapons he needed to fight the Iranians as they were selling them to the Afghans during the soviet era—something the movie *Charlie Wilson's War*[4] clearly demonstrates.

I was advised time and time again that I was going to be killed or captured and tortured by Saddam's loyalists or worse, by terrorists. It seemed that terrorists had become the greatest threat to humanity and were responsible for killing more people than cancer, domestic violence, drug abuse, and the many diseases in the modern world that our nurses, doctors, and scientists are fighting with every day in our overfilled hospitals.

However, having worked for the British newspaper tabloids, my understanding that our media was not immune from propagating our political leaders interests made it necessary to see for myself what we were not told or shown. Simply by following my basic instinct to learn the truth, I was now labelled a traitor; a madman; a Saddam sympathiser; a selfish prick; a terrorist; a raghead; and an array of other condescending terms merely for wanting to know the truth.

I began to understand how the apostles must have felt when they wanted to learn more from the wisdom of Jesus Christ and had to face a barrage of criticism from the mostly ignorant society of that time. Perhaps the prophet Mohamed or Islam in general was also victimised by what I learned to call 'the regime of the English law'—which could not operate if the simplicity of Sharia Law was implemented.

---

4   *Charlie Wilson's War* is a true story of U.S. Congressman Charlie Wilson who partnered with CIA operative Gust Avrakotos to launch Operation Cyclone, a program to organise and support the Afghan mujahideen during the Soviet war in Afghanistan.

But, I was no apostle. I was part of the ignorant masses following what the mass media had me believe. The media policy to incite fear amongst the Western populations to justify an invasion was successful, and I too was now terrorised by the fear that terrorists were going to lynch and torture me. Sleep was now impossible, so as everyone on the airplane slept, I read the newspaper.

What I read was an article about the voluntary Human Shields. I couldn't believe that some people were so opposed to this war that they were willing to risk their lives to stop a war. Who on Earth would be willing to die to protect complete strangers? 'Loonies' the newspaper called them.

When I turned the newspaper page there was an article highlighting the UNICEF estimation asserting that ten million children were being abused, traded as sex slaves, and prostituted *every year*.

Did that mean there were ten million paedophile terrorists lurking around to pay tens of thousands of dollars for the sickening privilege of corrupting such divine innocence? Wasn't this statistic far worse than the Jewish Holocaust? I was truly going mad and out of my mind.

Were not the Western tourists who visited third world nations to prey on children for their sexual pleasures a greater scourge than terrorists? Wasn't world hunger a greater threat to humanity than a handful of crazed lunatics we labelled as terrorists? Like so many others, I simply did not buy the Bush administration's propaganda. So I went to Iraq.

"Ladies and gentlemen, please be advised that due to recent terrorist activities in America, all Muslim passengers visiting the United States may be fingerprinted, photographed, labelled, numbered, and filed as potential threats to world peace," a courteous young female voice read out across the personal address speakers on the flight. But it was my imagination, and instead she said: "We will be landing in Jordan shortly, please fasten your seat belts." Reality snapped back.

It was Valentine's Day. 14 February 2003. A day where love was celebrated worldwide and I should have been thinking of love, not war. I was already saddened to be leaving Sydney, the city of love and romance, on this St Valentine's Day, to visit Baghdad, the city of peace and war.

Fortunately, I had the intelligence to understand that there was more chance of being killed by a poor and ignorant criminal in the West than by a terrorist in the Middle East. So shortly after the plane touched down in the Queen Alia Airport in Jordan, I jumped on a bus to the main centre and quickly organised my taxi ride to Baghdad.

I paid fifteen dollars for the 500-kilometre taxi trip to Baghdad. In Australia, fifteen dollars was what we would pay to go from the city to the airport, about ten kilometres. However, I had to share it with three other Iraqi men also going to Baghdad. I was instantly mortified at the thought that I would be lynched along the way. *Perhaps they are Saddam's spies monitoring my movement or Al Qaeda operatives who would decapitate me along the way*, I thought in fear, as we started our journey to Baghdad.

When we arrived at the Iraq-Jordan border, I was expecting a body search, interrogations, fingerprinting, photographs of me taken, and my details recorded in a data base of a policed state. But none of that happened as it happened when I visited America. Instead, the Iraqi guards greeted me in broken English and welcomed me to Iraq.

"What is the purpose of your visit?" a young Iraqi border guard asked me.

"To study," I replied.

"You are a student?" he asked me.

"Yes, a perpetual student," I replied, perplexing the young guard.

"Oh—okay, enjoy your visit to Iraq. Welcome to Iraq," he greeted me, and that was it. I crossed the border.

One older guard, the only one dressed in army greens, looked at me with the serious contempt of a battle-hardened fighter. The scars on his steel face seemed like credible evidence that he had seen war and fighting first-hand. But he too welcomed me and managed a welcoming smile.

When we left the border crossing, the first impression was stunning as we left the poorly-built Jordanian roads and drove onto an immaculate concrete road three lanes wide, heading into Baghdad. A similar road ran parallel in the opposite direction with clear road markings; well-measured safety rails; strong, well-built bridges; power poles that extended as far as the eye could see; and regular resting places along the road to Baghdad. As a truck driver and tourist around the UK and Europe, I qualified to assert this was amongst the best road I had ever driven on. Iraq was definitely not a third world nation. The government had spent large amounts of money on these roads, that was for certain.

As our taxi reached speeds in excess of 180km/p.h. I was now certain the taxi driver would kill us before the terrorists. I was given the front seat as the honoured guest so I tried to enjoy the mostly flat desert scenery. I pictured camel trains crossing this vast space of wasteland, watching lunar landscapes unfold and looking in awe as the setting sun cast spectacular shadows across distant hills and plateaus. I tried to calculate the millions of dollars it must have cost to have the thousands of kilometres of large towers that supplied electricity to remote desert locations. I wondered how the nomads and herdsmen could continue their ten thousand-year traditions and not have adapted to modern living. It seemed that time had stopped and frozen in Iraq. But her science and technology were threatening world peace with weapons of mass destruction.

When the taxi stopped to refill at a crossroads, my first revelation concerning the real reason for this war was clear to me. Oil was cheaper than water in Iraq. It cost $0.05c of refined, clean fuel in your tank per litre. Yes, five cents per litre of super high-grade gas. If I could sell that to the Western world, my mathematical brain calculated over 200% profit. Any money-hungry thief or criminal would see the logic of killing civilians to make such a profit. This crossroad stop was operated by several small family businesses competing with each other which allowed us to get a good feed and drinks for just a couple of dollars.

It was dark when I arrived in Baghdad and the bright orange streetlights illuminated the main roads that led to the centre of the city. I was surprised to see the main streets were well-kept, and people went about their business like any other city. For some reason, this was not what I was expecting.

I had never seen any modern film or documentary about Baghdad; such was the censorship in our Western media that I was expecting camels, tents, romantic oases, public executions, floggings, a policed state where people feared to venture into the streets. I expected to see military personnel stopping us at check points and secret undercover spies watching my every move—or at least, police check points stopping the traffic to inspect our documents or randomly breathalyse us.

This was supposed to be a brutal regime according to Richard Perle, the American Secretary of Defence that now acted as a main advisor to the Bush administration. Richard Perle was also the same person that in 1970 had given Israelis secret American military information, and later alleged in the 1980s that the Russians were breaching the nuclear treaty whilst all the American seismologists and American personnel disagreed with him. Indeed, Richard Perle had a demonstrated track record of manufacturing information to suit alternative agendas. So I was not surprised to see that now in Iraq, all my expectations were instantly shattered. It was simply astounding that the American intelligence agencies had not detected a psychotic madman in Richard Perle.

My first impression of Baghdad was that of a modern city built in the middle of a vast desert, where people roamed freely and children played along the streets as their mothers talked with neighbours or swept dust from pavements. Shops, restaurants, cafes, and merchants traded into the night. Traffic flowed in a controlled and orderly manner, and gangs of youth played street football as romantic couples walked hand-in-hand along the riverbanks.

People in Baghdad were indeed content to be living in peace.

By the time I arrived at the Palestine Hotel, I was exhausted. I checked in and quickly found my room. This was a five-star hotel yet all the furnishings, the carpet, and curtains were no less than thirteen years old. It was, nevertheless, so peacefully comfortable that I slept through to the late morning the next day.

After a long, warm bath, I went downstairs to the foyer and I realised that I was a day early for the NASYO convention. Yet, the excitement was already in the air as organisers and hotel staff hurried along with last minute preparations. So I decided to go for a walk.

Introducing myself to one of the men who seemed to have some authority, I asked him if it was okay for me to leave the hotel. He looked at me firstly with a surprised expression and then with a curious pity, as if not understanding why I should ask for permission. I never told him of my fear that I expected terrorists and hard-line Muslims to be waiting outside ready to lynch me.

"Mr Al," he said. "You are in Iraq. Here you are safe. We do not have gangs and drive-by shootings like America," he reassured me with broken English, and walked with me to the entrance of the hotel. "Please feel free to go anywhere you like. But please be sure to attend the opening conference tomorrow. We will leave here at nine tomorrow morning. Enjoy your visit." He walked me outside and waved me goodbye. *This may be the last person I talk to*, I thought in my growing hysteric paranoia that made me understand how Richard Perle must think.

It was now Saturday 16 February 2003. I stepped into the Baghdad sun and my pupils dilated to greet the clean, crisp, perfectly blue sky. I asked a taxi driver to point me toward the city and he guided me in the right direction. As I walked away from the Palestine Hotel, I noted a large bronze statue saluting in the same direction of the city centre. There was no mistaking that monument as a salute to Saddam Hussein. This was a high-density population area with apartment blocks surrounding the neighbourhood. If that statue was ever toppled by coalition forces, this plaza would fill with tens of thousands of anti-Saddam demonstrators, I reasoned as I walked passed it. This was also the same statue that an American GI covered with an American flag and only a few months later several hundred demonstrators toppled it.

My most memorable first impression when I walked along the streets expecting to be kidnapped, shot, or lynched by the secret police, was that nobody took any notice of me. It was unlike the Sudan experience; people here all went about their own business of shopping or traveling to work; busses carried commuters; taxis negotiated traffic; children played or went to schools; and shopkeepers attended their businesses. Did anyone know there was a war looming? I wondered this as I continued my walk.

It seemed like any other city, only the visible signs of neglect from a failing economy made one aware that things were not all right in Baghdad. As I walked toward the centre I stopped at shops to look at the merchandise and study the brands, the quantities, the prices, and the stock. It was obvious that this city was surviving on a minimum of rations.

There was a complete lack of modern technologies like mobile phones, computers, satellite dishes, and other electronic equipment. Automatic Teller Machines were obsolete and an internet café was not even invented here yet.

The cinema theatres showed old Arabic films, mostly romance and comedy. Bottle shops stocked a handful of alcoholic beverages. Single bottles were placed on display in mostly empty shelves: scotch whiskey, Russian vodkas, and French champagne perhaps smuggled in or unsold as the Muslim majority would not have purchased alcoholic drinks.

Fashion shops mostly displayed simple garments and mannequins often remained naked, waiting to be adorned with new clothes. Most of the fashion in this wealthy nation had remained in the eighties.

The one business that seemed to flourish was the newspaper stands and the print media. While curb-side libraries sprawled a healthy supply of newspapers, magazines, and books in a variety of languages, Arabic reading material dominated the stands. Was all this print media censored or did the Iraqi people, who invented communication, law, order, and civilisation, also practice the freedom of speech? I began questioning what I was seeing.

As I walked further along I saw a Catholic church that was well-preserved with stained glass showing the twelve apostles beneath a rising sun. The doors were opened and some elderly ladies slowly walked in peace to the outside world.

Another striking observation was the Iraqi police force that slept in their cars at main traffic intersections. Booted feet hung out front police car windows, and police caps covered their eyes. During peak times these traffic police would stand in the midst of traffic acting out the human traffic light functions. However, the Baghdad traffic often disobeyed the police instructions, running through clear indications to stop and sounding their horns in the process as if the police officer didn't know what he was doing.

Like any other city built around a desert, the streets were dusty and some litter could be seen in the gutters. However it was not unusual to see the same amounts of litter at this time of the day in any modern city. The street cleaners were visible but mostly in the early morning and then later, after the evening traffic. Council workers repaired paths and broken water pipes and cleaned the streets.

The one confronting difference between this and any other city I had visited along my travels, was that Baghdad seemed to have remained in the eighties.

It didn't take long to realise it was not Saddam Hussein's regime that impoverished these people, but something far more sinister, far greater an evil than the hard-line government of the Iraqi Ba'ath party; it was called economic sanctions. Were other countries with economic sanctions like Cuba, North Korea, and Iran destined to suffer the same fate of forced impoverishment?

After an hour walking around Baghdad, I stopped at one of many tea-serving carts and when it became evident that I didn't speak Arabic, the local men gathered around me like a novelty act. I braced myself and prepared to meet my fate as I expected to be knifed. "This is where I get lynched," I thought. But instead, they talked to me in broken English and some translated our conversation to other men who did not understand English.

"I am Mohamed," a young man introduced himself, offering me his hand in friendship. I told him my name and we shook hands. Soon, I was shaking hands with all the men that had gathered. But paranoia was still strong in my mind.

"You are American?" Mohamed asked.

"No!" I quickly answered, hoping I would not be killed just yet. "I am Spanish-Australian," I replied, wide-eyed, awaiting an assault.

"Spanish-Australian?" he asked, surprised at my answer.

"Yes. I was born in Spain, but I am an Australian citizen," I explained.

"Oh, I see," he said, and then translated to others that were gathering around me.

Pre-emptively, I started to review my street-fighting tactics, ready to strike and run for my life. So I looked over their shoulders and prepared my getaway plan. But others asked questions, which were translated from Arabic to English by the main speakers.

"Why are you here?" I was asked.

"To attend the NASYO conference," I replied.

"Ah, NASYO." Some seemed to understand the word NASYO. It was like a password, and suddenly they were more interested and they continued to ask more questions.

"You are teacher?" one asked.

"No," I answered quickly, releasing a nervous laugh. "I am student."

"What do you study Mr?" another young man asked from the back of the crowd.

"Humanities," I answered.

They spoke in Arabic amongst themselves as this answer was translated and discussed amongst them. Soon they all understood and continued my interrogation.

"You like Iraq, Mr?" another man asked.

"Well, it's my first day here."

The answer was translated and some laughed whilst others greeted me with warm welcomes.

"Welcome, Mister." They all seemed to know the word welcome.

"You speak good English?" I asked in return, to learn something before my capture.

"Yes Mister," he assured me. "Everyone here learns another language."

"Oh, I see," I said, dumbfounded.

"Tell me, why don't I see many women on the streets?" I asked, changing the conversation to the subject I knew all young men liked to talk about.

"They all sleep too much." Those that understood English laughed whilst the others awaited the translation and joined in the laughter later.

"Here, too many women lazy," Mohamed acknowledged with cynical laughter.

"When it's hot day like today, they stay inside and sleep," another man told me. "But you see at night, too many woman," he continued.

"You come to my house and eat, yes?" one invited.

I was instantly horrified. That would be a trap. I had only just met these men and I was being invited to their house for dinner? No way! That was a certain trap, I thought. I was well aware that tens of thousands of people went missing in the Western nations. Many were raped, tortured, and killed simply for sexual gratification whilst many others suffered from drug-induced mental illnesses or alcoholism, or hid to avoid family court impositions. Perhaps as many children went missing in Iraq as did in the US of A. I pondered, knowing that missing kidnapped children was a national disgrace in America. So I did not want to disappear in Baghdad.

"No, I'm sorry, I have dinner with important people in the hotel," I lied.

"Ah, I see," the disappointed invitee acknowledged. "Maybe another time okay?"

"Okay," I said as I pulled out some notes to pay for the tea.

"No!" My interrogator screamed. "I pay already."

I looked around the crowd of young men that had gathered and realised they were all smiling. This was a test, I thought.

"Yes, it's okay, I can pay," I said.

"No Mister," said the same guy that asked if I liked Iraq. "It is our custom to invite and pay for guests here," he explained.

"Oh." I grunted again like the ignorant barbarian that I realised I was as these men welcomed me with genuine interest in learning about me as a foreigner and a Western white man in Baghdad. Would they ever know how they would be humiliated, isolated, and threatened as wogs in Australia? Or fingerprinted and labelled as terrorists in the USA? The irony stunk.

As I walked aimlessly around Baghdad, I would turn around to see if there was anyone following me. But I could not see anyone. Then I thought about hidden cameras, but there was no way that this government could afford to import modern traffic lights, let alone high-tech surveillance equipment to keep a track on a student backpacker. Nor was I going to be bombed by a terrorist: terrorists had never bombed Baghdad at this stage. My ignorance of Iraqi people was absolute. The American media had successfully convinced me that Iraq was a brutal regime. Yet people here seemed happy, hospitable, and at peace.

It took about four hours to get over my media-induced paranoid psychosis and realise that these people were getting on with their lives as usual. They were not going to lynch me, or stone me to death, or arrest me for no apparent reason. I began to feel more at ease and was soon walking along the back streets of Baghdad in search of poorer and more disadvantaged people, to draw comparisons between wealthy and poor suburbs, to understand better the social and political environments at the street level in Baghdad. So I continued to walk anonymously. Like a hardened street-fighter, I was armed with a small pocketknife and I knew I would not hesitate to use it. The need to fight in the streets of Sydney, London, and Barcelona that I had experienced would never unfold in any Muslim nation I visited.

The backstreets and alleys of Baghdad were filled with children playing games, oblivious to the mounting coalition army of grown adult men that would soon start sending missiles in their direction. The paradox was now making me sick. These children would be oblivious to action war heroes, like Rambo, G.I. Jane, and the string of Hollywood fantasy heroes. Heroes that would influence the American military personnel to join the army and kill or destroy whoever their commander-in-chief wanted to kill or torture, irrespective of the truth or justice.

I remembered the misunderstanding we had in the Western world about the Muslims. How we believed that Muslim men demanded their women to stay indoors and cover their bodies from head to toe with shawls. As the sun went down and the temperatures dropped to cooler levels, more women, mostly younger girls, started to walk along the streets. Most of them wore hijabs, however the younger generation of girls showed of their long hair and wore tight, long slacks and more modern dresses. It seemed the elder ladies who I later learned were hajjis, wore all-black burkas. So I was surprised to learn that the hijab was a woman's choice and not the men's decision to make.

The truth was that we in the first world were more exposed to the policed state of George Orwell's 'big brother' than the Iraqis. We had special departments to monitor our taxes and our spending habits; cameras monitored our traffic speeds and our movements; we had departments to check our credit activities. We lived in bipolar existences with one law for the wealthy and another law for the poor. We had a private and exclusive education for the wealthy and a basic or rampant public education for the workers. We had traffic officers to book us if we parked illegally, council rangers that fined us if our dogs went astray, and road inspectors to ensure our vehicles complied with strict rules that at times seemed unfair for those who may struggle. The Western way of life was a policed state with two values: one for the masses and another for those that invented the laws.

In contrast, I learned that Iraqi and other Islamic states had the same laws and free education across the board. There was one basic and common law known to all the people. Sharia law was unambiguous and the same across the Islamic world. Iraq, like Iran and every other Muslim nation, had courts of law where the natural law of God rather than the man-made English laws or the European civil laws were used to pass judgements and sentences. The harsh penalties from Sharia law were now making me feel more comfortable and thus I began to feel safer. In simple terms, we had nothing to fear if we were not criminals in the Islamic world. However, George W. Bush knew too well that he could get away with murder or even genocide with his capacity to manufacture, invent, or adapt laws to his advantage.

As I continued to walk around Baghdad, the antique shops particularly interested me, as did the jewellery stands. In our Western nations jewellery was a product treasured and highly protected behind screen doors, monitoring devices, and in some cases special and private security guards would patrol the jewellery stores.

In Baghdad, however, shops that contained gold, diamonds, and assorted jewellery remained opened and inviting. It was as if thieves did not exist in Baghdad. There was gold in abundance and the antiques were sold at bargain prices. The Iraqi people lived relatively free lives, and only the obvious economic sanctions impoverished and crippled their lifestyles.

As the sun descended, the universe cast a sleepy eyelid across the Baghdad skyline. Tired workers returned to their homes and the marketers packed and stored their merchandise. Now the suburban streets came to life as more women and children came out onto the streets to talk with neighbours and friends or play street football on near-empty back streets. Many shops remained opened and restaurants now hosted families, lovers, and young university students that seemed to meet for discussions and debate that filled the cafes.

However, the American-led coalition of the willing were amassing and surrounding these peaceful people. American soldiers tuned their tanks, aiming their missile launchers and sharpening their knives in preparation for an invasion. I stared at some children and prayed to God that none of these children would be caught in the crossfire of what would later be called the 'shock and awe' tactics of the American military machines.

It was well after dark and I had walked continuously for most of the day. My first night in Baghdad would forever live in my mind as the personification of the free world: a city living in peace and enjoying the fruits of an educated population.

That night I walked along the Tigris riverbanks beneath a magical, clear night that shone with the same stars that all our ancestors had stared upon. Only now, the condemned people of Iraq lived oblivious from the amassing new-age crusaders surrounding their country.

The laughter of children playing, the romance of young couples wooing and talking along the Tigris river levy, and the old men and women that congregated in small groups made me sad to know the truth. The Tigris River flowed silently toward the waiting coalition of battleships in the Arabian Sea that now waited to bomb Baghdad.

By the time I arrived at the hotel, I was tired and had appeased my curiosity sufficiently to feel more comfortable in Baghdad. The Palestine Hotel lobby was now buzzing with more international students, academics, and media gathering for the conference. It was an exciting place to be and I walked around, smiling courteously at the multi-coloured faces from Africa, China, Japan, Europe, and the Americas. It was like the world was amassing here and I was amongst them.

Chapter 8
NASYO

The Non-Aligned Student Youth Organisation Conference
Hosted by Dr Huda Salih Malhdi Ammash
Deputy to Saddam Hussein
17–20 February 2003

The following morning a cosmopolitan breakfast was served by the hotel and then we were told to join some busses waiting outside. My Western media-influenced psychotic paranoia began to make me sweat, thinking that we were going to be taken to a concentration camp or a large open hole to be buried in a mass grave. Maybe they had gas showers here too. Saddam's evil regime would surely torture me first, I reasoned, as I walked to the waiting buses. After all, these people were primitive, unlike the sophisticated, intelligent, and military-disciplined Western world.

So when a young Middle Eastern man approached me asking me with a strong accent, "You speak English or parlez vous Francais?" I immediately thought he looked like a terrorist.

"Soy Español," I said, instinctively defensive.

"Huh?" he asked, looking puzzled.

"I am a Spanish-Australian," I replied, correcting myself.

"I am Ghassan, what is your name my friend?" he said, extending his hand in genuine friendship.

"I am Al," I replied suspiciously.

"Al. My friend, are you Australian or are you Spanish?" The interrogation had begun.

"I am both," I corrected myself. I had him confused now. I could see it in his face. *I have cleverly confused Saddam's secret police*, I thought now with internal pride, and smiled at him.

"Oh. I see. Okay well if you have any problem, please come see me okay friend? I am the NASYO English and French translator," he said. "Now you must please get in one bus there." He pointed in the direction of the waiting three yellow busses.

I felt ashamed. He wasn't the dreaded secret police at all, but rather, the English and French translator. Did I hear right? English and French? Oh well, maybe it was a mistake. So I followed the rest of the delegation onto the last bus. I thought the first bus would surely be the one to take the hit from the waiting terrorists.

As I sat alone in the back of the last bus, ready to break the back window at the first hint of an ambush and ready to run, I noted a beautiful young lady in her early twenties accompanied by an equally impressive young man. They both could have passed for Spaniards in their dress styles and manners. So when I heard them ask if there were any Spanish speakers in the bus, I quickly answered.

"Si, por que?" I asked and they approached me and introduced themselves in Spanish.

"I am Shaima, Sir," the girl said in perfect Spanish.

"And I am Ammar," the young man followed.

They explained that they were my translators and guides. I learned that all the translators were language students from Baghdad Central University and were given the opportunity to improve their language skills with foreigners as a way of gaining work experience. Their pay was in kind, as they would eat in the five-star hotels for free and practice their chosen language with foreigners.

Shaima sat next to me, which made me feel uncomfortable as I expected women and men to be sitting apart in public, but after looking around the bus I noted men and women sat together at random. My understanding of the Islamic world was incredibly shallow and wrong. Soon after, her fluency in Spanish had me feeling relaxed. I learned the main aim in Shaima's life was to visit Spain and continue her Spanish history studies at a Spanish university. I also learned that I was the only Spanish speaking delegate in the entire conference, which made me sad to think how the Spanish speaking world had too many problems of their own to afford to send a single delegate to this conference. Or perhaps they understood the uselessness of attending a condemned nation to avoid a war.

The buses took us to a large theatre hall. This was the first time the entire NASYO delegation had been together, and it gave us the opportunity to see academics from almost every nation seeking the answers to the many questions that remained to be answered so that we may understand why on Earth the Americans were going to war with Iraq.

It made me feel proud to be amongst Indians who sat next to Chinese; who sat next to French; who sat next to Germans; who sat next to Africans; who sat next to Japanese; who sat next to Arabs; who sat next to Jews ... in fact it seemed the whole world except for the Hispanics was sitting together for this lecture.

When the hall had filled, a band played the Iraqi national anthem and a small lady wearing a green army dress and semi-transparent shawl over her head stepped up on the stage and stood behind a podium with the posture of a university professor about to start a lecture.

I was sitting in the front row next to the exit door and was ready to run from the terrorists when they stormed the building, so I could see her perfectly.

She seemed to generate warmth and her aura was almost visible as she looked around, calmly absorbing the crowd and waiting for the national anthem to finish. When it finish, a man stood up and shouted something in Arabic and all the local population applauded whilst the international representatives in the conference sat watching, bemused, not understanding what was being said. Then another man stood, shouting something before all the Iraqis soon joined, breaking into a chant, clapping hands in a unified tempo. This went on for a while before a woman stood and shouted something and they all joined again for another chant.

"What are they chanting about?" I asked Shaima.

"Sir," she said with a broad grin on her face and a sense of national pride, "with our lives and our blood we will defend Saddam Hussein." Then she also started clapping and chanting.

After a few minutes, the petite lady wearing army greens spoke out and the hall went silent and listened. I could not understand a word she spoke as it was all in Arabic. But then she started again and seemed to repeat the earlier spill in near-perfect English. What impressed me the most was that she didn't read from cue cards; her speech was from the heart unlike others who needed speeches to be written so they may read what they didn't necessarily feel in their hearts.

"Ladies and gentlemen, NASYO-invited guests, students of the world, and friends of Iraq and observers for peace: welcome to Baghdad." She paused. "I am Dr Huda Salih Mahdi Ammash, the deputy member of the Ba'ath Party and I will be the host over the next few days. Today, we invite you here to see for yourselves our beloved city of Baghdad. We welcome you here to study and to learn more about the unjust nature of economic sanctions upon our people and we wish to show you how sanctions are a violation of human rights and a crime against humanity."

As she spoke, it occurred to me how little I knew about economic sanctions. So if my understanding about economic sanctions was minimal, and I was an addict for information, then how much did our leaders, or our intelligence agencies like ASIO; CIA; FBI; Mossad; MI5; CNI; AFP; or even our normal populations know?

"Iraq has pleaded for the international media and governments around the world to end the sanctions. We have been disarming and complying with the United Nations Security Council that we do not have any weapons of mass destruction and we have been disarming in accordance with international law so that we may have the economic sanctions lifted without further delay."

She continued to clarify that the Iraqi people needed peace and desired to resolve all confrontations amicably, through debate and diplomacy. She noted that Saddam Hussein had requested to debate with George W. Bush on international media but Mr Bush had denied this request. She spoke about Iraq's destruction of the al-Masaood missiles, which was the last line of defence, which now made Iraq completely defenceless. I knew this was being done with UN supervision as it was well-covered by the BBC just before I left Australia. She pleaded for the international delegations to make it clear to the coalition that Saddam had complied fully and possessed no biological or chemical weapons, let alone weapons of mass destruction as alleged by the Bush administration. She acknowledged that Iraq was the most invaded and most attacked country in history and thus had every right to a defence force; what the people of Iraq now wanted was lasting peace. Peace with Iran, the Kurds, and the Americans.

"No war. Yes peace," she said clearly in an exhausted tone and paused to gather her composure. At this point, the entire auditorium broke in applause, standing in united ovation. After the applause, someone stood up and repeated the words, screaming them in a chant.

"No war, yes peace, no war yes peace …" and the entire hall erupted to the same chant that went on for minutes as I looked around and everyone chanted with genuine optimism.

"No war yes peace," I chanted along with Shaima and Ammar, clapping to the beat. This made good sense to me. However I knew that the 'coalition of the willing' were prepared to defy the unanimous vote and go to a war with Iraq, and that they were surrounding us.

"We Iraqis have seen too much war and that's why we want to stop war," Dr Huda continued. "Over the next few days we would like to show you the devastating consequences of Economic sanctions on our people and our country. Much of my studies have been focused on learning about the long-term effects of American uranium depleted bombs—the shadows of which have been cast on our land for more than a decade.

'So we want to share with the world the immeasurable suffering of our people so that we may end the embargoes forever and make Americans accountable for using banned nuclear depleting bombs against our civilian population," she said sternly. This allegation was not just a violation of war crimes committed by the North American military, but a gross crime against our global environment.

Dr Huda went on to prepare the conference for the events of the next few days. She outlined the activities that were planned and concluded with the reassurance that there was not going to be a war as Saddam had agreed to all the UN demands and was complying in full. She thanked everyone and walked offstage to loud applause and a second standing ovation.

For a moment I believed her that there was not going to be a war. Such was the optimism from the Iraqi Ba'ath party.

After the conference, we returned to the hotel where Dr Huda hosted a more private conference with the international media and members of the NASYO delegation. I was sitting with Shaima and Ammar in the very middle of the front row of a passageway, as always ready for the quick exit, when a young and stunningly beautiful girl walked in and sat three seats away from me. She was accompanied by a tall, handsome man about my age, and a small, more rounded girl wearing tights, which seemed odd for a conference of this nature. They sat, attentive to the conference, taking notes, oblivious to the many stares they attracted as the youngest attendants of the conference.

Dr Huda gave a more detailed speech, mostly in English, as the convention was specifically for the international guests. Again, she spoke about Iraq's need and desire for peace, and how they had learned from the 1991 Gulf War and were complying in full and unconditionally with the United Nations to reach a peaceful solution. She spoke about how the embargo had crippled their country, causing immeasurable harm and suffering to the Iraqi people and the country's corporate sector; about how Iraq had paid compensation in full within seven years to the Americans, Kuwait, and the United Nations post the 1991 war.

As she spoke, she backed every aspect of her speech with dates, facts, figures, and resolution numbers. The international audience seemed impressed by this fragile lady who spoke without using notes or cue cards as her lecture was from the heart.

"On the sixth of August, 1990, the Security Council Resolution 661, 2nd paragraph forced Iraq to withdraw from Kuwait or economic sanctions on Iraq would be imposed," she stated as a matter of fact. "This was made by American officials and is arguably the most comprehensive regime to impoverish a country in our collective history," she continued.

"Iraq completely pulled out of Kuwait by the 28th of February 1991 and the economic sanctions should have been lifted. However, the American officials then asked for the disarmament of Iraq. The world turned a blind eye to the continuing violation of human rights faced by the Iraqi people as the rights to development were denied," she added. "We are the most attacked and invaded country in Earth's history and yet we agreed to disarm—but with rightful caution. Remember, we are surrounded by enemies that continue to attack our people, and now our once-ally America is joining our list of enemies simply because we made peace with our Iranian neighbours and stopped buying American weapons," she added sternly.

"On the 3rd of April 1991, Security Council Resolution 687 linked sanctions on Iraq with weapons of mass destruction and ordered the destruction of such weapons. We Iraqis fear the weapons of mass destruction possessed and used by the Israelis and Americans against Iraqi people. We have pleaded to the international community to end the persecution, the genocide, and the systematic killing of Palestinians by the Jewish military, yet the international community responds with bias and prejudices. We agreed to a ceasefire by the 1st of March 1991 so Iraq had no other option but to surrender and accept Security Council Resolution 687, under duress from the Americans.

'This was at the expense of destroying factories, exposing national security secrets and the destruction of many other weapons that made Iraq virtually defenceless against our enemies. If ever we did possess WMD now was the time to use them, but we simply did not have them as we have claimed time and time and time again," she asserted.

"By 1998, President George W. Bush insisted that presidential sites bigger than Washington are harbouring weapons of mass destruction and Tony Blair claims that these sites are bigger than Paris and supports the outrageous comments being made to justify their obsession with Iraq," she continued.

"We allowed UN inspectors into every location they chose, including Saddam's palaces. Should we also inspect Israeli sites for these weapons? Or Buckingham Palace?"

As the lecture continued, I drifted off into my madness, and remembered why I had come here in the first place. The world media seemed to be blindly taking sides and never once questioned the mental health of George W. Bush or Tony Blair. Was it possible that these were megalomaniacs that had lost the plot in their possession of such power? They both knew how much wealth in oil was at stake. Was this going to be the greatest theft ever in the history of mankind?

Was I mad? You bet! Mad with rage at the painful truth that Iraqi leaders and the Iraqi people were exhausted with war and they truly wanted peace.

Perhaps Saddam Hussein would lead by example and really did disarm the alleged weapons of mass destruction as he had repeatedly claimed.

Doctor Huda was an inspiration as she continued to talk from the heart, with her emotions contained and the interest of peace and disarmament as the premise of her speech.

"The UN weapons inspectors have visited all locations requested by the Americans, including the privacy of Saddam's palaces, but have found nothing. The Americans then insisted on universities. Eighteen universities inspected, and nothing was found. To date, no chemical or biological weapons or WMD have been found in Iraq. And we know they cannot be found because we simply don't have them. We have been disarming and we want lasting peace," she said, sounding exhausted.

"Should we now also inspect the White House or American universities? Perhaps the world should remember that the Israelis invaded Palestine by force and now are in possession of such weapons of mass destruction. We know for a fact that Israel has nuclear weapons and we also have evidence that they have used chemical weapons on Palestinians. Do we need any more evidence than is already available from the Palestinian people and the victims of Israeli war crimes?" this little woman challenged openly, before continuing. "By the end of 1998, Kofi Annan ordered a comprehensive review of the disarmament and Security Resolution 427, and transferred to UNSCOM the responsibility of making official inspections—where only four cases of non-compliance were found. Despite a 99% level of compliance, the American military decided to launch 460 cruise missiles into Baghdad over a four-day period, killing hundreds of innocent civilians in the process. But apparently these attacks are not terrorist attacks as they are military-launched. Is that justice? Or is that institutional terrorism?" she asked, knowing that this action had spread terror amongst the Iraqi civilians.

"Security Council Resolution 687 stipulated the lifting of sanctions upon the removal of the weapons of mass destruction. As we have demonstrated time and time again, we simply do not possess these weapons and now seek for the good of our people for these sanctions to be lifted," she said, believing that the United Nations would soon act to let Iraq back into the world market.

The fact was that if Iraq was allowed to enter the world markets, the entire world would have benefited from a great reduction of fuel costs that would have reduced food, transport, commodities, and all manufacturing. However, oil companies and weapons dealers would not have profited as much, as they represented the corporate competitors of Iraqi oil fields.

By the time she finished, Dr Huda had earned a third standing ovation, then she thanked her audience and invited everyone to ask questions. I wanted to ask if she knew that the Americans were already going to invade irrespective of Iraqi compliance with the United Nations Security Council. Instead, I asked about the terrorists and the disunity of the Islamic world if terrorists didn't end their reign of terror. Her reply was based on the multicultural diversity of the Islamic nations and outside influences that continued to infiltrate and divide the Muslims.

It dawned on me that there were many in the Muslim world that knew and understood how the United States of Islam would dwarf all superpowers and truly take Islam into the third millennium: hence the need for the West to keep the Muslim world at war.

After question time we were taken to the Baghdad Equestrian Club for dinner and entertained with local performing artists who consisted of musicians and male and female dancers dressed in traditional Iraqi costumes. Our guides were, as always, invited to the feast, and we shared a great night dancing, clapping, and rejoicing with the local Iraqis who truly believed that this war was never going to take place as long as they continued to comply with the United Nations.

The most striking feature of that night was watching that young girl I had seen during Dr Huda's speech. Her presence was not only magnetic but also admirable as she walked among other delegates smiling, socialising, and dancing, oblivious to the attraction her beauty had for all the delegates in the club. She was truly the life of the party.

During the traditional dancing I looked around the reception hall as several hundred guests discussed ideas, exchanged thoughts, and projected visions of things to come. For most of the night, I remained in silence, knowing the coalition armies were not going to retreat. All the necessary preparations for war were in the final stages, and the American-led forces would soon be destroying this precious hall. What would happen to all these performing Iraqi artists? I thought sadly. It was a tragic situation to be in knowing these young Iraqis that danced, played music, and sang for our pleasure would soon be struggling to stay alive.

That night, when I arrived in my room at the Palestine Hotel, I stepped outside onto my thirteenth level balcony that overlooked the Tigris River. It was a clear night and the stars seemed to shine like sparkling confetti pasted on the black backdrop of a theatrical stage. The Tigris seemed lifeless, casting a mirror reflection of the West Bank. The city of Baghdad was truly a beautiful city. This vision of Baghdad would be how I would always want to remember her: cleanly glistening with sharp silent lights and peacefully awaiting the invasion of yet another megalomaniac.

As I gazed to the west, I understood why the four main prophets Abraham, Buddha, Jesus, and Mohamed had all visited this region. It became clear why the three wise men that travelled to Bethlehem had come from Baghdad. It was now obvious why Alexander the Great; Ghenghis Khan; Saladin; the Babylonians; the Hebrew Jews; the Romans; the Persians; the Arabs; The British; and now the North Americans wanted to rule this land. This truly was the centre of world domination, the symbol of power, and the birthplace of civilisation.

Chapter 9
Saddam's Children's Hospital

George W. Bush flags wider war on Iraq, Iran and North Korea, the axis of evil.

The Age
January 31, 2002

The following morning at 10:00 am, we were taken to Saddam's Children's Hospital. When we arrived the sound of screaming children and the smell of disinfectants reminded me of visiting the daughter of my dearest friend at Sydney's Children's Hospital in Westmead, near Parramatta.

Anthony El-Chah was a Lebanese-Australian with an extraordinary outlook on life. He was blessed with the stability provided by a loving, well-educated family, and was a natural-born leader. In the true fashion of an alpha male, 'The Great Lebanese Elk' as we liked to call him stood tall wherever he walked.

What I admired most about him was the ability he had in dealing with racist Anglo-Australian boys that ridiculed his Lebanese appearance. His diplomatic nature allowed him to laugh at those who called him the derogatory name 'wog' and upstage them with his wit rather than turn to violence.

Above all, the Elk had a natural ability to unite people from different walks of life. On several occasions I saw people with racial bias towards each other united by the Elk. His ability to make everyone laugh in distressing times and the genuine interest and paternal care he had for people made him an outstanding true friend to anyone who crossed his path.

As I remembered my mate, the screams from Saddam's Children's Hospital reminded me of the day I visited Elk's eldest daughter Madeline.

Madeline was strikingly beautiful and like her father she was an outrageously witty teenage girl at the prime of her life when she contracted meningococcal at a school dance. So when I visited her in hospital I was terrified by the obscene image of this little girl who now rested in a coma with her delicate face swollen beyond recognition. She was in a deep sleep and I knew from experience that she would not be in pain at that moment. The pain was yet to come if she survived and at that realisation my heart sunk.

"Look at this," her father said, pulling the hospital blanket from her feet, and I saw the deep purple bruising around her feet and legs. It was as if Satan himself had taken a baseball bat and continuously battered Madeline until only her fair skin remained blotched like white bruises.

I stared at her father and I could not even imagine what pain he was experiencing from the watery look in his eyes. Here was one of the hardest men I knew, a man whose nose had been splattered across his face as the captain of our rugby team and wanting to continue to play the game. He would almost always top the tackle count as he threw his body and soul at charging men twice his size and then get up as if enjoying the pain. One day I saw him stand up to a man that was literally twice his size, smiling at what would surely have been a painfully torturous defeat. I remember thinking he was a true masochist when I saw him tempting death or excruciating pain by charging running bulls crazed with fear in the Spanish City of Pamplona to prove that he was a Saint Fermin[5].

Yet, never had I seen him endure as much pain as that day in the hospital; it was that day that I realised he was not a masochist. The Elk, the once proud, fearless Lebanese warrior, was now a sensitive parent. An emotional man! One that like the many millions around the world would endure immense internal pain watching his child suffer and perhaps die.

Later that day, Elk and I walked around the grounds of the Westmead Children's Hospital and talked for what seemed like a decade. We talked about memories, recalling the good and the bad. We discussed the meanings of God, life, and the universe, which at that moment revolved around his daughter. Yet, with the grace of God and the wisdom of an angel, the father of five beautiful girls and with a role model wife could only ask me one question.

---

5   Saint Fermin of Amiens is one of many locally venerated Catholic saints. Fermin is the co-patron of **Navarre**, where his feast, the '**San Fermín**' in the capital **Pamplona**, is forever associated with the *Encierro* or '**Running of the Bulls**' made famous by **Ernest Hemingway**. Fermin was long venerated also at **Amiens**, where he met martyrdom.

"You know what really gets to me about this whole experience with Maddie?" he asked rhetorically as we came to the end of our tenth lap around the grounds.

"What?" I asked, thinking that this was probably not enough pain for him to handle.

"That it doesn't matter how bad my daughter Maddie is at the moment, there's always going to be another child, another father or mother feeling exactly what me and my family are feeling now all over the world ... and some are worse off than us," he said, in awe of the human suffering that existed on Earth.

As I recalled visiting Elk's daughter Maddie, I realised that angels did walk our Earth. These were all the underpaid and overworked nurses, the life-saving and pain soothing doctors: all the necessary hospital staff that mostly went unnoticed. It was all the scientific researchers who spent laborious years searching for cures for the real terrorists like AIDS; cancer; tuberculosis; diabetes; haemophilia; meningococcal; or malaria, which still exist in our brave new modern world.

Why on Earth would we justify a war when there was medicine to be researched and a greater world to be developed?

Now in Saddam's Children's Hospital, the Elk's selfless words echoed in my mind: *It doesn't matter how bad my daughter is right now, there is always going to be some other parent somewhere in the world, whose child is worse off ...* And now here I was at Saddam's Children's Hospital understanding the wisdom of the Elk's prophecy.

As much as I hated the painful truth of Elk's humble wisdom, in Saddam's Children's Hospital I found the parents and the children that Elk understood.

Saddam's Children's Hospital was in urgent need of modern technologies, funds to upgrade facilities, and more complicated medicines and monitoring computers or x-ray equipment.

"Why don't you upgrade your machinery and equipment?" I asked one of the young doctors. "Doesn't Saddam buy any technological equipment?" I asked again.

"Yes, Saddam wants to buy more equipment like this—look." He walked me to a nearby room and when I walked in I saw an enormous collection of ageing computers and medical equipment. "You see!" The young doctor exclaimed. "But sanctions do not allow us to import such equipment."

"But why is it all here in storage?" I asked the obvious question.

"Because we cannot import any more technology to fix it up, some things are broken and we cannot buy and import spare parts or computer software. That is why economic embargo is very bad," the doctor acknowledged.

"I see," I said, amazed at only one aspect of the inhumane crippling consequence of the embargo.

"We see economic sanctions like terrorism for these children," he added. "Only this kind of terrorism is a long, slow, painful death that tortures not just the dying children but

the mothers and fathers that have to see their children die and there is no government in the world that can stand up to show America that their foreign and economic policies are worse than any terrorist action. If they invade our country against the will of the Security Council it will demonstrate that the world lives in terror and afraid of America like we are afraid of their military and economic power," he reasoned. It was easy to see why these people saw Americans as worse than terrorists.

I began to wonder how much human suffering would result in any country burdened with economic sanctions. As the excursion continued, we understood more why the Iraqi administration had brought us here to the hospital.

The few chemical labs and factories that the Iraqis had were destroyed or made redundant by the American bombs—with the claim that they were manufacturing chemical bombs. What this children's hospital needed was medicines and technology, not sanctions.

As I walked around the hospital wards, I looked around in awe and wondered at the satanic hypocrisy of the West, as saintly children everywhere seemed to be pleading with muted stares for their hellfire suffering to end. *Who are the real terrorists?* I was now asking myself as the expressions on these innocents' faces reflected the torturous truth that they were being terrorised by the American imposed economic sanctions.

Was Cuba, Iran, or North Korea suffering the same fate simply because they did not buy American weapons or trade in American dollars?

There was no doubt that this was a good tactical move by the Ba'ath party government to shock the mostly Western contingency. They made it well-known that it was exactly their intention to show the world what the American economic policies and sanctions were doing to Iraqis.

"In the West, you call a suicidal madman a terrorist, so what must we tell our people about the people who stop us from buying medicines, technologies, and medical equipment?" the Iraqi doctor asked me. My face reddened in shame.

I remember the embarrassment as Shaima and Ammar gazed at me for an answer. Their watery eyes demonstrated that this was not orchestrated. It was their first time in this hospital as well. I compared numbers and thought about the three thousand people that died in the 9/11 New York towers and compared the numbers with the estimated one-and-a-half million innocent Iraqis that had died since Saddam attempted to reclaim the historically Iraqi state of Kuwait.

What was worse, is that Saddam played no involvement in the 9/11 terrorist attack.

Suddenly we heard a loud, hoarse scream from a nearby ward. A nurse and a doctor rushed to the screaming lady that sat cradling her child. Shaima and Ammar were with me as we looked to see the doctor attempt basic life-saving procedures with his mouth on the child's and the nurse desperately attempting to spark the heart beats with the downward pressure of her hands. All the while, the mother stood aside screaming and wailing, now being held by another nurse who attempted to sooth her with comforting words.

As we stared mesmerised for a few minutes other delegates arrived and more nurses now started to push them away. But the expressions of that young doctor and nurse said everything that needed to be said as the mother screamed again and fell to the floor holding the young nurse by her waist, crying and yelling some foreign words.

I had just witnessed a murder. Not a cold-blooded murder that kills the victim almost instantly, but the slow, torturous killing of a little girl.

Her mother's screaming and wailing were horrific as she punched at the doctors who tried to hold her away from her motionless daughter.

"What is her name?" was all I could ask of Shaima who stood next to me with tears welling in her eyes.

"Wait …" Shaima gathered herself. "I will ask," she said and asked a nearby nurse who seemed immune to this tragedy. When she returned, she told me.

"Zainab. She is three years old and she had pneumonia."

"Pneumonia? But that's curable."

"Yes, maybe, but the sanctions did not allow the hospital to import the medical x-rays equipment the hospital needed," Shaima acknowledged.

The nauseating smell of cheap disinfectants mixed with the aroma of medicines and the realisation that it was us in the developed world that were creating third worlds by imposing economic sanctions. The deep-rooted truth was that we in the first world were the greatest threat to life on Earth and lived oblivious to the human suffering we were causing. The horror of seeing dying children that could have been saved and knowing thousands if not millions were dying the same slow painful unnecessary deaths, made me want to vomit. I wanted to be sick and went searching for a bathroom.

As I walked around the wards searching for the toilet, I separated myself from the group, thinking of the young girl, Zainab, who had just died in front of me. I remembered what it was like to be truly sick from disease rather than from my inability to cope with this disgusting truth.

I remembered three Ethiopian children whom I stood over, watching in a horrid fascination, perversely witnessing their death. Now this little girl called Zainab re-ignited those feelings. With the constant screaming in the distance, the dumb, expressionless look on desperate doctors, the overworked nurses, and an international delegation of NASYO representatives watching I ran away, holding back the tears.

Entering the disease-infested toilet cubicle of the Saddam Children's Hospital ward, my tears exploded. The stench of stale urine mixed with fresh faeces made my guts churn. This was a humbling moment; a moment when I really understood the courage of third world warriors. The tough street-fighter was now a whimpering coward, crying and vomiting as the pains of the terrorist truth tortured my soul. Crouching over the stale urine stench that came from a hole in the cracked porcelain floor, I vomited my breakfast and wept unashamedly. I was coming to terms with the fact that I was a weak and pathetic coward, a modern-day slave incapable of breaking away from the chains of my masters, a pathetic fool paying my taxes so that my governments could pay the weapons dealers absurd amounts to destroy our precious planet. I had become an idiot who lived to work, lost touch with my natural environment, and sacrificed my freedom to be materialistically wealthy. The truths tortured my soul.

When I returned to join the main party I walked along next to some journalists and photographers. I could hear them speak in English as we returned, back to the waiting busses.

"This is how we get trapped; they show us the bad stuff to make out like they don't have money," an American journalist said to his counterpart.

"You wouldn't want to be sick here would you?" I heard the other journalist ask.

"Can you imagine what it's going to be like if the war breaks out?"

Chapter 10
The Australian Spirit

Australian Prime Minister John Howard was censured by the senate for misleading the public in his justification for sending Australia to war with Iraq.

The Age
October 8, 2003

After visiting the hospital we visited the Baghdad Museum for a private tour of Iraq's national treasures. This was a welcoming relief, to take our minds away from the hell we had just visited.

Along my travels I had been to the Cairo, Athens, Madrid, London, Rome, and Istanbul museums. But this was by far the greatest collection from our ancient world I had ever seen.

Entering the museum we saw the skeletal remains of a Neanderthal woman fully intact and protected in a fragile glass tomb. I looked in awe at this fragile woman's skeletal remains, which now rested in peace. Perhaps she should have been named Eve, as she was the oldest remains I had ever seen, and was likely to be a great grandmother to all humanity.

The journey in this museum started some 33,000 years BC and ended with the beginning of Islam in 500 AD. We saw amazing stone sculptures, preserved metals, and mud pottery that dated over seven thousand years old. We travelled through epochs like Mesopotamia; Assyria; Bronze Age; Phoenicians; Hebrews; Greeks; Romans; Christians; Mongols; Persians; and Byzantium. It seemed like every great power had occupied and ruled this cornerstone of our human existence.

There were hundreds of artefacts: bowls; carvings; implements; coins; medallions; spears; knives; swords; amour; sculptures; and scriptures. But to me the most daunting and enlightening discovery was a large black rock with the oldest man-made laws in the world inscribed on it. I looked at the carvings but my untrained eye refused to see any logical meaning from the carvings. This was called Hamblin's Rock.

As I looked closely at the oldest man-made laws in the world, that were so clearly inscribed on this black rock—a rock that symbolised the origins of Law itself—I became transfixed. My thoughts swirled around the origins of religious laws, natural laws, international laws, and other the man-made laws like The English law regime of the Commonwealth and the religious laws of Sharia; native Indian and Aboriginal laws and the laws of physics; the differences between European and American civilian laws; or the universal law of opposites. These were all laws that should have served a purpose for understanding, for rationalising logic, or for natural justice to prevail over evil deeds. My thoughts were sinking deeply into the realm of consciousness and justice.

Suddenly, it was Ghassan, the suave young man I had met earlier in the Palestine Hotel foyer, who was a translator of French and English, that interrupted my deep thoughts.

He asked me, "You can read those scribbles?"

I looked at him, wondering if he was serious or joking. But he seemed serious.

"No, I'm just amazed at how the origins of man-made laws begun with carvings on this stone and I'm trying to imagine the stonemasons engraving these symbols with stone tools, wondering what cause of events led them to write these laws down," I replied, in honest bewilderment.

"I'm not a historian, but I am a language student and sometimes I like to imagine how our ancestors made peace with people they didn't understand," he replied with a half-smile, and I returned a warm, understanding smile.

We instantly knew we would have an academic bond and thus a lot in common, and from that moment on, Ghassan would be the man I trusted the most in Baghdad. We shared the common fascination with our past and how we came to be who we were as a modern society. We walked and talked for a while as we quizzed each other about our academic backgrounds, origins, and vocational passions. Ghassan was a Middle Eastern Palestinian-born Iraqi Muslim and I was a Western Spanish-born Judo-Christian Australian. Two completely different men, yet we both had English degrees and both shared the same passion to make the communications between the East and West as effective and as clear as possible so that one day our dialogue would unite us, rather than divide us through the misunderstandings that occurred and what was lost in less effective translation.

For the rest of the tour I walked near Ghassan, listening to his translations and looking in awe at the priceless collection of historical evidence stored in the Baghdad Museum.

You didn't have to be a connoisseur of ancient art or a historian to know that this museum was an authentic collection of true, historical artefacts that could never be bought or replaced—only robbed. There was a distinct possibility that the coalition of the willing may know of this priceless collection and were already planning the greatest heist in recorded human history.

Later that night, after dinner, Ghassan and I remained talking until the early hours of the morning. I learned that Ghassan's family were Palestinian refugees that had migrated to Iraq in search of peace and a new home. His family was expelled from Jerusalem at gunpoint. He recalled how his father had been given an option by a Jewish military commander.

"If you stay here, we kill you and expel your family. If you go, you can live with your family," Ghassan said, imitating the Jewish commander. In any court of law, this was called 'duress' which made it illegal.

"So you came here? To Baghdad!" I asked in disbelief at the audacity of any Jew to repeat the injustice of the Holocaust.

"Where else could we go to?" he asked indifferently. "You see Al, we are all brothers of the same family but sometimes our big brother is too strong and we cannot fight him … so it is better to walk away. Don't you agree?"

The analogy was amusing as I remembered beating my smaller brothers into submission with my unfairly advantageous strength. Perhaps the people who inscribed these laws on the rock realised the importance for fairness and justice to prevail over brute violent force.

"Surely you could have taken legal action against that commander?" I said, not fully understanding the prejudices of the Israeli courts.

He smiled and diplomatically asked, "What do they teach you in Australia? Or is it Spain my friend?"

"Um, in Australia we learn a lot about cricket, rugby, AFL, beer, pop music, or royal visits—and in Spain we learn about football, bull fights, wine and flamenco or religious festivals. But why? I don't know," I said jokingly.

"Don't you learn history?" he asked me.

"Yes, of course. But that's a selective subject in our curriculum. Only a few people choose to study that," I admitted, acknowledging what my schoolteacher said I would one day regret: my failure to learn history. "But I learned a lot about fighting," I added stupidly as I recalled the bombardment of war and violence-related Hollywood films.

"Ah. My friend ... you have too much to learn," he patronised me. "You must come and speak with my father. He is a professor at Baghdad University, of Arabic literature and history. He will teach you many things and you can ask him anything you want, okay?"

"Okay." I jumped at the opportunity to learn.

At this point, I noticed three Western men and a distinguished looking lady. They were easy to identify as Westerners. I had seen them walking around as individuals, and like the many international delegates who braved torture, lynching, and being blown up by the cursed terrorist, I immediately admired their courage—in particular as they seemed so relaxed amongst the terrorists that surrounded us.

Yes, I was still losing sleep and spending my time restlessly walking around looking over my shoulder for Saddam's secret police. After all, these people did not live in the free world as we did in the West, I thought.

"It's bloody outrageous," I heard the lady say with a strong Australian accent. "To think the bastards can get away with it? Who do they think they are?" she asked rhetorically as they walked by and sat down in the corner of the hotel lounge.

"You know those people?" Ghassan asked me as he turned his gaze to where I was looking.

"No. But the lady is Australian," I said to Ghassan smartly. "I can pick an Aussie a mile away."

"Really?" he asked me. "And what about the men, where do you think they are from?" he asked me.

"The young guy with spiky hair and a camera bag is either an Englishman or a Frenchman. The older guy with a digital camera and grey hair is an American filmmaker or German artist, and the one carrying the big writing pad and a serious look on his face, he could be from anywhere—say international," I said, confidently asserting my uncanny ability to pick characters.

"Oh. You are so wrong my friend. Come let me introduce you. They are all Australians," Ghassan said, smiling.

"Australians? Here?"

"Yes," he said, and proceeded to approach the group with me grinning behind him at the thought that I would not be lynched or perish alone.

"Hello friends, how is your evening?" Ghassan interrupted the group with a casual confidence, like a suave Arabic version of James Bond.

They nodded, smiled, hummed, and yawned, then Ghassan introduced me as a fellow Australian. "This is a country man Al, also from Australia," he said with one hand on my shoulder and making way for the scheduled handshakes.

"Hi. I'm Rosemary Gillespie, a human rights lawyer, but my Aboriginal name is Waratah," she said as we shook hands firmly.

"George Gittoes," the man who could have come from any country on Earth said as he placed his writing pad aside to shake my hand.

"Hello, I'm Wayne Coles, filmmaker," the youngest of the three men greeted me with a warm smile and a comforting tone.

"And I'm Mike Hartnell. I'm just a computer systems technician," he said half-jokingly to make me feel more at ease.

"It's nice to see other Australians here," I said, genuinely relieved.

"Yes it is. It's just a shame that there aren't more of us here," Waratah added.

"Have you being here long, Al?" George asked me.

"Third day!" I replied.

"Are you here for the NASYO conference?" Mike continued the questioning.

"Yes," I nodded.

"How long are you staying for?" Wayne completed the round of questions and I sat and joined the Australians with the secret relief of knowing that there was safety in numbers—and there were none safer to be with in a moment of crisis than Australians.

Australia was truly a futuristic global nation. Every Australian understood the value of multi-ethnicity from the day they were born. In fact, every Australian had two identities; one from our ancestors, and then Australian. Although we had an extreme minority of Australians that had not been educated to understand the greater value of dual identities, the vast majority of Australians knew their origins and now lived in harmony and tolerance with people completely different from themselves. Once traditional enemies were now united by the same Australian identity.

In other words, you had English-Australians; Irish-Australians; Chinese-Australians; Japanese - Australians; Aboriginal - Australians; Italian - Australians; Indian - Australian; Vietnamese - Australians; Palestinian - Australians; Israeli - Australians; Mexican - Australians, and so on … just about every nation on Earth populated this great land Australia. Thus, every Australian had a point of origin and a cultural background that enriched the Australian identity. Thus it was that diversity, acceptance, and tolerance were ingrained in the Australian cultural identity, making Australia the Switzerland of the Pacific.

Consequently, Australia was the home of an Aboriginal-Australian people whose cave paintings date back almost 40,000 years. Made up of the new immigrants that mostly came as convicts, and the cheap labour from Europe, Africa, and Asia, this melting pot of languages and cultures that now share Aboriginal lands in peace is the reason that Australia is a neutral nation with the entire world as allies. The cultural diversity also makes it a financial safe haven with wealth for toil, and as such, Australia is well-placed to lead the world into the third millennium.

It was this quality that drove and motivated Australians to help other people in times of adversity, hardship, and crisis of any magnitude.

As the Switzerland of the pacific and a neutral country with the entire world as her allies and no natural enemies, Australia could afford to not waste money on expensive depreciating weapons. Yet the divisive forces between the ruling British royalists and the Australians continued to keep the people ignorantly paying tax to acquire weapons of mass destruction to enrich the few manufacturing families in foreign lands.

Perhaps it was the spirit of the convicts that united Australians, as we learned of the injustices and the hardship suffered by many convicts expelled by the British Empire. Convicts were victims of the English law regime, serving life-long sentences for minor offences like stealing food or not paying taxes or rent. From such injustices, Australians have evolved to become compassionate, caring, and genuinely empathetic people.

"I don't believe that it is the peaceful loving Western world that is now the aggressor?" Waratah asked rhetorically to continue the conversation these Australians were having before I joined them.

"It's all to do with manipulation of the media," George replied.

"To think that the cost of just one American aircraft carrier can educate an entire African country for a generation!" Waratah added.

"Not just one country, Waratah, it's more like most of Africa," Wayne interjected.

"I think it's half of the continent," I contributed.

"Whatever it is, it is still a hell of a lot better than the alternative of wasting that money on blowing up people's homes," George concluded.

"I think it's a crime against humanity if we continue spending wealth on destroying the planet rather than rebuilding countries," Mike said as we nodded our agreement.

"Do you think the Americans will really invade Iraq?" Wayne asked.

"Oh! Without a doubt," George answered confidently.

"I hope you are wrong, my friend," Ghassan rebutted.

"So do I," George agreed.

For the rest of the night we talked mostly about ourselves as we got acquainted. I learnt Waratah Gillespie was a retired human rights lawyer and a proud grandmother who had been given the Aboriginal name Waratah by the Australian indigenous elders as recognition for her humanitarian work with the native Australian ancestors.

George Gittoes was an artist who had probably been to more wars than any living mercenary, marine, commando, or legionnaire of any rank in our modern history. It was his vocation in life to witness the injustice of war to document in his big writing pad, where he scribbled notes, sketched images, and doodled abstract and surreal impressions of the horrors a few men could inflict on so many. His filming was later shown in Michael Moore's award-winning film *Fahrenheit 911*.

Wayne Coles was also an award-winning documentary filmmaker who was more comfortable shooting film than bullets in the line of fire. Later, Wayne, Ghassan, and I would spend time sightseeing, but Wayne remained committed to his film like a true ethnographic reporter, mostly shooting all the film he could in the little time he had.

Mike Hartnell really was a computer technician but above all, he was a family man. So perhaps he didn't know of the dangers that the American propaganda were promoting as the greatest threat to world peace: the Iraqi secret police, the hordes of terrorists, and even the suicide bombers waiting in the wings to get on our bus and blow us all up till kingdom come.

Indeed, none of them seemed to know about the dangers that those experts from the Western media was reporting. Ironically the only reportage that seemed to be permitted by the Western media interests and that was paving the way for the arrival of the US Marines, was that Saddam Hussein had weapons of mass destruction and was a threat to world peace.

This small group of Australians were truly fearless, I thought, after a long night talking and sharing our stories. We parted and agreed to meet each night at the same time, 7:30, to sum up our findings and share any information that could help us learn the truths we were all seeking.

It was the good fortune of all Australians to have two national identities. It really was empowering to the individual and enriching to the country. So why didn't The Jewish Palestinians and the Muslim Israelis simply understand that we were all the same children of Abraham? We were all on this same planet together and we were all going to suffer the same tragic asphyxiation if we didn't make dramatic changes to the way we thought or felt about our national pride. We needed to make the world environment our one great common wealth, and the time was nearing when we would all be at war against global warming.

Perhaps, the handful of Zionist and Christian megalomaniacs could play their games of power using Jewish, Christian, and Muslim pawns to fight each other and kill each other in the name of a flag … however, most Australians simply did not buy the lie.

Most Australians were well informed, as the recipients of free education that further allowed us to distinguish between truth and lies told to us by our governments or our media. In fact, most Australians opposed sending Australian troops to Iraq, but such was the power of The Crown that, by controlling the media, the British colonials would repeat the Gallipoli history and take orders from the Queen of England's representatives.

No questions asked by the Queen's servants, and only the hardened Australian spirit, stood fast against the John Howard Government; irrespective of political belief.

Chapter 11
Eleventh Commandment

The advice that was given consistently in the foreign office is that the war would be unlawful without a second UN resolution.
Sir Michael Wood
UK Foreign Office's most senior lawyer

The following day we were taken to the Baghdad University main campus. We were encouraged to walk freely and speak to any student at random. I was instantly surprised by the vast difference in female student to male student ratio. It seemed that there were more girls than there were boys by three to one.

In the university, most of the girls wore hijabs, but many others let their hair down or wore ribbons in ponytails, plaits, and styles. Perhaps this was the Muslim student's way of demonstrating against conventional thoughts. Or maybe these girls that didn't wear hijabs were not Muslim and exercised the right to free speech and expression in this alleged policed state. Needing to know more, I approached a group of girls with Shaima and asked her to translate after the initial greeting.

"Salaam Alecum." I was now also keen to learn Arabic before meeting Ghassan's father. "What do you study?" I asked them.

One said science, one said economics, and the third, who was not wearing a hijab, was a law student.

"How much does it cost you to attend university?" I continued my interrogation, thinking that I should be asking them for any top-secret information on the infamous WMD or secret police.

"Cost?" the one studying economics asked.

"To study?" the science student asked.

"Yes, I mean how much do you pay for educational fees?"

The law student seemed to have a better grasp of English and giggled at me—it seemed I asked a stupid question.

"In Islam, all education is free and paid for by the state," she answered.

I asked Shaima to translate properly to make sure there was no misunderstanding. Indeed, I learned that for Iraqis, as in many other countries, education was free to every man, woman, and child up to a doctorate level. It was very much a part of the Qur'an, and the Islamic tradition that the state should pay for all educational needs. Saddam was a Muslim and complied by providing free education to all Iraqi nationals. But why were we not told in the Western media?

"We have fifteen universities in Baghdad," the economics students said with immense pride.

"And the oldest university in the world is also here in Baghdad," added the law student.

"Um—yeah—I know," I stuttered a lie.

I had no idea that the educational epicentre known as a university had its origins in Baghdad. Later I would confirm that the institute of a university, that global phenomena that united all thinkers, researchers, and the best minds in each nation to study and find solutions to our existence as a human kind, was started in Baghdad.

The three Jewish astronomical kings that followed the falling star to Bethlehem travelled from Baghdad. *So why are these people now the axis of evil according to George W. Bush?* I wondered in silence.

"What did you study?" the law student asked me.

"I have an arts degree," I replied.

"Oh, an artist," she said, genuinely interested.

"Yes, but not a painter," I explained. "I like to write."

"Oh, a poet, very romantic," she flirted with me and smiled.

I was embarrassed to think these girls understood the significance of an arts degree whilst most people I knew in Australia found little of any value in an arts degree.

"No, just a humanities student," I said, shattering her illusion.

"Oh, you are humble, we know all artists are the teachers in the public class room of society," she added. I was astonished at the accuracy of her statement.

"Do they teach about Islam in your schools?" the girl wearing the hijab asked me, with a glimmer of hope in her eyes.

"No," I answered bluntly.

"Oh, that is sad, maybe your people don't know what it means to live a spiritual life if they don't learn from our prophets," she concluded.

"What do you think of Saddam Hussein?" I asked them.

"He is our leader," the legal student answered first. "Sometimes he makes mistakes but he is a good man."

"We don't like his son Uday," the economics student butted in, and they all laughed. It was clear that Uday was a rotten egg; the consequence of nepotism.

The Iraqi students were proud and delighted to show me around their campus. We walked through long corridors and entered classrooms freely. The library was full of books, however there was an obvious lack of computers and a stark reminder and evidence of the embargo. Shaima at one stage asked me to please do something about sending university books. That was all she ever asked of me in the entire time I was with her.

"Books? What kind of books?" I asked her.

"Any books will do," she replied. "For me, I like Spanish books of love and romance," she admitted to me quietly.

The effects of economic sanctions on the student of a country were obviously detrimental. Perhaps colonisation involved keeping the populations ignorant and starved for information as well as starved for technology, I reasoned.

Baghdad University was relatively small in comparison to other universities I had visited. The lesson I learned was about the resilience of these students and teachers who continued the learning process amid the sanctions.

As we left the university I saw one of the girls I had met holding her hand high with a peace sign toward the bus, screaming, "No war, yes peace!"

I was beginning to feel that I was in solidarity with these peaceful people. My paranoia was now subsiding.

Our next stop was the Amiriyah Shelter, a bomb shelter in the outskirts of Baghdad where over 700 women and children took refuge from American bombs in 1990 and were incinerated when two fancy million-dollar bombs the American military proudly called 'bunker busters' ripped through the ceiling. There was conveniently very little reporting of this war crime committed by the American military.

As the tour guide showed us around the bunker we could see the walls were black with burnt carbon, and all that remained was pictures of all those who died inside this burning oven. The similarities between the Jewish Holocaust ovens and this shelter were staggering. Both were man-made and in both the beautiful and the innocent were burnt and smoked to death.

"If you look at the walls you will see the scratch marks created by those trying to crawl out of the fire through the concrete," Ghassan translated from the Iraqi tour guide's lecture.

When we looked closer for the signs he was referring to we saw human scratching on the concrete and in some places there were broken fingernails, imbedded with dried blood, burnt into the walls. The sickening horror those women and children must have experienced was beyond measure as they tried to claw their way out through the reinforced concrete.

This site was kept preserved as a burial monument with pictures of all those who died lined around the walls. Some of the ladies in the delegation wept and others walked out, enraged, to breathe in fresh air. We held a minute's silence to respect those that died. Silently I prayed for the human race to end its own culling and get on with the act of making this star-ship planet Earth the safe refuge for life in this universe that it should be for all who inhabit it.

"God bless us all," the Iraqi tour guide said, breaking the silence. It sounded sweeter and fairer than the single-sighted view we heard from those who said, "God bless America."

***

Later that night, after a feast for dinner at the hotel, we were taken to a fashion parade to see Iraqi contemporary and traditional embroideries and designs. The fashion parade aimed to show us some of the beauty of Iraq, and beautiful it certainly was. The models, both the men and the women, were young, healthy, tall, slender, and graceful, with perfectly clear skin and broad, clean smiles. The garments they paraded were many and varied. Some were traditional while others were more contemporary—yet all were tasteful and elegant.

What was most striking was the sexual appeal of some garments, which simply did not equate with my narrow Western perception of what the Muslim world was about. As a Western person exposed to pornography, prostitution, and a blossoming sex industry from a young age, I was led to believe that the Muslim world was sexually oppressed. I was told of stories about women who had been beaten for exposing their hair or showing too much skin in public. Meanwhile our local newspapers in Australia advertised brothels, adult shops, and taught our young daughters about lingerie well before they reach puberty.

What I was not told, was that sex was also very much a part of Islam. However, it belonged in the private realm behind closed doors and was not a public concern. This explained why some Muslim women dancers and performing artists could do belly dancing in private venues like restaurants and cafes. It also justified some of the provocative garments that were now on parade.

I had been to other fashion parades, but this was my first Islamic Fashion Parade, and some garments were absolutely sexy. Beautiful models paraded seductively along the stage with their mouths and noses covered in near-transparent shawls, exposing flat-toned stomachs and long slender legs through well-cut splits in skirts or tightly bound garments that showed perfect curves and exposed only the right amount of skin to arouse our imaginations.

To be sexually aroused by an Islamic fashion parade was the last thing I would have expected to find in Baghdad before a war. But as I stared around the large room, I noticed it was not only me—everyone was gawking, wide eyed and in silence, confirming that some of the garments were absolutely breathtaking. These Iraqi models were as perfect as the imagination could conjure. They had large, brown, deep-pooled eyes that made the heart pulsate, and their firm and muscular yet slender curves hypnotised the admirer. There was no way to deny one's arousal, as all the audience sat in an uncomfortable silence with the deep-rooted desire to be with those that who preferred to make love, not war.

By the end of the fashion parade the NASYO delegates and our translators had experienced one of the most beautiful exhibitions of colour, music, art, and mild erotic seduction in our lives. This was evident from the encore of applause and the newly ignited energy that erupted when the show finished.

After the fashion parade, Ghassan and I stayed up again talking about Middle Eastern history and ways to resolve a looming war peacefully. As we walked into the main hotel bar, most of the NASYO delegation had retired to their hotel rooms whilst the student translators were up, listening to that strikingly beautiful girl I had seen amongst the NASYO delegation.

She was talking about Saddam's compliance in disarmament and the lifting of economic sanctions. She seemed convinced that there was not going to be a war.

Ghassan made the introductions. "Rema, this is my good friend Al," he said. We shook hands and I instantly argued with her that she didn't understand the likes of George W. Bush or the Western obsession with colonisation.

"Bush is like a poor little rich boy who gained power from his daddy's influence," I said to her.

"But what does that matter?" she asked naively.

"More than you can imagine," I answered.

"How?"

"Do you remember Hitler?"

"Yes."

"Well, he was a megalomaniac, right?"

"What do you mean?" she asked for a translation.

I described a megalomaniac as a person who was obsessed with power, as any man or woman who needed to be in full control, not only of his or her own destiny but the destiny of others around them, at all costs. Ghassan needed to translate my definition to her, and soon she agreed.

"Yes, I understand now," she said.

"Well, do you think Bush, Aznar, and Blair are any different to Saddam if they chose war before peace?" I asked her.

"Um ..." She seemed speechless and Ghassan, the ever-ready diplomatic gentleman, went to her rescue.

"Al, my friend, don't be so harsh, you can't compare the three musketeers with the lone ranger," he kidded. "They are all good guys, it just depends which side you are on."

"You know what the problem with Hitler was?" a Polish delegate who sat nearby listening to our discussion interrupted with his question.

"He was a mad man," I said.

"No," continued the Polish man. "He never finished his job!" That was the punch line, but only he seemed to laugh.

The group broke off into different discussions, leaving the Polish man sitting silently to realise that not even in the heartland of an Islamic state did the Muslims appreciate the atrocities Hitler forced upon the Jews.

Rema looked at me, puzzled, and Ghassan again diplomatically shrugged off the bad joke. I would have thought that Ghassan with Palestinian background would have laughed, but even he remained dignified, knowing that his people, the Palestinians, were the only people on Earth who welcomed the Jews when Hitler was ethnic cleansing Germany to get rid of them.

"Where are you from?" Rema eventually asked me.

"I'm a Spanish-born Australian," I replied with optimism, thinking that this beautiful girl took an interest in where I came from.

"Oh, like I am a Jordanian-born Palestinian, huh?" she smiled.

"And I am an Iraqi-born Palestinian," added Ghassan with a broad grin on his face, nudging me.

The three of us talked through until late that night, before Ghassan retired to join his patiently waiting wife.

Rema and I spoke long into the night. In one night I would learn more about the Palestinian struggle than throughout my entire Western-educated life. How little of the truth we were told about the Palestinian-Israeli conflict. Up to now, I believed that all Palestinians were terrorists. I knew little about the things that Rema was telling me, like the fact that there were more than five million Palestinians living below the poverty line as refugees in the neighbouring countries of Syria, Egypt, Lebanon, and Iraq. She told me how the Israeli government refused the Palestinian exiles entry into Israel to visit their own family. I didn't know about the construction of the dividing wall at this stage, but Rema explained the significance of this wall as a way of taking more land from the mostly defenceless Palestinians and creating the world's largest prison. The inmates of the prison, however, were also innocent women and children persecuted and incarcerated simply for being Muslim Palestinians.

"You know what I find most frightening?" I asked Rema before we retired for the night.

"What is that?" she asked, puzzled.

"That the Palestinians are mostly portrayed as terrorists in the media, but when Israelis kill Palestinians it is portrayed as military strikes and thus justified." I shared my realisation of the biased reporting on the Israeli-Palestinian conflict.

"Maybe your media is guilty of, how you say … inciting? Is that correct, inciting violence against Palestinians and maybe Iraq if your country attacks Iraq?" she asked before standing to her feet.

"Maybe …"

I hated to admit the real possibility of the truth. But what could anyone do against a media that incited violence or a war to boost sales and profits?

That night, I felt my spirits uplifted/ and went to sleep with Rema clearly on my mind.

***

The following morning the NASYO organisers planned an excursion to the old city of Babylon. Ghassan ensured that I joined his bus, which contained the young crowd, and we were bound to have more fun. I looked for Rema but couldn't see her when the bus drove away from the hotel.

I was seated near the back of the bus where mostly the young male students sat, and a few young romantics sat in the middle. There was a beautiful Japanese girl who I met earlier. Her name was Yakiko; she was a Japanese traditional dancer that sat with four other Japanese people in the middle, with other Iraqi female students occupying the front seats of the bus. Yakiko was an exceptional-looking Japanese lady. Strikingly beautiful and overtly feminine, she wore lace and frills, silks and short skimpy dresses throughout her stay in Baghdad to defy Islamic traditions, yet she was never challenged by the authorities as I had expected. Perhaps it was her refined, well-educated Japanese manners, or maybe it was her petite feminine form that allowed her such liberties that she could walk anywhere she wanted and doors would open for her or the best seats were offered to her. Yakiko was the sweetheart of the NASYO delegation as one of only four Japanese representatives and with a school girl innocence that made everyone protective of her. She was always surrounded by people.

I was overwhelmed by the fact that these young men I sat with were all oblivious to the sexy Yakiko and the mounting military hardware surrounding Iraq. I tried to explain that the Americans and their allies were getting ready to strike, but they were totally convinced that war was avoidable as Saddam was now destroying the al-Masaood missiles. Then they started singing songs and clapping their hands whilst others romanced their sweethearts in the seats in front of me.

I was no longer paranoid about the Iraqis. Now, as I sat looking out the window, watching the poverty-stricken suburbs on the outskirts of Baghdad, I imagined the growing American military machine that was mounting on the Mediterranean and the Red Sea and the Gulf. It was all like a bad dream. The paranoia now turned against the Americans and the coalition of the willing.

The buses stopped about half a kilometre from the gates of Babylon. We were surprised to see what seemed like hundreds of young school children wearing uniforms and creating a kind of guard of honour for the NASYO visitors. They started singing and chanting as we walked along the road to the old city.

"No war, yes peace, no war, yes peace," they chanted before breaking into an Iraqi song.

I was saddened to see that some of the children wore dirtier uniforms and older shoes. A handful wore civilian, stained second-hand clothing. I assumed that these few were the poorest of the poor. My heart went out to them with sympathetic understanding, as they looked on with sadness or shame in their eyes.

There were also some children with old, worn shoes and no socks, and I remembered my own shame when in our poverty I too had gone to school without socks. Other kids stirred and mocked me for not wearing socks. Then I wore odd socks and again they mocked until the shame drove me to steal a pair of socks from a large department store as a nine-year-old.

As we walked through the old gates of Babylon, we joined tour guides that would tell us stories of the kings, the prophets, the architecture, and the building techniques used by Babylonians.

Amidst this Babylonian ruins, civilisation began. It was here in this epicentre of human existence where began laws; trade; irrigation; domestication of animals; agriculture; language; mathematics; astronomy; and medicine. But above the recognition that our universe was singular like a single God, it occurred to me that over time the eleventh commandment had emerged: thou shalt care for the natural kingdom—which included the environment.

It was perhaps the most significant revelation that infiltrated my thoughts in this city that united all humanity in some way with the people of this region. It was truly a blessing to walk in the steps of our forefathers. To think that the three greatest prophets, Abraham, Jesus, and Mohamed, or the three wise kings, and now the three dominant religions, had all sprouted from this region. Now, at the beginning of the third millennium, I began to appreciate the significance of the third world warriors. I stood staring into the same hills and the same horizon, the same sun and moon that our forefathers had once seen. I recalled the coalition of the willing's armies surrounding this great city, exactly as so many other empires had done previously, only to be driven away with time.

Suddenly, I saw Rema in the distance with her admirers following closely as she looked at me and waved, with a warm smile. My heart fluttered as she approached me. She wore tight jeans, a T-shirt, and a denim jacket. Her hair was tied in a ponytail and there were running shoes on her feet. She looked like an angel in disguise, with a small, fragile porcelain-white face and deep, dark eyes.

"Al, hello. How are you?" she asked with a warm and genuine smile that made her face glow.

"Good, how are you?" I said, still depressed and amazed by the Babylonian's legacy in Iraq and in the world at large. I was thinking about how it was possible that these people could threaten anyone.

"I am fine," she said. I stood and glanced around the ruins in an uncomfortable silence for a little while.

"I—enjoyed—talking—to you—a lot—last night," I said, breaking my words so she could understand me clearly.

"Really? Me too" she said. Then she did the most unexplainable thing—she grabbed my arm gently to steer me away from the rest of the tour. I found this odd, as I didn't think Muslim women could touch a man. My ignorance about the Muslims continued.

"I liked talking to you last night," she confessed as we walked away.

"I haven't stopped thinking of you," I admitted to her.

"Really?" she asked, surprised.

I nodded silently, unable to speak.

"How long will you stay in Baghdad for?" I asked her after a short pause.

"I leave tomorrow," she said with a saddened tone. "When you go?"

"I'm not sure, maybe a week or two. It depends on how long my money lasts."

"Oh, I see," she said as we reached the Gates of Babylon.

The delegation was gathering and her friends started calling for her and waving at us as we waved back. "I must go with my friends," she said. "Maybe we talk more tonight okay?"

"Okay, but wait. Here. Give me your camera." I asked someone to take a picture of us. I had a strong feeling that I would see this girl again, and my Western instinct was to snap away and picture the moment. We posed like tourists in front of the blue and gold gates of Babylon, where civilisation had begun, and parted soon after, agreeing to meet later that night.

As we left Babylon, all the school children sang a sweet-sounding Iraqi farewell song. My heart cringed at the thought that the world's best-equipped army, the most fearless fighters, and the most disciplined killing machines were gathering and preparing to mount their assault on these unsuspecting children.

Chapter 12
God's Will

Before the throne of the Almighty, man will be judged not by his acts but by his intentions. For God alone reads our hearts.
                                                                Mahatma Gandhi

We arrived at the Palestine Hotel in time for what seemed like a traditional Iraqi dinner and a dessert of local sweets. There was an air of excitement among the NASYO delegates as the organisers and the hotel staff prepared for Dr Huda, who was due to arrive for a more private discussion with the high-profile foreign diplomats and senior academics.

I was mostly interested in finding Rema and spending more time with her, as she seemed to re-ignite an old flame in my heart that I thought had been extinguished a long time ago. I was walking around the hotel grounds in search of Rema when I saw Dr Huda casually walking along with a small group of delegates I recognised as the German and Japanese representatives.

I followed them for a little while, acting as if I was inconspicuously sightseeing and appreciating the architectural designs of a shoebox room and admiring the fading white paint on the walls like a connoisseur of fine art. I was engrossed by the mesmerising designs of the Persian rugs when a burly Iraqi security guard approached me and asked what I was looking for and if I had lost anything.

I was going to reply that I had lost my mind, but I didn't think the translation in Arabic may have had the same meaning. Instead I said, "I'm just looking around."

"You like looking round?" he asked me in broken English better than any Arabic I could muster.

"No, I sometimes like to look square," I kidded.

But he wasn't amused and looked at me questioningly. By the confused look on his face, I knew instantly that he did not appreciate my smart remark, and I thought I was going to be grabbed and hurled out on to the street. Instead, he continued to interrogate me. I was doomed now, I thought.

"Where you from Mister?" he asked.

"Spanish-Australian," I answered, now more seriously, realising this big man was not about to joke around with me.

"Huh?" he grunted.

"I am in-ter-na-tio-nal," I said slowly, thinking it may make this big ape understand me. "International," I echoed. "You un-der-stand me?"

"Oh! NASYO?"

"No, in-ter-na-tio-nal," I corrected.

"Yes, but you are with NASYO," he said as a matter of fact, making me feel stupid.

"Yes."

"Ah. You come to meet Dr Huda?"

"Yes," I lied, thinking it may save my life.

"What is your name?" he asked.

"Al," I said.

"Okay Mr Al. Wait, I ask," he said, and walked to the other guard standing at the entrance to the door where Dr Huda and her guests had entered. He seemed to whisper to the other guard who looked at me, smiled courteously, and walked into the room. He was in there for a whole minute when he emerged and approached me.

"Your appointment with Dr Huda will be at 10:30 tonight," he said. "You are lucky man. You are the last one she will see today," he said.

"Oh, okay. Thank you."

I puffed my chest like I had seen the great man himself do before he talked about national homeland security and his tough stand on terrorism, and then walked away with my arms out like a cowboy ready to draw. Only, my mission was not to see myself as a war president, but more as a romantic looking for a Palestinian angel.

However, Rema was nowhere to be seen, and I shared a table with an English professor and a French doctor. During dinner they joked about the upcoming world rugby cup, football, and women generally, before settling down to the more serious business of the effects economic sanctions had on the entire Iraqi population.

"No wonder Saddam is disarming," the English scholar said with a strong Oxford accent.

"You really zink he can have dis weapon of mass dixtruction?" The French doctor asked, to appease his curiosity about our understanding on the matter.

"Yes," I said, chewing on a carcass, convinced that a madman like Saddam would have just about anything in his home cabinets.

"I don't think so. Look at his army. I mean they don't even have uniforms or modern weapons. How could he possibly afford chemical or biological weapons?" the English professor questioned.

"Why you zink he has dis weapons?" asked the French doctor, looking in my direction to pick my brainwashed mind about Saddam.

"Because I saw it on the CNN and FOX news," I replied smartly.

"But did you know that CNN stands for the Christian News Network and they clearly report with biased and prejudiced anti-Islamic reports, or show the face of Islam as terrorists, the greatest threat to the Judo-Christian relationship?" the English professor asked me, as if I should have already known that.

"Eh—um. No." I hesitated to answer in ignorance.

"You see in ze news how terrorists are always Muslim and not IRA or BASQUE or corporate executives zat profit from starving millions of people in Africa and in zey own countries?" the French doctor asked me in shock.

"Well, um, yes I do, but, um—we don't think terrorism is the solution to the problems of American and Western national security," I said naively.

"Oh, dear me, you really are an extraordinary chap, do you really think that terrorists would want to invade America, or any Western nation for that matter?" the professor asked me with a look of pity now expressed by the squint in his eyes.

"Yes, isn't that what terrorists want?" I asked smartly to challenge these intellectual thinkers.

"My dear boy, I do believe you are the very reason for the state of affairs in our global socio-political environment; if you don't mind me saying that. But I think you need to open your mind to the real possibility that terrorists are not an army but rather embittered individuals who have no other way of fighting a vastly superior army." The English professor paused and I nodded dumbly for him to continue.

But the French doctor continued as if he already knew what the English professor was about to say. "It seems to me zat you have to learn more about our human history to understand why we have evolved to where we are as a global humankind before you parrot or echo ze same words like young George Bush Junior," he added, to make me feel more ignorant than I already was.

"But Saddam has weapons of mass destruction and biological weapons that he can use to hold the world at ransom," I said, thinking this to be an ingenious answer. "That's enough evidence to wage war. Isn't it?" I asked sarcastically with a madman's smile. "Isn't that a good reason to destroy a country and create another third world nation?" I added.

I thought I had managed to convince them. As they finished their meals in silence I felt the looks on their faces telling me that they feared the madman sitting between them more than Saddam Hussein or George Bush. Indeed, I was mad! Mad at the realisation that colonisation of a now defenceless nation may become the greatest threat to our global economy and a war against Iraq may cost thousands of lives, jobs, and a detrimental damage to our natural environment as we misappropriated funds to deliberately destroy a sovereign state with prejudice.

After dinner, they politely stood and hurried away, leaving me alone with my blissful thoughts about Rema. Where was she, I wondered, knowing she had missed dinner altogether. The world was going to go to war and all I could think about now was Rema. Was she scared of me too?

I went up to my room and washed before putting on my best attire; a white, wrinkled, long-sleeved cotton shirt and a blue pair of faded jeans that I pulled out of my rucksack. Unfortunately, I only travelled with the same desert boots I had bought over a year ago, and they looked a bit out-of-place, with well-worn scratches. I was now ready for what was to become the most important date in my life.

"Hello Mister Al," the English-speaking guard greeted me as he defended Dr Huda's room. "You are early. Yes," he said, smiling.

I looked at my watch and realised it was 9:25. "Oh, yes," I said as if I had known the time. "I was just making sure she was still here."

"Yes, but now she has African guest from Nigeria and after she has fifteen minutes break then she meet Canadian friend. Okay! And then you can meet her at 10:30, okay?" He seemed to ask for my approval.

"Okay," I approved.

Suddenly the doors opened and a young, distinguished looking black man emerged with an African rounded cap on his head, followed by a bigger and older black man. Both men were wearing long robes and wide grins. I had seen them around the sites, in the conventions, at the Almeria shelter, and in Babylon, but we were never introduced, so I immediately extended my hand, and in my coolest Afro-American black speech, introduced myself.

"Hello brothers, I am Al," I said, shaking the hand of the smaller man first and the bigger later.

"Hello Al, I am Prince Dr Godwill O. Richman, of Nigeria, and I am the World Youth Peace Mission President," he said in perfect English.

"And I am his minder," the bigger fellow smiled as he crushed my hand with his bear-like claw.

"Oh," I muttered. "Where are you from?"

"As Prince of Nigeria, I'm from Nigeria. And you?" he smiled.

"I'm Australian," I said, feeling more at ease.

"Excellent."

He seemed to say the word excellent from within his heart every time he said it, pronouncing it as X-sell-ant, and I smiled, remembering an Eddie Murphy film and thinking, this was the guy who he imitated.

"It's good to know that not all the Australians support Mr Bush. I know there have been many demonstrations in Australia. But why does Mr Howard not listen to his people?" he asked with deep concern.

"I'm not sure," I answered truthfully. "That's why I came to Baghdad. To see for myself and find the truth."

"Excellent. You are a teacher?"

"No."

"An NGO?"

"No. I'm a humanities student."

"Ah. Very good," he said, nodding approval to his minder, who nodded back.

"How was your meeting with Doctor Huda?" I asked, trying to make light conversation as we started to walk toward the main foyer.

"Excellent," he said again. "We believe this conference will have positive outcomes and we want to ensure more money is spent on humanitarian relief than weapons," he said. "Dr Huda is a smart lady and as the deputy to the Ba'ath party, she could become the first woman to govern Iraq."

"Excellent," I found myself echoing this man's word.

I noted he smiled at my use of the same word. Or was it something else? I looked down my shirt for a possible stain, but only saw wrinkles. I looked up, and it dawned on me that he had introduced himself as a prince. But I thought I may have misheard him and asked him, "What do you do?"

This was a popular question to ask when you mix with Westerners but perhaps a dumb question to ask a prince.

"I am the General President of the World Youth Peace Mission," he said, nodding an approval or code to his minder who reached in his briefcase and handed him a business card. "We are holding many meetings and conferences to raise awareness of the many problems our youth of the world face these times. If you have any interest in this matter you may contact me any time you like," he said, relaying the business card his minder gave him to me.

"Cool," I said, trying to sound hip.

"Are you scheduled to meet Dr Huda now?" he asked.

"Yes. Well, in about an hour," I said, trying to sound more important than I really was.

"Excellent. Well do you want to join us for a cup of tea?" he invited.

"Sure." I accepted the invitation to spend time with a prince and we walked and talked at the same time all the way to the main foyer, where we were seated, and chatted some more.

He discussed the problems of illiteracy in African countries. He talked about child slavery, abuse, homelessness, AIDS, and the many children that were used in the front lines of warring tribes. He had a genuine passion for helping children not just from his country but from Africa and around the world. As we spoke, I was drawn to respect this great man as a true prince. Perhaps a time would come when he would inherit a throne and I was pleased to know that not all kings or sultans were as docile, apathetic, and cowardly as other monarchs we already knew about. Individuals were more obsessed with the importance of their kingdoms than the welfare of the children within them.

"You see Mr Al, child abuse is the real terrorist!" he said with a look that could kill.

I nodded and agreed with him, realising that there were other forms of terrorism that we were not addressing, like child abduction in America, or child slavery in India. What were we as a people doing to eradicate or save these children from condemned, painful lives?

"We believe there are ten things we must address if we want to make the world a safer place for the majority and the mainstream and not for the few people in privileged power," he said casually before spelling each one out for me in point form and holding up a different finger as he did so. "First, today's children are tomorrow's leaders. Second, the youth are the investment of a nation. Third, a nation's wealth is in its youth, not their stubborn and aged that are unwilling to change or accept alternatives to co-existence. Fourth, we believe that the youths are the real reservoir of peace. Fifth, is the obvious no to violence and yes to peace in every country on Earth.

'Sixth, is to say no to weapons of any kind and resolve to promote knowledge and dialogue as the key to the future of mankind. Seventh, the youth are the prerequisite to the elders' health as the youth will ultimately care for their elders. Eight, the youth can be self-reliant, self-disciplined, and are fast thinkers so we must teach them well and learn to rely on their judgements—the judgements we will have taught them to make without prejudices. Ninth, our youths are the catalyst for social, economic, and political development, so it is vital we invest as a priority to their education. And finally: the tenth point is that no nation should ever despise their youth or promote drugs, violence, or crime as a means to survival. Rather they should provide free education and promote healthy lifestyles to all its youths at any cost," he said sternly.

"It is impossible to argue in favour of any war knowing it will be the children who suffer the most. Yet, the English law regime and the George W. Bush administration were able to convince the world with blatantly manufactured lies about weapons of mass destruction so that a war was justified. How do we, the people of planet Earth, let this happen?"

"You are an amazing man," was all that I could mutter at the reality that here was a true and noble prince that cared more for his people and others on Earth than for his assets, his reputation, or his military supremacy.

"Thank you, but tell me truly, what do you think about our beliefs?" he asked humbly.

I paused to think and could only recall how the youth in developed nations were manipulated with meaningless and un-educational entertainment. Violent video games, sexually-arousing music videos, provocative clothing, and the glamourisation of alcohol or nicotine were Western values promoted on television screens for the uneducated and vulnerable youth.

Yet the consumption of these products would ultimately result in crimes that would destroy lives and benefit mostly those who upheld the laws: large international corporations, legal practitioners, and the crown.

The revelation was uplifting and all that came to mind was to echo this prince in helping the African youth and I replied, "Excellent."

At that moment, I felt like Moses must have felt when he received the Ten Commandments from God. What a privileged man Moses was. How ironic that it would be Prince Godwill from Nigeria who would share with me ten crucial points, like commandments, for the real benefit of the greatest majority of us and our children on Earth.

However, with the amassing armies surrounding Iraq, my mind snapped to the reality that other more sinister forces were about to send the world into turmoil over Iraqi oil.

Suddenly, I looked at my watch and realised an hour had passed and now I was running late to meet the little lady who stood next in line to govern Iraq, the deputy of the Ba'ath party, Dr Huda.

"I must go, I'm running late," I said to the young prince hastily before running off, shouting at him from across the main foyer, "we can chat more tomorrow!"

"Excellent!" he shouted back, smiling.

Chapter 13
Democracy with Prejudice

*For us, terrorism remains the great evil of our time,
and the war against this evil, our generation's great cause ...
There is no middle way for Americans: it is victory or holocaust.
These ideas are foundational elements of neo-conservatism.*

Richard Perle
Former Secretary of US Defence

I hurried to my scheduled appointment and the two talking giants made it clear that I was now ten minutes too late.

"But it's only five minutes late," I tried to play it down and buy five minutes from the ten minutes by their watch.

"Mr Al, Dr Huda have bee-see day you know," he started, but was stopped when Dr Huda's assistant opened the door and called for me to enter.

"It okay, Mr Al, Dr Huda will see you now but it will be briefly okay?"

"Okay," I agreed and smiled courteously at the two guards.

When I walked in, Dr Huda was sitting behind a long table with only her assistant in the room. She stood to shake my hand, then sat and remained perfectly poised as she was every other time I had seen her speak throughout the convention. Her back was straight and her hands touched at the fingertips. She looked tired and serious yet spoke with the passion of a future leader. It became clear that a woman of this nature should be destined to be the deputy of the Ba'ath party and next in line to rule Iraq. She had time not only for all the foreign diplomats and academics she had seen during the day, but also for an unknown entity such as myself.

"Thank you for seeing me," I said, as we shook hands and I took a seat close to her.

"It is my pleasure," she said, welcoming me.

"You may appreciate that my life is on the line," I said, thinking from my paranoid state of mind.

"Oh." She seemed to gasp. "Why is that?"

"I'm going to be a Human Shield if America invades," I said, trying to sound brave, honourable, and as dignified as any Human Shield should be.

"That's very honourable. But not necessary. There is not going to be a war," she said, comforting me. "But let me see. Are you Australian? Or are you Spanish?"

"I am an Australian that was born in Spain. So I call myself, a Spanish-born Australian," I explained.

"You are a truly international man!" she flattered me.

"No, I am an Australian. You see, all Australians have at least two identities, since we have an international origin as well as an Australian origin. That is what makes Australia a neutral country in all conflicts. Do Iraqis have two nationalities also?" I asked her.

"Well, in some ways yes. But we are more like the indigenous Aboriginal people of your country. We have always lived in and occupied Iraq."

"But our Aboriginal people now live under English rule, which makes them dual nationals as well," I said.

"Yes. We know how that is. Iraq was once ruled by the British, and that is what we fear the American-led coalition really wants. To control and rule Iraqis under the pretext of democracy! But they do not speak the truth, and as we Iraqis know only too well, the truth will always prevail."

"But doesn't it bother you that the Americans are getting ready for war and have made it clear they will strike even if the United Nations says no?"

"No," she echoed what all Iraqis seemed to believe. "But we have faith in the United Nations and the international courts in The Hague. Above all, we believe in Allah, the most compassionate and the most merciful. So we have firm beliefs that with the truth, justice always prevails," she affirmed. "But tell me, why is your government supporting to attack my people unilaterally with the coalition but without approval from the United Nations?"

"I'm not sure. That's why I came to Iraq: to learn more about the real reason why we would start another war when we already know that modern warfare is futile."

"And what have you learned?" she asked.

I explained to her that in the West, the news reports were all negative about the Saddam regime. We were never told the positive aspects like the free medical and health care or the free education. I was never aware that Iraq was not an extremist fundamental Islamic state like

Afghanistan under the Taliban, but more secular like Turkey and Iran were—freedom of religion was a legal right. Nor was I aware that the system of democracy in Iraq was the fundamental basis for an Islamic state, or that Saddam really wanted to achieve peace for the Iraqi nation that had only ever known war. In fact, most Western soldiers never knew or did not understand how it was the Americans who in the first place sold Iraqi weapons of mass destruction so they could be used to combat and fight Iranians on behalf of American interests. That is why, from what I have seen of Iraq, I am tempted to become a Human Shield," I concluded.

"You think your governments will listen to the Human Shields?" she asked.

"Yes. We have democratically elected humane governments and they would never attack or bomb their own people."

"Yes, I understand that we are the same in that regard," she said.

"But that's not what we hear," I challenged her. "We understand that you used chemical weapons against your own people up in the north?"

"Really, and you believe it?" she asked as if surprised.

"Yes. And we saw the film footage and photos in the news as evidence."

"My God—and you believed we would kill innocent people for no reason?"

"Well, yes, at first, but not exactly everything. That's why I am here, to get the truth," I said confidently.

"Does your media show you the dying and suffering people that American bombs have killed?"

"No," I admitted.

"I can see you are an intelligent man," she flattered me some more, "so let me ask you a question. What would our people gain if we bombed our own people? I mean, do you think Saddam would have the support he has if he murdered his own people?"

"Maybe if he manipulated the media coverage."

"Do you believe that our journalists would report lies?"

"I don't know. There are many regimes that censor journalists or news coverage and in some places they face executions, imprisonment, or deportation for reporting the truth," I said smartly.

"Executions, imprisonment, and deportations for reporting the truth, you must think we are barbarians?" she asked as a pretext to her most revealing statement that prophesised what was to come. "Look at your own media and tell me, are they really telling you the truth? I mean, you yourself came to Iraq in search of the truth because you understand how the media works. So when you return, try and tell the story from an Iraqi perspective and see if your media will communicate it to your people. But please make sure your people understand that what we really want is an end to economic sanctions and to continue living in peace, not in war," she added.

"Okay." I agreed to her test, and with this book I comply.

"As you know, every government faces opposition and sometimes the opposition attempts to kill leaders that are as successful as Saddam has been for Iraq since he came to power. Here in Iraq, we call those who try to kill Saddam terrorists, and under Sharia law, they would face certain execution," she explained. "You see, these are regional problems we face as leaders of this nation. We do not need or ask for a foreign intervention, rather for understanding and now lasting peace."

Perhaps I was now being brainwashed by a wave of logical thought as Dr Huda talked reason and common sense. I understood immediately why she was the Ba'ath party deputy and next in line to govern Iraq. She had an acutely sharp mind and a completely serene and relaxed manner that could only inspire those who would come to contact with her.

"I am certain that the educated and learned people on Earth understand that every regional leader, no matter how great or small their region of governance is, can only be deposed by their own people and not by foreign military intervention or foreign propaganda. So if Iraqis wanted Saddam ousted, we could do that amongst ourselves, but the fact is, the majority of Iraqis continue to support our leader. But I am certain that is not what your propaganda media would be broadcasting to your people."

"Does Iraq have weapons of mass destruction?" I asked her point blank.

"No," she said firmly and confidently. "We have seen too much war in our history, we just want peace and to be left alone and trade in the world markets," she answered frankly.

"So why did you invade Kuwait?" I challenged her.

"As you know, Kuwait is traditionally an Iraqi state and before 1990, Kuwaiti government was trading against the interest of Iraqi and Arab states. So we felt the only way to reclaim our land after many failed attempts to negotiate with the American sponsored Kuwaiti oil merchants, who now call themselves sultans, was war. We invaded Kuwait with the understanding of American diplomats that they would not interfere. But we have learned an expensive lesson and now know that war was the wrong action. We have since paid our compensation and endured the thirteen years of economic sanctions. We have paid the penalty and now we want to get back with the business of governing our people. That is why we want peace," she answered.

"I guess it makes sense," I said, truly believing that this woman could not possibly be as evil as our Western media had portrayed her to be.

"I will be surprised but delighted to hear from you again further down the road to see if your findings and our side of history is ever told in Spain or Australia, let alone the other Western allied countries," she challenged, not knowing her destiny would be cut short by the invasion against her government.

"I'm sure that we will. We have free speech in our country."

"So do we," she answered with a concerned look on her face as if trying to work out my questions.

"But what about the executions and tortures that take place in Iraq against those that speak against the Saddam regime?" I asked now more frustrated and anxious get at the truth.

"Mr Al," she paused, and I could sense that I was getting to her and now hurting her with the truth. Or was she genuinely tired after a long day, at now almost eleven o'clock at night? "It is late, and as you can imagine, it's been a long day and I am tired. I would love to continue to speak with you and answer all of your questions. But that would take a lot more time than we currently have. So unfortunately, we will need to end our meeting now. Okay?"

"But what about the mass graves?" I asked her bluntly.

"This is Iraq, we have had many wars and the Americans have killed many thousands of Iraqis over the past thirteen years. We have criminals that under Islamic Sharia law are sentenced to death for rape, murder, treason, and infidelity. But unlike Iran and Pakistan or Saudi Arabia, we don't always have public executions. We feel these criminals need no respect. And as you know, Islam is about the future of our children and how they will share what we leave behind for them to inherit; it is not about burying our dead in monumental graves. You should not forget that the American bombardment of Iraqi soldiers killed tens of thousands of Iraqi soldiers during the 1991 war. And yes, we buried many of our fallen in mass graves along with the many innocent women and children the American bombs have killed," she concluded.

I was horrified by this admission but it gave a reasonable explanation for why the Iraqis now lived in peace and in a relatively crime-free state. Hardened criminals would be sentenced to death and many escaped to live in the West where their crimes would be untold. Many Muslim criminals have prospered in Western civilisation where they do not face the harsh punishment of Sharia laws.

"But tell me one last thing," I said as she stood to walk me outside. "You know that the coalition forces are going to attack, don't you?" I asked as we approached the door.

"No. I don't know that, and I don't believe they will go against the United Nations resolutions. They are not that barbaric," she said humbly.

I couldn't believe that for such an intelligent woman she could be so naïve that the coalition led by the George W. Bush administration would not attack one of the most oil-rich nations on Earth when it was impoverished by sanctions and defenceless from the disarmament process.

"I will pray to God that you are right," I confessed my earlier prayers. "But I believe your country will be attacked," I said as she stood and showed me the door.

"Mr Al. We are Muslims, and we believe everything that happens is God's will. So if you are right, it will be the will of Allah. It will be your duty to do whatever you can to ensure such a crime against humanity never happens again as you have attended the NASYO conference and will walk away with your own knowledge. But please don't forget. We Iraqi have known war throughout all our history; we are in our own country, our own lands. I am sure if the Russians or Chinese invaded your lands and occupied your countries, your men, women, and children would unite as one and resist any foreign occupation. Correct?"

"Yes. I suppose so," I nodded in agreement.

"Well our people would simply continue to retaliate and defend our country in any way possible. Even if we need to resort to terrorism like our Palestinian brothers and sisters have needed to do in order to resist the illegal Israeli settlements. And I assure you our people would continue until *all* occupying forces were gone. Isn't it legal to defend your life from an aggressive attacker in America?" she asked, showing me the opened door. "The right to self-govern is fundamental to world peace. And we Iraqis have our own elected government and our leader is Saddam Hussein," she said, stepping outside.

"Well, why doesn't he surrender?" I asked her.

"Why should he? He is our leader and we Iraqis don't want to surrender. We simply want to live in peace and enjoy our own natural wealth. Not have it stolen from us …"

"I can't believe what you're telling me," I confided.

"Then perhaps you should question who is reporting in your own countries and question again who the government spokespeople are in your media. Do they have a name or a face?"

"I don't know," I realised.

"Well, there is a good challenge for you. Sir, now I must really say goodnight and thank you for taking an interest in our plight for peace. Salaam Alecum," she said as we parted.

"Salaam Alecum," I wished her peace in return.

Walking away from the meeting with Dr Huda was an awakening experience. I recalled feeling a bit like I had spoken to a queen. But how could the Western media have portrayed this kind and gentle lady as the doctor of death? Or was it Dr Chemical, or Mrs Anthrax? It was impossible to imagine that a woman of such values and principles could ever condemn anyone to death. If she were as bad as the Western media made out, surely she would use chemical and biological warfare against the advancing Americans. A cold chill ran down my spine, thinking I had once again escaped the claws of death from this notorious killer with an angelic face and immeasurable wisdom. Was she the devil in disguise? And Bush the saint? Or was it the other way around? I wondered these things as I walked away.

I wanted to find Rema and tell her all about my unexpected meeting with Dr Huda. I puffed out my chest as I walked past the two guards still defending Dr Huda's temporary classroom and like the coolest cowboy that ever lived, ready to draw my guns at the twitch of an eye, I strolled around the Palestine Hotel with arms out by my sides and swaying like John Wayne. I was feeling important. I was proud to have a new challenge to test our very own Western media and the values we imposed on the world in the name of democracy and world peace. So I searched for the only person I could share this new challenge with but Rema was nowhere to be seen. *Has she gone already?* I wondered, losing the puff in my chest and slowly returning to reality.

How on Earth does one learn of the many evils that roam our planet and then teach those who don't want to learn how to stand up and fight against those evils? I began to ask myself.

That night, I went to sleep late, as I stayed up thinking and writing the conversation with Dr Huda in my diary and reading some material about the Iraqis and their deep-rooted history. It made some sense that they would have a military man who had fought in the frontlines as their elected leader.

If the American administration really wanted to promote democracy in Iraq, they would have invited the Ba'ath party into the elections. The truth was that the Americans had no real concern for the Iraqi democracy.

Chapter 14
Anything but the Truth

Beware of false knowledge; it is more dangerous than ignorance.
George Bernard Shaw

The following morning I awoke late and ran downstairs looking for Rema. Her bus was leaving at one in the afternoon so I lingered around the hotel lobby talking to Ghassan who noticed my attraction toward her. At about twelve thirty, I saw the fragile feminine stature of a girl carrying a heavy laden backpack. Her friend Abirr accompanied her.

"Al, where were you?" she asked.

"Looking for you!" I admitted.

"Really?"

"Yes."

"Me too. But you not here last night," she noted.

"I was talking with Dr Huda," I said, puffing my chest again with pride.

"What you talk about with Dr Huda?" she asked, perhaps wondering what I was doing puffing out my chest as if I were a Silverback Gorilla.

I explained and retold our conversation briefly, but by the time I had finished she was being called to mount the bus. I wanted to kiss her, but that was disrespectful with a Muslim woman unless she was your wife or a family member. In fact, it was disrespectful to kiss any person we didn't know intimately in public, no matter what religion or gender. But it did not deter from the natural urge we feel when we want to kiss someone who is genuinely and sincerely innocent of the feelings of love they provoke within our hearts.

I had already learnt that it was left to a Muslim woman to decide if she wanted to shake your hand, either in private or in the public space for all to see, as the power was with her. Above all, I had learned that Muslim women were deemed untouchable unless she allowed you that liberty, which is why under Sharia law, a rapist faced imminent death. So I was happy when Rema extended her hand in friendship, allowing me the opportunity to squeeze her fragile hand firmly; as the most subtle emotional gesture that a man is permitted to express publically in the Islamic states.

"Can I contact you when I get to Amman?" I asked her as we shook hands. Our eyes firmly locked, our senses oblivious to the turmoil that surrounded us.

"Yes okay," she said, looking flustered, and suddenly turned to go.

"But I don't have your phone number," I cried desperately after her.

"Oh, here." She took my notepad and pen and scribbled it on the back cover of the pad. "Call me when you come to Amman okay?"

"Okay. See you in Amman," I said as she walked away with her friend Abirr hurrying her onto the bus. It felt ridiculous to stand alone by the side of a bus gazing at her until she sat down by the window. But I had been paralysed by the crippling grip that a gentle woman can have over the vulnerable heart of a single man. Who would have thought that it is our governments, the people we vote and entrust to represent us, that have the power to break families and tear hearts apart? *What world were we creating for our children where war, materialism, and spiritual ignorance would determine the fate of the majorities*, I thought.

When the bus turned the corner away from my line of vision, I sat on a stone ledge near the parking lot. From here I could see the great statue of Saddam Hussein saluting in the direction of Baghdad city. What will become of this grand city if the G. W. Bush administration decides to bomb her people?

Shortly after being dumb-struck by the germinating sensations of love, reality awoke my consciousness to the fact that I was in the very centre of the East and the West in the prelude to a modern day war.

From my vantage point, I could see as the remaining NASYO delegates were ushered into buses and I was waved in to join them.

We were then taken to the great hall where Dr Huda was going to sum up and close the NASYO convention. However, as she spoke, my mind was distracted by the thoughts of a platonic love for Rema and the knowledge that a war with Iraq was inevitable.

To understand why we, the self-acclaimed free world, would launch an attack on a now-impoverished and disarmed nation, was impossible. I tried to understand the kind of person George W. Bush was. But all I could think about was a man I had fought many years ago in Sydney's affluent suburb called Double Bay. In this suburb was the Golden Sheaf Hotel, which was where the mostly wealthy private school students would meet every Thursday and Friday nights. These schools included Scots College; Cranbrook; Sydney Grammar; St Andrew's; and Waverley College from the boys' side, and King Copple Rose Bay Convent; Kambala; Ascham; S.C.E.G.G.S; St Vincent's; Holy Cross; and St Catherine's, which made up the girls.

Having grown up amongst the poorer Aboriginal community in Redfern with the elderly unemployed and the housing commission working families, the drug dealers and the alcoholics, as my peers, I accepted the invitation from some friends to see how the other half lived. Or perhaps I was more drawn to the possibility that I may meet that illusive princess so we could live happily ever after, as television screens repeatedly showed our generation how wonderful it was to be married to the beauty queens of the more affluent suburbs and how sad and ugly the other alternative can be. When I reflect on those days, it makes me realise that poverty truly is the seed to our success, or it can be the cancer that eats our self-esteem and drives us insanely toward the consumption of mind-numbing drugs so we may live in anything but the sad truth to our existence as the poor.

However on this night, I would also learn how the spoiled children of a selfishly wealthy parent could be so obnoxious and self-righteous that we called them brats. These were children that grew up in the same environment as the likes of George W. Bush and Saddam Hussein's son Uday; children that gave nepotism its true meaning. Kim Jong-Il from North Korea, Saif al-Islam Gaddafi from Libya, Prince Charles from England, and so on … these were children who grew up never experiencing hunger, hardship, injustice, or abuse.

Hence we use the term 'brats' to distinguish these self-righteous people that employ servants at will from the day they are born, as opposed to the rest of us who understand the painful truth that our destiny is paved as a long road of seemingly endless hard work. What empowers us to label these individuals as different to the rest of us, is the knowledge we have that it is these brats that may decide if we go to war or live at peace. Or more to the point, these are the brats that have the ability to be the most abusive with the power they yield; a power they were given, rather than a power earned.

As I recall, this was my first visit to the upmarket hotel, and I was not dressed suitably to match the expensive tastes of Sydney's wealthiest youth. As I did my best to imitate a cheap version of a James Bond secret agent amidst the ocean of real hardcore 007 agents, I was spotted by the presiding chief-of-staff who walked toward me with his chest puffed and arms out. I was completely ignorant of his dominance amongst the Thursday night crowd as the alpha male lion from Scots College. Not that that would have mattered as I toyed and played with the beautiful princess I had just met.

"What are you doing here chatting to these ladies that are well above your class?" he asked me, sitting himself down on the other side of the teenage beauty queen.

I guessed it was my desert boots that gave me away—or was it my flannelette tartan shirt? Perhaps my torn, faded jeans did not agree with his immaculate, expensive fashion labels.

Nevertheless, the insult burned my pride and I could only retaliate with an offensive line, not knowing about his dominance amongst the Thursday night crowds.

"I'm doing what you can't do," I challenged him stupidly, "being a man!" I said this thinking that now according to the English laws, I was eighteen and legally a man. In many third world countries, boys became men as soon as they could fire a rifle, prostitute their young bodies to wealthier lords that paid for their sexual services, or work to earn a meagre income for their families—all mostly before they reached puberty.

"Oh, you're a smartass as well," he acknowledged.

"Only with those that want to cut my grass unsolicited," I reasoned, trying to impress the sexy young girl who now flirted with me. Her age was deceiving. She had small breasts and the face of a child, yet her lip-glossed makeup and her provocative clothing made every man and woman turn to look at her.

"Listen mate!" he said, hitting the table hard with a closed fist that caused my drink to spill over, pouring its contents over my best and only jeans. "If I wanted a smartass, I'd go west to your suburbs to find one!" he asserted, challenging me.

"Well, maybe you should go west, young man." I echoed a famous line with my madman's grin to hide my shame that was now raging inside me and making my face flush red.

"Oh you're a real cowboy aren't you? Coming out here, trying to be what you're not." He answered his own question like I had seen young George W. Bush Junior do.

"Look, he's going red," one of the girls noticed my shame, and the laughter that followed made my face burn to a darker shade of red.

"Mate, you really should go. Your time here is over," this brat suggested as I looked to see where my friends were, but they seemed busy with their own conquests.

So I leaned over to this son of a greater man than he, and whispered, "Look mate, just leave me in peace. Can't you see I'm making progress here?"

I was thinking this would qualify as my first warning as a subtle man-to-man message. Perhaps Saddam Hussein had also warned George W. Bush of the disastrous consequences when he warned of the dangers if Americans invaded Iraq. Perhaps Saddam Hussein was also enticing the ignorant brat that G. W. Bush was into his trap for the greater good of Iraqis, who now had very little to lose and only gains to be made.

In any case, this brat continued the verbal assault, which made me realise that I was now going to encounter another pig-headed megalomaniac in the shape of a young spoiled brat.

"Progress ... with her? Mate, she's way above your kind. Aren't you baby?" he asked the blonde aloud so that the world would know his superiority in wealth and social status. Or perhaps it was simply to discredit my reputation, like I had seen the Western media discredit governments that opposed the wealthier influences of American foreign policies. Propaganda truly is a double-edged sword that can slice through any truths at the whim of a brat. I knew this girl was well above my kind, which was perhaps why it was more challenging a conquest.

The girl I now called Bambi sat back, watching the spectacle with amusement as his coalition of wildcats began to gather around. The herd of young, beautiful, stupid girls, some too young to be drinking the alcohol they now consumed, were laughing and giggling while waiting to be pawed by the other cats that now seemed to be circling our table.

"I don't mind him," Bambi interrupted this alpha male, looking at me with her fluttering eyes. "He's more handsome than you, so piss off!" she said with hearty laughter at her friends who were watching with gleeful amusement, and they all laughed.

"He's not going to look good after I rearrange his face," he threatened indirectly, looking at the gathering crowd for support. *Why do cowards and the guilty always provoke with lies to gain temporary support?* I wondered. *Or worse, why do the lords of our destiny invent laws that we must keep and they can break?*

"There's going to be a fight!" one of Bambi's friends said aloud.

I wished that girl had remained quiet and not added fuel to the mounting fires. She was like the media who boasts loudly 'WAR' or like a pack of school kids that shout 'Fight, fight, fight!' hoping to add some excitement to their miserable lives as they encourage two fools to fight each other over a girl. Or two oil merchants that employ entire armies of servants to go and kill each other over their oil.

"I think we should go," I said to Bambi as I grabbed her hand and stood to exit the scene.

"She's not going anywhere with you," this global dictator commanded.

"Oh, aren't I?" she said, now rising and getting her things. "See you girls later," she dismissed herself from her allies and joined my ranks as if she understood that a global dictatorship was not what she required in order to flourish, within the frustrating and sensitive environment that was striving for world peace.

However, this must have aggravated the boy, who continued to reason and justify his superiority over my third world existence in the working class suburbs. So I walked hand-in-hand with Bambi whilst this nagging, spoiled brat continued to nag and now allege that I had a knife or some hidden weapon in my back pocket.

"You've got a knife in your back pocket, haven't you?" he alleged with a question that would convince his coalition.

Clearly, he was using his political influence over the materialistically rich and spiritually poor crowd to win their support, using his sharper command of the English language as verbal propaganda to falsely discredit me and muster support from the gathering coalition. This was a coalition that remained apathetically oblivious to the truth. And his verbal humiliation continued as we walked outside followed by his friends that now surrounded me, wanting to see a fight.

"Mate, I'm not going to tell you again, but if you don't go away, I will hurt you," I said, looking at him over my right shoulder as Bambi held my left hand. This was now my second warning, and I was clear that after the third warning, it was God's will that I retaliate with an insurgent attack to defend what I now held in my hand, the oil-rich Bambi, with the honour I needed to defend my sovereignty. It was like governing my own nation without an American government telling me what I could or could not do with my natural wealth.

"Oh, the cool cat is smooth, I suppose you carry a hidden weapon, don't you? That's the only way you can hurt anyone, right." He sensed my pre-fight fear and continued to relentlessly use anything in his power to discredit me and indirectly seek to reassure his safety concerns that I would not pull out a secret weapon to pulverise his stubborn megalomaniac ego.

"I don't need weapons," I said as we reached the rear lane exit of the Golden Sheaf Hotel.

"I bet you have; don't you, boys?" he asked his blind followers who seemed to agree with everything he said without question.

Remembering Ticker the Turk's Islamic wisdom, I replied casually, thinking that perhaps with the unbeatable strength of the human spirit and the unconditional faith in Allah, the spoiled child of a wealthy father would go away and leave me alone.

I replied, "I will warn you that if you are asking for a fight, I will hurt you."

This statement seemed to aggravate him.

As we stepped outside of the safety of the United Nations in the shape of a large Pacific Islander and a Russian heavyweight hotel security bouncer's jurisdiction, he stepped in front of me to block my path and prevented me from passing him as I stepped right, then left. I came to a halt at the end of the road.

"Mate, I don't want to fight you," I admitted, noticing for the first time that he was marginally taller, heavier, and broader than me. When I looked around, his coalition seemed to be gathering and circling around him. The pre-fight nerves began to tremble my hands. This was definitely my third and final warning. Another false accusation, threat, or hostile act would warrant my full and unconditional retaliation. Just as Ticker the Turk had once told me.

"But I hate your dirty kind coming here and taking our women, you greasy wog," he said, making it clear that he was not going to quit his assault as he dug his pointer finger hard into my chest.

Instinctively, I released Bambi's hand, clenched my fists with nervous anger, and like a madman swung a punch, connecting with my aggressor's jaw. That was enough to send him tripping across to a parked car, which held him up from completely falling to the ground. I turned and shaped up against any of the coalition willing to attack. But not one approached.

When I looked at the now dazed brat, I could see he was coming to his senses. So I completed the task of knocking him to the ground with a final combination, and again turned to see if any of his coalition would defend him. But again, they simply stared in shock.

As I remembered this brat who would never understand what it was like to grow up in the slums or wake up at three thirty in the mornings to work selling newspapers or mixing a batch of concrete and carrying heavy stones before school as I had done in my childhood. The similarities between the coalitions of the willing against the aging Saddam Hussein were daunting, making me oblivious to the concluding remarks that Dr Huda was making.

"We do not have any weapons of mass destruction and we are simply wanting peace for our people and the lifting of economic sanctions, so that we may restore all our international relations and continue trading with our partners…" She continued to repeat her mantra with desperate pleas for peace, while my thoughts shifted to the reality of our brave new modern first world.

When I first arrived in Iraq, my fear was expecting to be lynched or captured and tortured to death by a secret Iraqi police. Now I realised that the secret police were not in Muslim countries that left everything to the hands of Allah, but rather in our very own Western nations. I knew if I stayed and waited for the police, they would have arrested me for the battery or assault of this brat who clearly needed to learn some manners under the natural law that is as old as the origin of speech.

What I feared is that in the English law courts, justice would have favoured him simply because he could afford expensive legal representation, while my poverty would have condemned me to a criminal status. So I hurriedly exited the scene with the peace of mind that natural Justice had been served, and this brat would never humiliate another human in public again.

Paradoxically, the CIA, FBI, Mossad, ASIO, MI5, KGB, and CINE, among others, were all highly financed Western government entities designed to spy and lynch criminals or foreign threats to national security. Their agents are paid inflated salaries to spy and do as they are told in the same way that Police officers become trained to be good obedient servants entrusted to protect us. We should be reminded that it is our tax dollars that we employ these public servants, who in real terms are our employees. So what I needed to know is why I was seeing hordes of police lines heavily armed and overly financed to stop peaceful demonstrators from marching, chanting, and raising the public awareness of the crimes our governments were about to commit by invading Iraq? This was the question I needed to answer.

We already knew that some of these overpaid police and spy agents had the capacity to act corruptly. It was natural to say that every dog had a price, and some of these agents had the capacity to manufacture lies and perpetrate injustices beyond the tax-payers' understanding.

In the guise of national security, these entities have the power to arrest, incarcerate, sensor, edit, and kill any individual or government that threatens brats like Kim Jong-Un from North Korea, or G. W. Bush. We the powerless people either accept the payment and the work, or some other bastard will take the job of jumping on the high horse of morality from the perspective of a brat.

We The People should never forget that our governments and our police are employed to serve us. It is our taxes that pay them their salaries. It is our votes that employ them, and it is our world that we entrust them to govern. We do not pay taxes to protect brats, giant corporation executives, or in particular, brat's protecting the oil rich corporations that are ultimately polluting our natural environments rather than ensuring the future of our children.

It was well-known that individuals who lacked the capacity of surviving on their own intelligence became reliant on the public purse, such as police officers, politicians, and crown prosecutors, or else they were dependent on the state for a lifetime job. In the same vein, these government bodies were designed to protect us, the people. However, my fear was materialising, as they had become agencies that protected monarchs and an elite few dynasties who had more money than sense, rather than being the transparent public agencies designed to ensure corruption was eliminated, criminals were caught, and justice would prevail.

When I came to my senses, I realised I was listening to the closing speech of the NASYO conference.

"Saddam has asked Mr Bush repeatedly for a debate to resolve our differences but Mr Bush has denied us that peaceful measure. We have done everything in our power to prevent a war and we are all here today to seek peaceful resolutions on behalf of our people," Dr Huda explained.

She went on to plead for us in the international community to understand that Iraq was surrounded by natural enemies and would like nothing more than everlasting peace. But now with the American threats of war, once again Iraq needed to arm and prepare for war. Instead, they were disarming and respecting the wishes of the United Nations.

"This is our way of leading the world by example of our peaceful intentions," she said, with a tired tone to her voice. "If we want the world to truly live in peace, we must all disarm for the greatest of mankind and the future of life on Earth." The crowd erupted in a loud rapture of applauding, cheers, and chants, which again silenced the small lady.

"We have made peace with our Iranian brothers and sisters in the East, we continue to look for solutions with the northern Kurds, we have been disarming as requested by the Israelis and Americans in the West, and we have surrendered our state of Kuwait in the south as requested by the United Nations. Now, we simply do not know what else we can do to demonstrate to the world that we want lasting peace not just for the Iraqi people, but for our region and the world at large."

There was an eerie silence when she said that, perhaps because many Iraqis at that conference believed that Kuwait should continue to be a state of Iraq or because the Kurds continued to attack and terrorise the Iraqis from the north, or because there were threats of American invasion from the West. Even if these notions were a part of the picture, I felt that the main idealism of global peace was the main point. The international NASYO delegation and the Iraqi locals alike sat in silence, realising that what she was in fact saying was that Iraq had succumbed to the economic sanctions and was now surrendering to the world at large.

"So now, ladies and gentlemen, you can see that we the Iraqi people simply want for the rest of the world to follow the disarmament process to make the world safer, united and at peace for the better of mankind," she concluded, and again the hall erupted with chants, whistles, and applauding rapture.

The truth of the matter was that the world needed cheaper fuel offered by Iraqis and Iranians and not the profit-driven American corporations that continued to break records with all-time high personal incomes that were impacting global economies.

The world needed to give Saddam Hussein an opportunity to speak in the international media rather than destroy the environment with the consequences of a modern war. The truth was, a modern war would affect all life on Earth in the long run. With nine trillion dollars in the wrong hands, we could expect to hear anything but the truth. What greater evil was there than a global media that manipulates truths to protect the interests of a few? The truths were certainly going to hurt some monarchs, governments, and individuals whose grasp on power verged on psychotic megalomania.

In the years that followed, Collin Powell later affirmed and admitted he lied in his testimony before the United Nations Security council, saying it had been manufactured to justify the invasion of Iraq.

The truth was painfully clear much later, yet it was even clearer to those of us who were there at the time.

Chapter 15
Angels in Baghdad

Angel, *n. Divine messenger (one of a class of spiritual beings: lovely or innocent beings; attendants of God; obliging, kind person).*

The following day I went to Ghassan's family home. I was instantly amazed to see the striking resemblance with my grandparents' house in Spain. The overwhelming feeling of being home was soothing to my soul. There was a solid old timber door that hung on old steel hinges, and the walls were whitewashed with lime inside and out. The floors were paved with large terracotta tiles and there was a small entry foyer that opened with a passageway that led to a warm and welcoming sitting area or tea room with an open fireplace. The house may have been built several hundred years ago on the banks of the Tigris River. The Arab-Persian and Moorish influence was unquestionable in Spanish history. In Baghdad I saw the origins of the workman's cottages that would dominate European architecture, and most notably rural Spain.

Ghassan's mother was a gentle, caring, and fragile elderly lady who understood her culture and was raised with the traditional female values to serve and please her husband and nurture her children. She was simply happy to be a woman with a life ambition to serve her family. She covered her hair with a light shawl that she grasped with both hands as if to keep her warm. She greeted me at the entrance, giving me customary kisses to the cheeks and saying in broken English 'welcome, welcome'.

Ghassan's father was a medium-built man about my size but now elderly. His mostly white hair now receded and his mostly white beard reminded me of the pilgrim I had met in Sydney's International Airport. He had a peculiar way of looking at me as if to be studying my every word or gesture. There were times when he leaned back, brushing his moustache and beard with his right hand so that I felt like I was being scrutinised by a great wizard. Such was the aura of his gaze.

After a few minutes of cordial introductions and light conversation, we removed our shoes in the foyer and entered to sit in the warm lounge room where his family liked to spend most of their time together. The absence of a television would guarantee family discussion, games, and intellectual interaction. This was a common scene in the more educated families that I had visited. Perhaps these family gatherings were becoming increasingly absent in the Western world, where families were more likely to be divorcing—often to the delight of family lawyers.

"Ghassan tells me you like literature?" his father asked me with an accent, yet near-perfect English.

"Yes," I admitted my interest in learning from others through reading their stories.

"You know that literature was invented by our very own ancestors," he said, with a humble yet proud smile.

"No. I didn't," I admitted.

"Oh." He seemed surprised about my ignorance. "You didn't study ancient literature in your university?"

"Well, we studied Socrates, Plato, Aristotle, and Sophocles," I answered, wanting to sound smart and dropping the ancient names.

"Ah, the great Greeks," he acknowledged with full respect. "But they were more philosophers than romantic poets, don't you think?" he asked.

"You know about them?" I asked stupidly, thinking that this knowledge was only privy to us Westerners.

"Yes, of course," he said confidently. "Maybe you didn't know that it was the Muslim Arabs that salvaged Greek literature from the Christians and the Romans? They wanted to burn Greek philosophies and literature as they were considered Pagan and anti-Christian; devil's work," he continued my unexpected lesson.

"No," I confirmed my ignorance about the Arabs, Iraq, and Islam in general.

"Well then, maybe now is a good time to learn some things about our country," he advised me as his wife entered the room carrying a tray of boiled sweet tea to complement the sweets, serving us before she sat and joined, with a permanent, warm smile.

"Iraq is the birth nation of the Jews. Our fathers are Abraham; Moses; Noah; Solomon; Jesus; and Mohamed. All these good men came from our lands," he said proudly.

"But Arabs are Muslims," I said, correcting this wise old history professor.

"Yes, that is right. We are mostly Muslims, but not all Muslims. As you know, our father Abraham was Jewish. He gave us the first holy book, the Torah. Abraham is not only the father of the Jews, but the father of the Christians and also the father of Muslims, did you know that?"

"Yes," I said, recalling this from before.

"And did you know that's why all Muslim are Jews first, Christians second, and now thirdly Muslims?"

"Yes, I did," I said, asserting what I had already learned from Sheik Ali.

"So what is it that really brings you here Al?" he asked politely.

"Well, I am ashamed to admit that I am really quite ignorant about Iraq," I admitted. "So I came here to learn more and see for myself what we are not told about this region. Perhaps I may understand the problems that may justify a war," I added.

"I see, but the great problems of the world are not with religion. I think it is more to do with money and the ignorance of the majority of people on Earth who really don't want to learn anything after they have reached a certain age. I have seen this problem in many schools I have taught in, both here and abroad," he continued, sharing his wisdom. "You see, after we reach a certain age, many of us stop learning." He paused to sip his tea. "Many discover the pleasures of sex or drugs or wine or perhaps a computer game in today's modern world, and that replaces the instinct to want to learn such boring things as history, science, language, or God forbid, religion," he said, with a joking tone and a smile.

"I know what you mean," I said as I recalled many people I had known who stopped studying after high school, believing that they knew everything they needed to know, ready to toil endlessly for the rest of their lives.

"Perhaps if more people on Earth understood the logical progression of mankind and the evolution of religious and spiritual wisdom, then perhaps we could make the world a truly safer place for all." He paused to sip on his tea again. "After all, it is absurd to think that God would only bless America. Don't you think?" he asked like a true scholar who was always searching for answers to the great mysteries of the world and our universe.

"Mm," I nodded, taking this chance to sip on my tea.

"As we learn more we must change. That is God's will. Many Jews changed and accepted that Jesus Christ is the son of Allah after reading the wisdom contained in the holy bible, which we see is the second book of the Holy Trinity," he added calmly.

I thought I was in for another lecture from a Jehovah's Witness about what I already knew and accepted as truths in both the Torah and the Bible. So I braced myself and sipped some more tea. But Ghassan looked at me, sensing my discomfort, and encouraged me to listen some more.

"Al, listen carefully. This may be the most important lesson you will learn from visiting Baghdad my friend," Ghassan presupposed. "Pay attention," he added, with an understanding smile and turning my attention to his father.

"To understand Iraqis you must first understand the history of our people. We occupied this land forever. We invented agriculture and irrigation over twelve thousand years ago. We invented writing methods and mathematics. Law, order, and the protection of the weak was first written in Baghdad. For the past five thousand years we have lived in peace using our minds to invent and progress so that we may survive together. But by creating riches, we also get attacked and invaded by every neighbour we have. They always come for the things they don't have. That is why we do not need to attack or invade. We have always learned to survive with what Allah has given us. But now we have what you people call, how you say it? 'Black gold'?

"Yes, I know." I confirmed the fact that this war was in the interest of Saudi Arabia, and that the Coalition of the Willing needed to take control of Iraqi Oil fields before sanctions could be lifted, allowing Saddam to remain in power of his sovereign nation.

'You know we were exchanging ideas internationally with Greek philosophers; Roman scholars; Persian poets; and even with Chinese merchants hundreds of years before the establishment of the United Nations. Pythagoras theory was being used in our lands one thousand and seven hundred years before Pythagoras introduced it to the Greeks. Civil engineers first started building tall towers and complex structures here in Iraq. You probably already know that the oldest traces of civilisation in the world are found in southern Iraq. From here you will also find the oldest cities in our world. We domesticated the animals, became horse, camel, and goat breeders, and started grazing and weaving.

'We also established the first school of astrology in Baghdad. This school gave three wise men the guidance from Baghdad to follow that famous star to Bethlehem where they witnessed the birth of the Jewish Palestinian born Jesus Christ, one of the prophets of Allah. We have the Al Mustansiriyah School, which is the oldest university in the world. You probably should also know that around the time of Al Rashid and Al Ma'amoun we searched the civilised world and extended invitations to professors to come here and teach their learning in medicine, mathematics, religion, law and literature … the Jewish father Abraham was born here in Babylon," he uttered, taking a deep breath and a sip of his cooled tea, creating a moment of silence.

Pause.

Reflect.

The Father of the Jews was born in Baghdad.

"Yes, I know some of the things you are saying," I said, breaking the silence. "But I didn't know everything you are telling me," I added, seeing that their attention was focused on me and there was a silence.

"What are you thinking?" Ghassan asked me as we silently sipped our tea and absorbed this information.

"I just wonder how many people in the West know all this," I asked rhetorically.

"Sadly, education is for the lucky and the privileged in every corner of our world," this third wise man confessed.

He looked sad and fragile. I pictured this vulnerable old man as a personification of everything that Iraq and Palestine had become. An ancient old man, filled with academic knowledge and meaningless patriotic pride. Now, impoverished with pain from economic sanctions and without the ability to defend himself, he stood alone, surrounded by thieves who desired his vast wealth. Then I saw America like a giant, young, strong bully mustering support from the schoolyard to justify the crime of beating the little man down into complete submission in order to take that man's wealth. There was simply no way the bully would let that little old man speak or even defend himself. This bully wanted the old man disarmed, impoverished, and vulnerable, for an easy victory and complete domination.

As I thought about this analogy, I remembered my own father's words: "Al, if you see an injustice like a woman or an old man getting attacked, or if it is your own family being beaten, you must get in there and fight for what is right," he instructed after the beating when I saw my sisters in that schoolyard fight.

It was at this time that I realised my visit to Iraq was not futile. I had made this journey to see for myself and discover the truth. Now the truth was unfolding as it became clear that Saddam Hussein was disarming and wanting peace. The Iraqi people desperately wanted help rather than war.

As my street-fighting instincts began to burn like a flame that could only be extinguished with a fight, I realised this was not a street-fight. But I would have to fight the toughest fight of my life; a fight against a regime obsessed with world domination on behalf of a few vested corporate interests. It seemed that for some, financial gain was the moral high ground to be worshipped over the lower values of impoverished human life.

My dilemma was preposterous. How on Earth could any man fight against the might of the Western propaganda machine? All I could think about was the fable of David and Goliath and how under Islamic law, there was no impossibility under the sun, as it was Allah's will. So I temporarily puffed out my chest, but soon deflated it; the reality of the absurdity in my thinking hit me with a devastating blow as the truth hit home.

The world didn't want truths. It wanted jobs; fairer wealth distribution; good health; free dental care; freedom of expression; liberty; justice; and much more, I recalled as my lecture continued.

He told me about the 1980 war with Iran and how the Americans and the British fueled the war with weapons and ammunition. How they had sold Saddam Hussein hundreds of millions in dollars of weapons to fight Iranians. But more alarming, how he feared the same would happen as weapons dealers ensured war would take place to use their expiring merchandise and begin the production of a new range of weapons of mass destruction, like drones and non-discriminating robotic weaponry.

But then he told me how he had been captured by the Iranians in 1987 and escaped as the Iranian captors who got to know him deliberately looked the other way and allowed him to return safely to his family.

"When those Iranian Shiite soldiers let me go, knowing I was a Sunni, I knew in my heart they didn't want to fight us anymore than we wanted to fight them. It was I who told our president Saddam Hussein this story and shortly after we made peace with our Shiite brothers in Iran," he confessed with a hint of pride. "Look at his," he said, showing me a photo with Saddam Hussein shaking his hand in what appeared to be an awards ceremony.

As he spoke, I began to sense that angels were gathering in Baghdad. George Gittoes, for instance, was an Australian artist who had been to more wars than the highest decorated military generals in any army, and never needed to be decorated. Then there was Waratah Gillespie, a street-toughened, highly educated, and humble lady with an accurate understanding of international law. These two angels came to mind immediately, but there were many more. Prince Godwill from Nigeria and most of the NASYO delegates, the underpaid Iraqi doctors and overworked nurses. I thought about the many millions of people that had rallied in peace around the world and knew they would all visit Baghdad if they could afford it. The Australian artist George Gittoes was right—if all the angels on Earth could gather in this holy land, they could defeat the lies, the deception, and the aggression that an evil power could muster. But this prophecy would be overrun by war-hungry demons.

"But I believe they will," I said, thinking about an army of peaceful angels coming to protect this holy land. However, with the knowledge of my gathered intelligence, I knew it may be too late, and there would be an invasion of Iraq by the coalition forces.

"We don't think Americans can be so naïve," Ghassan's father replied.

"And you didn't think the Israelis would make Palestine a Jewish state that discriminates against the Muslims, did you?" Ghassan said, with an angry tone, to challenge his father.

However, Ghassan's father sensed his anger and ignored his son to advise me. "You cannot fight a superior army or you will be killed." He paused to sip his tea.

"At least I will die a martyr, not a coward," Ghassan said with pride.

"At best, what we can do is to learn and know the truth. And remind others that goodness will always triumph over evil. That is our task ... if you want to fight evil, you must be smart and sometimes you must fight fire with fire," his father advised both Ghassan and I.

"But America and her allies are also my countries!" I said, resigned to the reality that it was my very own friends, family, and allies that were going to commit this crime against humanity and the environment. "They are getting ready right now all around Iraq and they are going to bomb and destroy your country!" I said, getting more aggravated by what I already knew, feeling utterly powerless.

"Mr Al, don't worry. There is not going to be a war. We are doing everything that the United Nations has been telling us to do. We are disarming and we want peace. Trust me, my friend. There is not going to be a war," Ghassan interjected.

"Perhaps he is right," the father credited his son.

How could this romantic academic, this philosopher, the genius who had written seven published works of literature— texts that he showed me—and a man who had seen so much of life in the Middle East, be so innocent?

He was a man that had already lost his home at gunpoint to the Israelis, a man that knew perfectly well about the injustices of war; how could he possibly believe that the Americans would not attack? Or that peaceful action was the solution to preventing the American-led colonisation of Iraq?

"I will not be a traitor," I admitted, emotionally exhausted and defeated. "But you don't know what megalomaniacs are like," I said, remembering a fight with such a man.

"Yes I do," he said, softly gazing down. "But they are not alone," he added.

I began to understand why Muslim people regarded the Western nations as barbaric infidels that would kill for money or material possessions. It was no secret that infidelity, violence, alcoholism, and drug abuse were very much a way of life in the West, in particular as crime was a necessity for the legal profession that thrived on the ignorance of the masses to understand the 'double-speak' ambiguities of a biased legal system.

Now, as the Western armies massed and surrounded this nation at peace, I understood the Viking war-cry more than ever. 'Rape, pillage, and plunder'. Had we not learned anything?

"Perhaps there is a lesson that Muslims can teach the West," I said, realising that my very own families and friends were not aware of their own sad destinies.

By the end of our meeting I was intellectually exhausted. It was like attending a two-hour intense lecture on the history and evolution of human consciousness and the future existence of mankind and life on Earth as we knew it.

This elderly Palestinian man who lost everything to the Israelis remained forgiving and accepting of the Israelis. He showed no contempt for the people who expelled him from his family inheritance, nor for the Kurds, the Iranians, or the Americans who continued to bomb this great historic land, ensuring it remained in a third world existence.

Chapter 16
Human Shields

Saddam Hussein has stockpiles of chemical and biological weapons and is a threat to world peace ...
George W. Bush
Repeatedly, 2002

The next few days all I could do was walk around the city observing how Iraqis got on with their lives while enduring economic sanctions. They continued to attend schools, do their daily shopping, drink coffee, and play games. Sometimes I would catch a taxi, asking the drivers to take me for long scenic drives to remote outskirts where I was able to detect the first signs of an Iraqi military build-up.

I began to see old military trucks, antiquated cannons, and old-fashioned armoured personnel carriers on the city outskirts. The odd tank was visible under desert camouflage as if the thin fabric would protect the fathers, sons, and brothers from the guided missiles that would later destroy them. What was notable was that each vehicle was manned by young men who clearly did not want to be there.

More and more young soldiers seemed to be digging in along the highways that entered into Baghdad. Sometimes I could see an old tank dug into a pit or old cannons under desert camouflage. The Iraqi military were poorly dressed, and often I saw young men wearing what looked like black school shoes without socks, and their army greens seemed to be either too long or too short and in some cases, patched with normal civilian clothes. Most had old AK-47 or even older hunting rifles. The saddest thing I saw was an old man proudly holding a sword as if he were ready to fight the American military machine with it.

The economic sanctions and the subsequent disarmament had successfully reduced the Iraqi army into a third world military power. This tin pot army was preparing to defend their lands from a foreign invasion against the best-equipped military power in the world. The prevailing injustice compared to a colonising slaughter of Native American Indians, African Zulus, or Australian Aboriginals, by a ruthless regime.

What was clear to me was that the world needed to clean up the natural environment; educate populations about living alternative eco-sustainable lifestyles; employ inventive sustainable energies; engage in peaceful debate that allowed the less-educated people the chance to catch up with the more advanced minds; see the necessity of wealth distribution as a reason to break down borders; and understand the importance to travelling abroad to find ways of understanding our miserable lives as a universal right. These were some of my beliefs that if employed would result in our good mental, physical, and spiritual health. Thus, I believed it was criminal for the North American military spending to reflect an aggressive stance rather than demonstrating care for our natural environment.

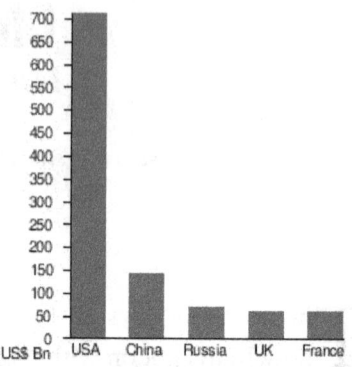

The world's top 5 military spenders in 2010. Figures sourced from the SIPRI Yearbook 2011

The carnage to come was predictable and perhaps this was a strategy designed over twenty years ago when Saddam stopped buying American weapons and made peace with Iran.

The following day I caught a taxi and asked the driver to take me sightseeing around the west of Baghdad. The driver spoke English fluently and introduced himself as Halim.

"Where did you learn English?" I asked him.

"I am English teacher," he replied.

"But why do you drive a taxi and not teach English?"

"Because embargo, many rich Iraqi family go to other country, and here only poor people. Now poor people learn to work, not to speak English, because maybe we never travel to English country," he answered.

What amazed me no end was that school children continued to attend schools, mothers did their shopping, and fathers went to work or looked for work, doing anything they could. Like Halim, taxi driving seemed to be a good way to earn a living as anyone with a car could turn their car into a taxi. The good will displayed by the Iraqi people in the face of sanctions was astounding.

As we drove I could see that many Iraqi people were either not aware of the surrounding military build-up, or were unaffected by the possibility of war. They simply seemed either disinterested in the looming war or were resigned to the infinite possibilities of fate they believed to be in the hands of God.

"Are you Shiite or Sunni?" I asked Halim.

"I am Shiite. But here in Iraq it doesn't matter if we are Sunni or Shiite, we are all brothers from the same family," he replied.

"But isn't Saddam Sunni, against the Shiite?" I asked him to confirm what I had learned in the Western media.

"No. No, Saddam is good man. He doesn't care if Muslim is Shiite or Sunni. No Muslim brother or sister worry for such thing. Only we are Muslim and maybe we pray different but we pray to same Allah."

"But why would Shiite and Sunni brothers fight each other?" I asked him.

"That is not true!" he spat. "Who tells you this?"

"This is what we learn on Western television," I revealed my source of information.

"No, that this is not true. Maybe your news wants to divide and conquer Islam, but this is not true—we are all Muslim and we all pray to the one same Allah," he rebutted.

"But didn't Saddam go to war against Iran because Iranians are Shiites?"

"No. This is not true. You are misled. Iran attack Iraq because America help us. But when Saddam made peace with Iran, America stop help Iraq, and help Kuwait. This why we fight with Kuwait brothers: because Kuwait is our brothers but they now get help from America like before America help Saddam," Halim said, convinced of his understanding on the matter.

It seemed to make sense and I had no other way of learning about the way these people perceived their history. As I listened I watched an antiquated army make desperate attempts, building piles of rocks to hide behind from the American missiles. It was absolutely clear why the Saddam administration wanted peace and to re-enter the global economic community.

"Why doesn't America spend more money to teach the world about God?" Halim asked me as we drove through a palm tree-lined avenue.

"I really don't know," I admitted.

Perhaps this humble taxi driver was right. Perhaps we could spend a fraction of the cost of a modern war by teaching our world the benefits of a peaceful God that taught many good things about co-existence, global care, and scientific research, to resolve all the problems that future generations would face in our wake.[6]

After seeing how unprepared the Iraqi military were to defend their land, I decided it was proper to do what I could to stop the foreseeable slaughter of these young men. Halim dropped me at the Palestine Hotel and we shook hands like two old friends parting. We farewelled each other with firm and long well-wishes to each other's families.

When I arrived at my room, I could see two red English double-decker busses. They were parked across the road and the words 'Human Shield Action Group' were painted along the sides. These were the people that our Western media had called Saddam sympathisers, beatniks, hippies, loonies, idiot crack heads, and other negative connotative nouns. What would the Western media have to say about me? I pondered the thought, knowing my untainted good reputation was strong, yet aware that my ghetto street fighting past and general interests in the dark nature of humanity would be easy to criticise. Yet, this was not about me, it was about justice, the natural environment, and all of us; in particular, our children and the future of life on Earth.

Unperturbed, I went down and across the street. When I approached the busses, they were empty and closed, so I entered the adjacent hotel that had a Spanish name—Al Andalus Hotel. This was a beautiful, modern hotel with a white marble foyer that gave it a heavenly brilliant white reception. It was like stepping into a cool, air-conditioned oasis in the middle of a hot, dusty metropolis. It was also where an international contingency of people sat in small groups of what could best be described as a global gathering of people.

---

6   **Institute for economics and peace** has several publications to provide further insight on the vast advantages for peace to reign over any further wars.

Asians, Europeans, Africans, Hispanics, and Americans united to prevent the catastrophe of a third world war or the creation of another third world nation at the start of this third millennium. They were seated in small groups and there was an eerie silence in the foyer of the hotel.

A distinguished-looking Arab gentleman greeted me at reception with a warm smile and then led me to a small makeshift office that had been set up in the back of the hotel's main foyer. There were two ladies inside who introduced themselves as Uzma Bashir and Donna Mulhearn.

Uzma Bashir was a British lady with all the English customs and manners, and her accent coloured her fluent Queen's English speech. Yet her Indian ancestry contradicted the snobbery one finds in so many of the women from the British gentry, a kind of snobbery that was fortunately unfashionable as more and more women opted to work rather than become stay-at-home ladies of leisure. Uzma looked to be in her thirties, but the beautiful, soft, dark skin of her face made her pass for a much younger girl. She seemed rushed and flustered with her work, handing me a registration form.

"Just fill in this form and afterwards you can come upstairs, where a meeting is about to take place," she said with a pompous English accent, gathering some papers.

Donna Mulhearn was sitting quietly behind a computer screen. She looked tired and concerned, and her hippie dress sense suited her surf-bleached blondish hair and strong, rounded shoulders.

Her eyes were fixed on the screen and when she gazed up softly toward me she said, "Good day mate, where you from?" it was obvious that she had to be Australian.

"Australia," I replied. It was all that had to be said. We both knew we were on the same team, and the wealth of Australia was the reason we could both be here.

"Great. I'm glad to know there are more of us with some common sense," she replied.

"Let's go," Uzma interrupted, inviting Donna to follow her up to the meeting, and both walked off in a rush, leaving me alone in the small office.

I sat down to write my details on the form and looked around the office to quickly recognise that the Human Shields were still in the process of establishing the group's structure and activities. There were notices pinned on the wall and the desk was overflowing with administration papers, notes, and clippings. I filled in my registration and went upstairs to the meeting, which had begun, so I sat inconspicuously at the entrance.

Ken O'Keefe was an ex-American marine who had served in the 1991 Gulf War. He was a battle-toughened man who knew from first-hand experience the full horror of modern-day war and the motives behind the American administration. As a peace activist Ken adopted the most extreme action, calling it the Human Shields Action Group. When I arrived, he was discussing the importance of choosing appropriate sites to shield. They were to be humanitarian sites and chosen for their necessity to everyday living.

"We need to go and inspect some of these sites to make sure we can live in them for a considerable time," he was saying when I walked in.

"We need to look at the April 7th water treatment plant and ensure there are adequate rooms for accommodation. We also need to locate food storage facilities like silos and distribution warehouses, as well as the whereabouts of electricity plants and all hospitals …"

As Ken spoke about the locations that had priority and the need to form groups to disperse the Human Shields evenly amongst the many sites, I noted a commitment and resolute determination of these peace warriors. The people in the room were normal civilians from across the world. They sat in silence and there was a peculiar presence of goodness in the air. It was as if Ken was the commander-in-chief of an army of peace warriors who would be going on a mission with no weapons and no desire to kill or maim. Rather it was a peaceful mission of rescuing whatever humanitarian sites they could before the dark empire with its military clones set upon and destroyed this peaceful city.

I estimated over a hundred shields at this meeting and their hearts were intent on standing in the line of fire to stop their own countrymen from bombing the basic necessities needed by the Iraqi people for survival. I still remember feeling spooked by the concept of bombs landing on my head. However, there was some comfort in the proverb that there was safety in numbers. So if hundreds of these international Human Shields were strategically placed around Iraq, then the world media would drive the final message home to the coalition of the willing that another war or crusade was not justified without the unanimous vote of United Nations Security Council.

However, the most haunting aspect was that these people did not have weapons and faced missiles aimed from hundreds of kilometres away from their enemy. What I learned was that the Human Shields were mostly an educated group of civilians—just like any other in any other country. Most had been to universities and those that hadn't took great interest in their world. All these people were highly sensitive and willing to stand against the military to stop a war. But above all, they had the humour and nobility with the understanding that they were able to stand fast against the greatest military invasion of the modern world. The courage these people demonstrated was unparalleled. Perhaps these were the few that understood that there would be a return of slavery if we allowed corporate giant executives to dictate who lived or died according to their corporation's needs.

For the first time in my life I understood the courage of David as he faced Goliath. These people would bear witness to the criminal intent of the American administration for many years to come all in the name of 'petro-dollars' traded between Saudi sultans and Western oil companies, with our obedient soldiers at the forefront of sacrifice.

I had always considered myself to be a fearless street-fighter, capable of fighting any man, irrespective of size. I had been shot, cut, beaten, bashed, battered, and had survived death. Fear was not a word I considered in my vocabulary as I feared no threat from criminal, military, or police oppression. I boasted a clean conscience and a cleansed spirit. But now, among these Human Shields, I realised that I was horrified, a coward, a white chicken, and a timid child amongst the most fearless warriors I would ever know. This was my introduction to real life third world warriors.

However, what really scared me the most was that this army consisted mostly of women: mothers, sisters, wives, aunts, and grandmothers whose maternal instincts seemed stronger and more defiant than the callous nature of war itself! As I looked around the room, I saw women from all over the world that had come to Iraq as voluntary Human Shields. The magic of seeing Asians conversing with Indians, Hispanics laughing with English, and Americans alongside Iraqis, was overwhelmingly inspiring.

As I looked around this large reception room I saw Waratah, the Australian human rights lawyer. She was amongst the first of the NASYO delegates to sign up and she was sitting next to Yakiko, the Japanese dancer whom I had met briefly at the Palestine Hotel.

"Have you joined also?" Waratah asked me, excited to see me after the meeting.

"Yes."

"Did you know that many Japanese are coming to join?" Yakiko asked proudly.

"Well I hope the world gets the message so that more Human Shields arrive before it's too late," Waratah added.

"Do you think the Australian television news will show this meeting?" Yakiko asked us, wide-eyed.

"I don't think so," Waratah said, sounding defeated and walking off into the shadows.

Yakiko looked at me for an answer but I could only frown, knowing that Waratah was right. Our television and Western interests would never tell the truth about these peace activists.

Our Western media had interests in promoting war for the purpose of increasing advertising revenues and military spending. The truth was, that our media reported to us the prejudices and lies of our editors and program directors, men and women who in turn were enslaved with conditions employed by private interests.

In other words, our editors and program directors were employed by the owners of the television stations on the basis of their values, their religious beliefs, their political ideologies, and their compliance with their employee's standards on all things.

Hence, propaganda was a two-edged sword and the sad truth was that the alleged free world was more policed and regulated than the rest of the world combined. Televisions around the world were sold to us with the promise of entertainment. The Chinese, Russians, Americans, British,

Germans, Indians and every other nation or government on Earth used the television as a means to 'teach' us about 'the truth'. So it was fair to say that while some content may be factual, at the same time some content was prejudicial or else information was edited out so we only saw the picture of what our leaders wanted us to see or understand. For example, Saddam Hussein's request to debate on the international media with George W. Bush over the rights for Iraq to have peace rather than ongoing wars, or Dr Huda's speech on the many reasons for abolishing economic sanctions, etc.

"In Australia we do have freedom of speech," I said to Yakiko, noting a slight confusion in her face. I tried to explain this international humanitarian right that we, the people of Earth, shared. "We are not like China or Egypt or Russia where people can be arrested without being charged and placed under house arrest for voicing or debating anti-government opinions or ideologies," I said. "In Australia you can say anything you want against our government or religious institutions or even against the Queen of England, because we are a free people to express our thoughts and ideas," I added.

"Really?" Yakiko asked genuinely curious. "In Japan also we can say anything," she added slowly as she searched for the English words in her mind. "But Japan people don't want this war ... but Japan Emperor like English Queen and Saudi sultans and many more kings ... they always do whatever they want and sometimes don't care about what people want," she concluded.

I explained to Yakiko how it was important for the future of all life on Earth for the world to be united in peace, and that monarchs were symbols of leadership that strived for peace.

I tried to explain that the Queen of England and King of Spain or Emperor of Japan or Sultan of Brunei or any other royal monarchs would know the futility of modern warfare and would join forces to stop this costly war and find an academic solution to the differences. But her limited English vocabulary made it near impossible for me to know if she really understood; especially as not a single monarch came to the defence of our natural environment or the creation of another third world.

This inability to communicate effectively with Yakiko frustrated me no end, and finally I quit. Walking away from her, my thoughts drifted to those foreign diplomats that need to agree and find solutions to complex problems when there was so much information lost in translation.

The fact was, international diplomacy should have been opened to ongoing open discussions, in particular when it was going to avert modern warfare. The truth was that there were a few billionaire dynastic criminals who gained absurd wealth from the business of war. But who could challenge them? Perhaps Saddam Hussein would pay the ultimate price for disarming and not buying any more American-made weapons.

What I was now learning was that the Human Shields cared more than any monarch, and yet the media managed to discredit these saintly, selfless people.

I spoke with Ken briefly and questioned his motives for initiating the radical action of becoming a Human Shield. His response was refreshing and authentic. He was not only concerned for the enormous human suffering that would be endured by the Iraqi civilians and the frontline soldiers from both sides. But he spoke also about the catastrophic consequences to the natural environment as a result of the uranium depleted American bombs and missiles; the animals in Baghdad Zoo that would die slowly from starvation; the war orphans that would be vulnerable to child sex abuse, slavery and destined to third world existences; and the impact on the world economy, to name but a few major concerns.

Ken was well-educated; he spoke softly and had first-hand knowledge from the 1991 war as he witnessed the environmental catastrophe of that war. He spoke passionately against the misappropriation of funds by the American administration. He acknowledged that war funds would be better spent in diplomatic debates, re-education programs, and making the world a truly peaceful world.

But what made me respect Ken was his undeniable commitment to preventing an illegal war by his own countrymen. He said, "I have friends in the US forces and they have no idea why they are going to war."

"But why would you volunteer to become a Human Shield?" I asked him, wanting to find the reason for this ultimate act of chivalry.

"Because I'm not alone," he replied selflessly. "If we have hundreds of Shields, or thousands, we can stop this crime from happening," he added.

Looking around the groups of grandmothers, mothers, wives, aunts, daughters, and sisters, with the occasional man amongst them, I saw a sad image of defeat. The world was too satisfied to be entertained in the comfort of their homes watching football, television commercials, and all types of mindless entertainment, including the spectacular entertainment value of foreign war, anything but the truth. These were the toughest group of individuals I had ever seen: people willing to stand in front of missiles to protect strangers. Yet their courage was never rewarded.

The dilemma I faced was that if I stayed in Iraq, my money would run out and my fate would be uncertain. There were no automatic teller machines as economic sanctions had denied Iraqis of such technologies. My instinct was to stay and help this raggedly dressed group of warrior women. Reality was unwavering, by the need for money to stay.

The next day, I went to the hotel early and sat in the lobby waiting for instructions. I approached Ken and explained that I would need to go to Jordan to withdraw sufficient funds if I was to remain In Baghdad for an extended period of time. He told me he was also short of money and gave me his credit card, entrusting me with the PIN number, and asked me to withdraw all the funds he had and bring them with me.

It was a simple task, so I returned to the hotel and prepared to head to Jordan determined to get, ironically enough, more American dollars. It was easy to get a shared taxi out of Baghdad, as more and more Iraqis were joining the exodus.

***

When I arrived in Amman I went directly to the Human Shields office at the Al Saraya Hotel. This was a clean and comfortable hotel chosen for its central location and reasonable budget rates.

It was late and I was anxious to get a room to sleep in. However, there was an air of excitement at my arrival as some of the Shields were awaiting visas and the world media were starved of information from within Iraq. Such was the strangulation of economic sanctions on a country that even reporting stories of the deaths, the suffering, the poverty, and the inhumane living conditions bestowed on the people of that country, were not reported to the outside world.

When I asked at the hotel reception for the Human Shields office, a tall, distinguished man introduced himself with an extension of his hand, and as we shook hands he said, "I am Fayez, welcome to my humble hotel."

Fayez led me away from the foyer and showed me the door to a warmly lit room where some young people sat around drinking tea and suddenly rising to welcome me, with genuine interest in hearing any news from Baghdad.

"This was my office but now it is yours," Fayez said, offering his hospitality as we entered.

"Hello, I'm Antoinette McCormick," a strong woman said with a distinctive American accent, shaking my hand firmly.

"This is Shane Mulligan. He is leading the Amman operations," she said, introducing me.

Shane was a tall, thin Irish man who seemed overwhelmed by his workload and the responsibilities he carried.

"Hi. I'm Sharon. I'm doing secretarial duties at the moment," a younger girl said with a strong British accent.

"And I'm Dieter, I'm the technical guy," a Scottish man wearing thin-rimmed glasses added.

"And I'm Tom Hurndall," a tall and distinctly handsome looking English man said, finally, to complete the introductions.

Antoinette seemed to have a better grasp of what was to happen in Iraq if her countrymen invaded Iraq. She had previous experience, having served in the American military strikes during the Gulf War in 1990. Over the next few weeks, we would spend many days talking and discussing the looming war and the human catastrophe that would result if the coalition invaded.

Sharon, as the group secretary, was stressed by the unpaid workload she was facing with the increasing volume of Shields adding more work to her already stretched working hours. Sharon was asked to register new Shields and help them try to get a visa from the Iraqi embassy. Her work was laborious and unpaid.

Dieter would later educate me on civil disobedience as a means of ousting a government that acted independently of their patriots. He understood that his action to join the Human Shields was not in itself illegal, but was an act of peaceful disobedience to his government in an otherwise democratic society. Thus it was legal and perfectly permissible as a valid democratic objection. Dieter seemed to be the more legally trained and had a clear conscience with his decision to become a Human Shield.

Tom Hurndall had already been in Baghdad and had left with the same plan as I had, to get more money from the Oman banks and return to Baghdad. But his plans had come undone when the Iraqis failed to issue him a second entry visa. So he was now contemplating going to Jerusalem as an alternative.

A meeting was quickly arranged and I was asked to brief a room full of anxious and excited people from every corner of the world. It was comforting to see that there were more and more Human Shields arriving every day. However, it was never my desire to be a public speaker, as any notion of fame terrorised me, so it was daunting to speak to a large crowd of internationals who now sat listening to my story. It was clear from the murmur in the room that my words were being translated into other languages, as some of the faces that stared at me or the multitude of fashions were clearly not English.

I explained why I went to Baghdad and spoke about the NASYO conference and our findings. I elaborated on the security situation, which at that point was safe. Iraq was a perfectly good place to travel whilst Saddam Hussein or the Ba'ath party were in control. I asked if they had heard anything about the letter sent by the NASYO administrators to the foreign media and the George W. Bush administration explaining the many reasons for peace and the long-term effects that economic sanctions were having on the Iraqi people. But no one knew anything about it, except of course the American and Western intelligence-gathering institutions like CIA, ASIO, FBI, MI5, and others around the world.

Then I explained the urgent need for funds as the Human Shields where self-financed by each individual and not financed by Saddam Hussein like the Western media were saying. It was obvious that all these people had travelled here with their own resources. The people of the world were not the ones hoarding wealth. We were the people who worked to earn what we spent. Our minor savings were mostly to comply with our banking lords' desires before they tempted us with loans, lines of credit, and bank cards. This amounted to expensive money and, as I learned, charging a compounding interest was not acceptable in Islam.

During my time as the speaker I looked around the room and saw the world represented by a collage of faces young and old, white and black, Asians and Europeans. There was absolutely no doubt on anyone's mind of the fact that we, the people on this planet, were the ones that had the most to lose if a third world war erupted. As such, a third world war was no longer an option. Weapons were becoming obsolete and weapons dealers or manufacturers were the future criminals we needed to punish.

When I finished telling my story, I was horrified to learn that the Iraqi embassy was making it increasingly difficult for Human Shields to gain visas, as many journalists, photographers, and possible spies or secret agents had infiltrated the Shields movement and were acting with ulterior motives to divide the group.

I was asked many questions that I knew answers to, and other questions I could not answer. We talked for what seemed like hours until Antoinette, the most experienced campaigner, suggested I get some rest and continue the following morning,

My mind, however, was on Rema. I wanted to see her and continue learning more about her as she was the only Palestinian person I had ever known. My understanding from the media was simply that Palestinians were terrorists and the Israelis were noble: an understanding shared by Tom Hurndall, as later that night before he departed, he told me his reason for going to the Promised Land.

Fortunately, I was trained to look for the truth from both sides of a story, understanding that propaganda had two sides to be told—as a result I wanted to hear the other side from a Palestinian. To understand her reasons, her history, her passion, and above all, to hold her close and make her feel loved rather than like a rejected Palestinian as the Western media seemed to portray. So the first thing I did in the morning was to phone her, and we arranged to meet at the hotel.

When she arrived she was, as always, dressed in the simplistic attire that became her trademark: tight jeans, a loose t-shirt, and on this occasion, a green woollen top, with comfortable running shoes. A practical and comfortable look that was far sexier than what many girls of the West wore, who flaunted their sexuality. Rema, as beautiful as she was at twenty-five years of age, took immense pride as a modern Muslim girl who opted not to wear the hijab yet covered her body appropriately.

We caught a taxi to the ruins overlooking Amman called the Al Cazar, where we walked and talked. I explained to her the things that I did in Baghdad and about my meeting with Dr Huda. She confided in me about the meeting she also had with Dr Huda and we both knew that there was more to this lady than the media were willing to tell. Indeed, Dr Huda was well equipped intellectually and politically to be the next president of Iraq. That would mean she would become the first woman to control the most hostile environment in the world: a feat that would put all white men in power to shame.

"What do you do for a living?" I asked her, realising I really knew very little about her as we walked along the Roman ruins of the Al Cazar.

"I'm editor," she said humbly, "for magazine. For students from Palestinian youth and Islamic youth." Her English seemed to be improving the more we spoke.

Editor! At twenty-five? "That's amazing," I acknowledged. "For which magazine?"

"It called, how you say? Um, Moaning Star?"

"Moaning?" I quizzed. Thinking, *What a great name for a magazine—it expresses the pain and suffering endured silently for so long by so many Palestinians.* "You mean like the star that is expressing pain and grief felt by you and your people?" I asked to clear my niggling doubt.

"No. No, I mean like when the sun rises, moaning star shines alone," she corrected me.

"Oh, you mean Morning Star!" I corrected.

"Yes, Morning Star," she said in her Arab-English.

"That's a nice name for a magazine," I admired. "And you write articles in it?"

"Yes. I do every-think," she corrected.

"Everything? But you can't do everything," I challenged her.

"Yes, it is my magazine. I invented and write and edit and other writers write for me," she said nonchalantly.

"Oh. I see. It's your idea and your magazine?" I asked, confirming the continuing misunderstanding between our language barriers.

"Yes." She smiled for the second time since I had met her.

"That's pretty cool," I said, attempting to be cool with the fact that she was far more intelligent and advanced at twenty-five than most people would ever be in a lifetime.

It was soon apparent that Rema was no ordinary woman. She may have been physically petite and fragile on the outside, but inside she was a burning fireball exploding with passion. She was a true journalist, willing to go the extra miles if needed to get to the very bottom of deeply painful truths. Whilst talking to her, I sometimes would feel a need to choose my words carefully or face her sudden snap as she corrected my ignorance.

"So what do you think about the terrorists?" I asked her, seizing the opportunity to speak with a Palestinian woman.

"Terrorist? They are martyrs," she corrected me.

"But how can you say they are martyrs when they kill innocent women and children in cold blood?" I asked her.

"Who kill innocent women and children and old people? Terrorist?" she retorted, questioning me.

"Yes," I said, dismayed at her ignorant retort.

"Then Israeli and American army are terrorist," she accused.

"But they are defending their people," I argued.

"Defending? Or attacking my people?" she asked, getting agitated with my naivety about the Middle East's problems.

"But terrorist are attacking them!" I said, feeling a bit apprehensive that this little girl with so much sorrow in her eyes was challenging my shallow understanding about the Palestinian people.

"Al, you come with me and I show you Palestine refugee camps okay. Then we go to Damascus in Syria and you talk to refugees and maybe you see the truth! Okay?" she challenged.

"Okay," I agreed, not knowing how much more there was yet to learn.

Chapter 17
Israeli Justice

The Goldstone Report ... and similar reports are simply a type of anti-Semitism.
Israeli information minister response when Israel was found to have committed war crimes against humanity 2009

The following day, Rema arrived at the hotel at the agreed time and carried a thick yellow envelope.

"In Australia, Spain, and America, they say Israel is okay because they have justice and democracy right?" she said as we sat down for a cup of tea.

"Well yes. But I think it's the fear of living under a harsh Islamic law that the Westerners fear," I said, trying to justify my Western way of thinking.

"They don't know Islamic law. You look at these pictures and tell me about Israeli justice," she said, giving me these pictures, which I promised her I would show the world.

As I looked through almost a hundred pictures of dead, dying, tortured, and maimed men, women, and children, I came to realise that we, the people of the world, were constantly denied the truth. We simply lived with the everyday concerns of survival while our leaders spoiled their children with expensive gifts; and what greater gift to give your child than to be the next president of the United States of America or North Korea? Nepotism had a dark side we needed to question more so than those who blew whistles when they witnessed an injustice.

Ironically, for those who did tell the truth, we branded them as criminals, terrorist sympathisers, or traitors, like Julian Assange or Edward Snowden or David Hicks. These were men who learned what I was now learning: the painful truths to the injustices of this war.

With this insight, I knew the time would come when some would want to discredit my good reputation and the authenticity of my story. So it was imperative that I design a plan that would allow me to complete my self-imposed mission to keep my promise to the dying children of the third world. I had already begun studying the dark side of humanity, and now I was diving head-first into the deepest pool of an unknown destiny that one could imagine. The most evil was yet to come.

As I browsed through the horrifying images, my heart sank with the atrocious nature of our creed. We were like animals that ravaged each other to death or predators that preyed on the weak and vulnerable. At least that much could be said about our modern warmongers.

The savage truth should hurt anyone of us who paid tax knowing that our governments were buying weapons to cull fellow humans in the name of oil, land, or worse—misleading lies. We were all dispensable. We were not free if we needed to work like slaves every day to pay bankers with mortgages or credit card interest rates. We were not free if our government was spying on our liberties. We were not free if there were prying police cameras that could monitor our every move. We were not free if the law was changed to benefit a privileged few rather than the poorer majority. With these revelations I concluded the Israeli regime was the most brutal and the least sympathetic to natural justice.

Our Western regimes were not much better. I was becoming motivated to fight against these injustices and my fighting instinct stirred as Rema showed me the rest of the photos showing maimed children and other innocent casualties of the Western-backed Israeli military regime.

These next sequence photos are only a few of the many I saw, but are the most depictive of Israeli justice and a brutal regime:

1. Palestinian youth arrested by Israeli military

2. Palestinian youth handcuffed and the witness taken away

3. The same youth stripped, searched, and questioned by Israeli secret police

4. Palestinian youth executed after questioning

"When Hitler was killing the Jews no other country in the world wanted to help them. But only the Palestinian people opened the door to the Jewish people because they are our brothers. You know, all the Palestinian people were once Jewish and then we all became Christian and then many more become Muslim. This why we help our brothers and we welcome them to Palestine to save them from Hitler. But after they ask United Nations to create a new state and call it Israel only for Jewish people. But we the Palestinian people, we said no, because we do not have any problem if Jewish people enter Palestinian democratic government. But Jewish people, they do not want Palestinian people in Israeli government. They do not allow Palestinian people to return to our homes. This called discrimination, yes?" she asked rhetorically, pausing for breath.

"Yes." I had no other alternative but to agree with the truth she spoke.

"And if the Jewish people, they have one law for them and another law for Palestinian people, this called apartheid, yes?"

"Yes it is," again I agreed, and now began to understand where she was heading. Previous North American President Jimmy Carter had also denounced the Israeli regime as an apartheid regime, yet the world media managed to censor his voice and the award-winning documentary film he made, "Man from the plains." The question we should ask is, what is the evil that censors such angels?

"Then why does America help Israeli people and not Palestinian? Is America a democratic country or is America like Germany was before Hitler, A Christian country, but her finances and her economy controlled by the Zionist Jews?" she asked, genuinely thinking that I would know the answer to such a complex question.

"I don't think so Rema, unless Allan Greenspan was Jewish."

"In that case I am right!" she said confidently. "Is not Jewish people that Palestinian have war, it is Zionist Jew. These Jewish Zionist have too much money and too much power in the world."

"But this was Israel before it became Palestine," I said, attempting to justify the Israelis' claim to their Promised Land.

"Yes. Al! All Palestinian people, we were all Jewish first. You know Jesus Christ was Palestinian Jew, and many Palestinian, Lebanese, Syrian, and Arabic people become Christian. But Mohamed teaches us that all people are born equal, and better way for living together. That is why many more become Muslim. You see, we all pray together. We all dress same when we do hajj. We all help each other. Muslim woman—we have rights to vote, to have business and bank accounts over one thousand years ago. But Western woman they only vote maybe fifty years ago. Islam is a very good religion for everyone, not only for some. That is why we help our Jewish brothers. But they come to Palestine after Hitler and now they take our farms or kill us and torture us—look at this photo."

The photo was horrific. It showed a young Palestinian man that had been tortured to death. His arm had been twisted so many times in the one direction that the broken skin and protruding bones made it difficult to distinguish that limb as a human arm. His body was covered in bruising, burns, cuts, and welts. His face was beaten beyond recognition and sunken where hammers or clubs had been used to beat him, and his teeth (those that remained) were completely shattered. It looked like his Israeli torturers had also tried twisting his leg but only managed a couple of turns as his foot and knee had snapped and now looked grotesque and inhuman.

"This Palestinian teenage boy after Israeli secret police tortured him," she said, restraining her deep-rooted anger.

She showed me many more photos of tortured Palestinians, destroyed houses, mothers in distraught grief, fathers in shock, dead children, and newspaper clippings of the enduring violence suffered by Palestinians. One article in particular caught my eye as it told of the trafficking of human parts by Israelis from young captured Palestinians who had been killed by the Israelis while in prison.

Israel Kills Palestinian Boys, Steals Organs for Transplants (JAN 2002)

AL-KHALIL (IRNA)—The Zionist state has tacitly admitted that doctors at the Israeli Forensic Institute at Abu Kabir had extracted the vital organs of three Palestinian teenage children killed by the Israeli Army nearly ten days ago.

Zionist Minister of Health Nessim Dahhan said in response to a question by Arab member of the Zionist Parliament 'Knesset', Ahmed Teibi, on Tuesday that he couldn't deny that organs of Palestinian youths and children killed by the Israeli forces were taken out for transplants or scientific research.

"I couldn't say for sure that something like that (taking out the organs) didn't happen."

Teibi said he had received credible evidence proving that Israeli doctors at the Forensic Institute extracted such vital organs as the heart, kidneys, and liver from the bodies of Palestinian youths and children killed by the Israeli Army in Gaza and the West Bank.

The Israeli authorities normally detain the bodies of martyred Palestinians for a few days without any explanation.

The Israeli Army on December 30 killed three Palestinian boys, aged 14-15 near Khan Younis in unclear circumstances.

The army issued conflicting reports on the killing, while Palestinian sources charged that Israeli troops murdered the three unarmed boys in cold blood.

The bodies of the three boys were handed over to the Palestinians for burial on 6 January.

However, shortly before burial, Palestinian medical authorities examined the bodies and found out that the main vital organs were missing from the bodies.

In July 2009 over forty Jewish rabbis were arrested in New Jersey for organ trafficking[7]. How many others around the world were getting away with this abhorrent crime? The answer to this question will never be known. What we did know was that human organs could be bought from third world citizens at a price only afforded by those with sufficient funds and an absence of morality. Or, those who believed themselves to be God's children, and as such could do whatever they wanted with the inferior class of people.

As Rema showed me these pictures and newspaper clippings of the atrocities the Palestinian people continued to endure since the state of Israel was approved by the United Nations after a marginal vote, 1948, I realised the horror that would soon be forced upon the Iraqi people if the Americans invaded Iraq. History was repeating itself and the common people would be the ones to suffer the most.

"You see Al; we are a poor people now. Israeli soldiers, they take our land and houses or they kill many Palestinian people. We cannot throw rocks against tanks and helicopters. We don't know what else to do. The world does not help us because we are poor people. But America and Israel have money and nuclear bombs so they can influence many countries to vote for them in any United Nations ... how do you say—assembly?"

"Yes, or the United Nations security council meeting," I added, thinking how ridiculous it was for her to assume the UN Security Council could be influenced with prejudices. Or was Rema right to understand the other laws that the civilised world had been trying to evade, namely, 'he who has the gold makes the law'?

"Palestinian people, we do not want war. We do not want to use terrorism to defend our country. But we do not want to become like Red Indians in America or Aboriginal people in Australia, or African Negro. We are Arabs, we are Jewish, Christians, and now mostly Muslims. But we do not want Palestine only for Jewish people. We want also to have Muslim Palestinian in government offices and to return to our lands and our houses and to have our wealth and our dignity ... this is our basic human right! This is democracy," she said, getting angry.

---

7   Article heading "Doctor admits Israeli pathologists harvested organs without consent" Ian Black, Middle East editor The Guardian, Monday 21 December 2009

"Rema!" I interjected. "I can understand what you are saying. But I don't think you understand what colonisation is," I said, realising that the invasion of Iraq by America would, in effect, be a modern-day colonisation if there was no United Nations Security Council mandate, and thus, an illegal occupation.

"Palestinian people, we now become like prison in our country. Only many young people don't want to be in prison. We want freedom. Freedom to go in and out of our country, to have business to go to university and to play games in Palestinian sport clubs, but Israeli government not let my people such freedom. Israelis they destroy our schools, our clubs, our factories, even our trees, they cut many trees to make Palestinian farmers poorer. They make us prisoners and torture too many men. Now they build a wall like a prison. This is not freedom. This is not justice. This is not people that want peace. This is a jail for civilian people that do nothing wrong but born. This is people who have guns and rob people that don't have guns. This is war. And Palestinian freedom fighters are not terrorist in their own country of Palestine, they are martyrs. Israeli soldiers in Palestine, they are terrorists. And if American soldiers attack Iraq, then America are terrorists!" she said passionately, with a sudden burst of anger.

It seemed unbelievable how we could perceive the truth sometimes in a way that suited our own needs. What Rema said to me was totally accurate and true whether we liked to hear it or not. For as long as we, the Western nations, sent our military to foreign lands, it was we that were the invaders: a fact that made us the terrorists.

To have peace, we needed to not bomb or colonise with violence. We needed resolve with peaceful dialogue, influential trade, and joyful cultural exchanges and sporting competitions. Here was the solution to peace that the mega weapons manufacturers simply did not want to know, and they would do anything to avoid achieving world peace.

"Rema, this is all too much for me to take in at once," I confessed to her.

Rema was not anti-Semitic, as she was not arguing against the Jewish religion. She was just stating certain facts about some of the evils of the Zionist regime that profited from selling weapons to Israel. Another clip that caught my eye, read:

> Rabbi Ginsburgh asked rhetorically: 'If a Jew needs a liver, can you take the liver of an innocent non-Jew passing by to save him? The Torah would probably permit that. Jewish life has an infinite value', he explained. 'There is something infinitely more holy and unique about Jewish life than non-Jewish life'.
>
> Prof. Israel Shahak and Norton Mezvinsky, "Jewish Fundamentalism in Israel", Pluto Press,
>
> London 1999, page 62

The truths she was sharing with me were painful. What made it worse was that she had photographic and archived evidence of facts. These were facts that our governments and our media chose to censor and not share with us. The truths were excruciating!

"Rema, there is nothing we can do," I said, defeated by the prospect of fighting the world's greatest threat to humanity and all those powers that ruled for personal glory rather than for all life on Earth.

"I understand. But you know, sometimes we need to fight fire with fire," she said, with a sad tone to her voice. "Israelis they call us terrorists and they are heroes because they have an army! But you tell me Al, how do we defend ourselves against an army with no army?" She paused, allowing me to answer what I couldn't answer. "With stones!" she said, exclaiming her point.

As I looked at her soft, pale skin, it was difficult to know how I would react as a man if anyone harmed my mother, my sisters, and now this woman that earned full respect wherever she went. Let alone if a person harmed a child.

"Peacefully and intelligently," I replied instinctively, succumbing to peaceful resistance rather than my street-fighting violent ways.

"Al, many Palestinian they already try to return to their home peacefully, but Israeli soldiers kill them," she said as a matter of fact.

"But Israel is a democracy," I said, not knowing the real situation of the theocratic state and the apartheid system that existed in Israel.

"You really believe that?" she asked me, dumbfounded. "You go to Israel. You look. You see. You go and you tell me what you learn okay," she challenged me.

For the rest of the day, we walked around the Roman Amphitheatre and talked about Palestinian history, Israeli occupation, and American intervention in their affairs. Rema new exactly how many American tax dollars were donated to Israel as 'aid' or charity, mostly in the form of weaponry. For the first time in my life, I began to feel a sense of terror at the thought that my revelations were prejudicial to the powers that governed our lives. We, the people of Earth were simply not free while enslaved to regimes that benefited less than 2% of the world's ruling elite. We were all simply modern-day slaves.

Later, Rema invited me to her home where I met her family. Amidst their poverty as refugees, they remained dignified, and her grandmother showed me pictures of their stolen farmlands now under Israeli control. It was clear from the pictures and their air of educated etiquette that they had once been wealthy Palestinians. However, when her grandfather was killed by an Israeli soldier, they were forced to leave and join the exodus of Palestinians.

"This is our lands," she said, translating her grandmother's words as she showed me old black-and-white pictures of olive plantations and a large white homestead.

"You mean this farm belonged to you?" I asked to ensure there was no mistake.

"Yes, until the Israeli army point gun to my grandfather and kill him then tell grandmother and mother to get what they can carry and walk away or die," she said in her broken English.

I was dumbstruck. It was well known that many Israeli soldiers shot to kill Palestinians who dared argue against them. But what Rema told me was clearly a crime. One committed by a brutal, powerful, and unjust regime.

The tragedy was that now it was the Jewish state of Israel who was perpetuating a holocaust on the Palestinian people. And by controlling the media, Hollywood and most weapon manufacturing, these few Zionist families truly believe they were the only ones chosen by God as 'God's children'. The rest of us were dispensable, like animals, including fellow Jews that could be sacrificed, like those left behind in Germany as the few Zionist families had the funds and capacity to escape the Nazis.

The thought that Hitler had motivated an entire nation against defenceless, good Jewish people while the few ruling Zionists escaped the Holocaust with their bullion to the UK, USA, and Australia, was nauseating.

Chapter 18
Talking Terrorists

In fact, the life of all mankind is in danger. Because of global warming resulting to a large degree from the emissions of the factories of the major corporations. Yet despite that, the representatives of these corporations in the white house insists on not observing the Kyoto accord, with the knowledge that the statistics speak of the deaths and displacement of millions of human beings ... mostly in Africa.

Osama Bin Laden

As the coalition of the willing made last-minute preparations to invade what was now the defenceless nation of Iraq, Western journalists were briefed by the military and were embedded into the coalition forces. These journalists were instructed and told what they could or couldn't report; freedom of speech in American media was censored. The fact was that We the People of Earth were also deprived of information. We the People of Earth were lied to and we would all pay the consequences in the years to come.

I knew many of the Human Shields in Iraq were running out of money and morale was low. By the 15th of March 2003, the Iraqi embassy in Amman had stopped issuing visas to the Human Shields. Many Shields had used all their funds and some were forced to leave Baghdad well before they wanted. All the Human Shields that were forced to leave early came and stayed at the Al Saraya Hotel. Then they would return to their homes, saddened with what lay ahead for the future of life on Earth.

With the bank restricting how much of my own money I could withdraw on a daily basis, it took me four days to withdraw the remaining three thousand dollars I had. I tried taking out money from Ken's account but it seemed he had also exhausted his funds, which meant he would be running short back in Baghdad. I rushed to the Iraqi Embassy and pleaded with the Iraqi staff to extend my visa.

"Mr Al, your visa is only for one entry, it is not multi entries. You will not be allowed to go back to Baghdad," a small overweight Arab-looking man told me.

"But I have to take this money to my friends from NASYO," I said, showing him the money after he first told me that I could not be granted a visa.

"Please Mr Al. It is for your own safety," The Iraqi consulate advised me. I wanted to scream and shout and fight this ignorant little man that had no idea what was about to hit his country.

"But I have to take this money to the Human Shields," I said, again waving the cash in American dollars.

"I am sorry. We cannot accept any more visas. It is our instructions," he assured me.

"But I have friends there that are waiting for me," I repeated, with a different, more humbling tone.

"Mr Al, please, we do not have any authority. We believe some spies have infiltrated your group and the last group of visas was approved already."

The last group of Human Shields to leave Amman for Baghdad were mostly women accompanied by a Scottish brave-heart named Rory McEwan and a large Afro-American radio DJ who seemed to tower over everyone, named Gerry, from New York. They were accompanied by two warrior women; one a Spanish Basque called Beatriz Almandoz, and the American ex-sailor, Antoinette McCormick. There were also some women from Argentina, Germany, Sweden, Japan, and France, and all would ride in three taxis.

I learned later that they each paid over one thousand American dollars cash to enter as tourists with the sole purpose of standing peacefully with white flags as voluntary Human Shields. Such was the courage and the determination from these peace warriors to prevent the man-made catastrophe. Yet the royal audiences cheered the cricket world cup.

Gerry, the Afro-American, was the most influential of them all. He had a deep baritone voice that spoke with certain humbleness and an inspiring calmness, respect, and attention to the detail of the wisdom he had to share. I was not surprised to learn that he was also a radio disc jockey, a poet, and a journalist. He was the kind of man that was needed and I feared the immeasurable loss to humanity if anything should happen to him. Gerry became like the big brother of the group, joking to keep the group's morale high:

"If my American brothers don't get the message that I'm in Baghdad with you guys and they start bombing, just stand behind me ... God knows I'm big enough to be a true Human Shield! But whatever you do! Don't let me fall on you or you're dead! Ha ha ..." His deep sounding voice added a serious tone of certainty to the laughter of the group.

Rema was still convinced that the Americans would not bomb Iraq and did not seem to see the seriousness or the humour of the situation. Perhaps she didn't understand Gerry's strong New York accent as she looked on quizzically at the gall of this international group of peace warriors about to enter the frontlines of modern-day warfare armed with white handkerchiefs and a good sense of humour.

As we stood around the Al Saraya Hotel waiting for the taxi drivers to arrive we cracked some feeble attempts at humouring the situation, and it was again Gerry who best calmed the group with his overwhelming presence and sharp wit. It was the most inspiring sight I had ever seen: a small group of peaceful individuals from around the world going to Baghdad on their own free will to stand against the ignorance of the American-led coalition military.

They paid a thousand dollars each and were happy to be going to defend the homes targeted by a terrorising regime. They each loaded their packs on the roof-racks and tied them off securely before cramping in for the long road to Baghdad. As the taxis drove away someone stuck a white flag out of the last taxi window that waved us goodbye.

***

The following morning of the 16th of March 2003 we all heard George W. Bush give Saddam Hussein a forty-eight-hour ultimatum to get out of the country. Under any law, this was called 'duress' and was thus illegal. "Leave the country or suffer devastating consequences," was what he said, which was not only a threat but blackmail.

I knew in my heart that the American military were now ready to destroy a sovereign nation that was on its knees pleading for peace and help. This was going to be the greatest criminal act our modern world would witness through the eyes of an imbedded and censored media, and We the People of this world were powerless.

The night before the invasion, nobody slept. We all stayed awake, pacing, playing backgammon, chess, cards, or writing in our journals. But unlike every other night when we rejoiced with the belief that the war was not going to take place and that peace would prevail, tonight we all remained in numbed silence.

The only sound came from the North American news broadcasters of the CNN, NBC and FOX coverage. It was like waiting for the start of a super bowl or a world cup final. I imagined how much popcorn, beer, and sweets must have been sold that night in North America.

Approximately 4:30 a.m. Amman time, which made it 5:30 a.m. Baghdad time, bombs and missiles would start killing and destroying the Islamic city of peace. Like every good film the Americans also managed to name this attack 'Operation Shock and Awe'. It was well-named, as we all knew that economic sanctions also had prevented any information from reaching the Iraqi people about the prelude to this bombing. So clearly, they would be shocked by the awe of the power the G. W. Bush administration yielded over world justice, our natural environment, and humanity at large.

"God Bless America to screw the world," I whispered to myself when the BBC news broadcast that Operation Shock and Awe had commenced. There was little doubt the world remained in shock and awe at the audacity of the American administration and the total ignorance of the coalition of the willing military to understand that what they were doing was illegal, criminal, and simply wrong.

As the bombing campaign continued over the next few days it became more and more obvious that now there was no way of entering Iraq until the Iraqi military was defeated or the war ended.

Rema and I continued to see each other on a daily basis after work, and about a week later we agreed to travel to Damascus, the oldest civilised city in the world. We were both tired and frustrated of watching the biased daily news reporting by CNN and FOX that told the world how well things were going for the American military killing so many bad people, i.e. the peace-starved Iraqis.

When we arrived in Damascus, Rema told me about Samer, A Palestinian friend she had who was studying his final year of a medical degree at Damascus University. Samer had a tremendous desire to help people and as a doctor would achieve his lifetime ambition to ease human suffering in a small but real way. When we arrived in his small student apartment, he let Rema sleep in his bedroom while he and I shared the lounge-room. I slept on the more comfortable makeshift bed on the floor while he slept on the smaller, less comfortable lounge with his feet hanging high off the armrest. Such was his hospitality that he would not have it any other way.

"This is my culture," he explained. "We must respect and treat our guests better than we treat ourselves. It is very much an Islamic tradition," he added.

The following morning, we went to Damascus University where we met other medical students from various Arab nations and were shown around the campus. It was one of my interests to visit major universities around the world in order to draw comparisons between the most important schools; those schools that were developing our thoughts, ideas, and national intelligence.

The similarities always fascinated me, between Damascus University; Baghdad University; Oxford; Cambridge; Madrid; and the Australian universities I attended at Sydney University, Macquarie, as well as the University of New South Wales and the University of Western Sydney. It was comforting to see how similar the mandate of each university was, especially as centres for academic research and as vehicles for teaching future generations how we could contribute to making a better world.

The fact was that the essence of a university was to continue developing, inventing, understanding, and improving our lives on Earth. For this reason, any university graduate was recognised internationally for his or her degree as an outstanding individual in our communities. This, however, was not to be the case in our Western 'free' world, as I was about to find out.

Like any other university in the world where truth, knowledge, and the quest for excellence is the essential element of the campus and the quest of its students, Damascus University's students were no different.

They conversed in small groups or walked between classes carrying books enveloped in their arms as if they hugged and nurtured the babies of wisdom. Like at other universities, there were small groups of students strategically placed in the entrances, raising awareness of any injustice or threat to mankind they discovered.

Today, they held signs in Arabic, English, French, and German, pleading, STOP THE WAR. They were showing graphic pictures of mutilated babies, dismembered children, displaced single mothers, and distressed male prisoners. These were graphic pictures that I knew would not be shown to the Western public in a great hurry. It was always the student who made the initial discovery of an injustice or a cure. For this reason alone, we had to ensure education was accessible to anyone wanting to study and not just those in the province of the privileged.

'God bless our universities' was what we all should have been saying, to benefit from the higher education we were privileged to had, so that we might contribute to making our world a better place. The reality was simple; education was the only doorway we could open together as one. Education was an industry that employed millions and an educated world could overthrow corrupt, criminal, or unjust leaders.

In China, the Tiananmen Square students stood fast against their Chinese government to show their freedom of speech rights. In Paris, the French students stood strong and united against corporations that exceeded pollution limits. Even in Georgia, the Orange Revolution students inspired their entire nation to march peacefully and oust their corrupt government. History was made by students who had learned ways to improve our lives and the future of our world rested on the shoulders of students' ability to learn from the past and invent a healthier, fairer, and a more just world for all. It was good to know that University students are, at times, the most advanced third world warriors we have to take action on our behalf. So why or who sends in the military armed police to stop them when they march? There alone is a question to resolve for greater thinkers than us.

It was enriching to know how important it was for all the students on Earth and those who aspired to the improvement of our world to have a truly free voice. The freedom to march and demonstrate peacefully was a fundamental human right that no government should suppress.

In fact, any good government would know the benefits of listening to the people, especially those students that were learning rather than stubbornly staying stuck in old ideals. It was the very essence of progress to change ourselves first if we wanted to change our world for the better. These students were changing and growing by studying. Now with their newfound knowledge, they demonstrated peacefully.

What I also learned was that in Damascus, the Syrian government provided free education to all those who chose to study, and the students were free to demonstrate and exercise their freedom of speech. It seemed that the Assad Syrian government understood the importance of listening to the students who were learning daily and inventing ways to improve our world, our medicines, and our economies. However, it seemed that the Syrian government of Assad had not learned anything from their students.

In the George W. Bush 'free world', tertiary education was only for those families who could afford to pay extraordinary university fees, or for a handful of a few prodigies who gained scholarships. Consequently, only a few educated people in the West understood the political mechanics of the world media.

Perhaps this was nature's way of eliminating the weak from the strong, which gave rise to the argument in favour of free education for all, justifying the inequalities we faced later in life as adults.

As we sat in the university cafeteria, I mentioned to Samer and Rema my desire to meet some terrorists so that I may understand what drove a person to commit such a horrendous crime. Samer said that was easy to do. He suggested we go to the family funeral of a boy that had recently been killed in Palestine by an Israeli soldier. He made some enquiries and soon we were in a minibus with other students driving around Damascus and heading to the outskirts of the city where the slums of Palestinian refugees now resided.

They took me to a ground floor apartment where a family was mourning the loss of a young teenaged son. Samer, Rema, and I appeared uninvited and as we walked toward the apartment there were men and women outside the foyer lining the corridor. Samer spoke to some men and we were allowed to walk in the apartment lounge, which was overcrowded as some people were forced to stand and those few that could, sat in a large circle.

The coffee table was covered with cups of tea and Lebanese sweet cakes. We were introduced to the grieving relatives and from behind closed doors I could hear women moaning and sobbing. The apartment seemed full of people. Some men looked at me with total contempt and now and again I started to fear for my life as the reality of my predicament came to life. These were hard men that had faced death and unimaginable loss and injustices. They were not happy with my presence.

Samer spoke in Arabic, and I couldn't understand what they spoke about, but an argument erupted between them and others argued amongst them. It seemed to me that our unexpected visit was not welcomed. But when Rema spoke, it seemed like everyone listen to her.

"Why you here now?" the elder of the group asked me abruptly with a harsh tone to his voice, making me the focal point of the rising anger.

"Because I am a writer, and it is important that the Western people and the world knows why they pay so much tax to destroy the environment and to create third world nations," I replied instinctively and defensively, unaware of the actual truth to my answer.

I explained that I was a humanities student now attending the university of life on Earth and that I was learning about the regional conflicts. I told them about my revelations in Iraq during NASYO and the importance for the world to understand the terrorists so that we may get closer to establishing the world peace that we all wanted. My explanation was translated and they discussed loudly amongst themselves, but I could not understand them.

As they were arguing in Arabic, it occurred to me that Jesus Christ had been a Jewish Palestinian Arab and sentenced to death by the Zionist Jews. Had anything changed in over two-thousand years of history?

As tempers flared and the tones of the arguments rose, I began to feel nervous. The men that argued were strong, well-built, and had reasons to be angry with me. My pre-fight instinct was to clench my fists as if getting ready to fight my way out in the true barbarian fashion that was so fashionable on Western television. With the palms of my hands sweating, I began to make my fight plans, preparing to hit the man on my right with a left hook to his temple, a right karate kick to the knee caps of the man opposite him to disable him, and a push of the man near the window through that window to cushion my landing as we fell to my freedom.

With my plan ready for action and now just awaiting the first sign of hostility, the fear in my heart was pounding the familiar beat that trembled through my body before every street-fight.

Then Rema spoke and again everyone seemed to listen to her and after the brief discussion that followed, I was told to sit down in the middle of the sofa as the very centre of attention.

"Why you want to talk to terrorist?" a man bearing a small scar on his forehead asked me.

"Because George Bush has declared war on terrorism but I don't know what terrorists are fighting for," I replied, staring him directly in the eyes.

"You are Australian?" a younger man asked me.

"Yes, but I was born in Spain. So it makes me a Spanish-Australian," I answered quickly as my anxiety mounted.

Spain was once an Islamic nation and the Muslim influence continued to be a part of Spanish culture. Flamenco; saetas; Spanish paella; saffron; universities; irrigation; sewers; grazing; mosaics; stonemasonry; and many government historic buildings were some of the legacies from the Muslims in Spain. To this day, many Muslims continued to visit Spain for holidays or retreats and many more to resettle. The Arab and Spanish ties remained strong as many Spanish people were constantly reminded of the goodness that Muslim scholars, architects, and merchants brought to the Iberian Peninsula.

Undeniably, many have argued that it was the Muslims that influenced Spanish customs the most. The Islamic-Spanish history was the greatest influence on the people of Spain since the Iberian Indians ruled the peninsula. To this date, we saw the Christian Arab Spaniards throughout Spain and Latin America. It was these Christian Arabs that Rui Diaz, also known as 'El Cid', summoned to expel the Muslim rulers. The mystery and the shame of the Spanish Inquisition had forever haunted the Spaniards who later turned on the Jews and Muslims with a satanic evil to make Spain a Christian state. In the same vein as Zionist Jews aiming to make Palestine a Jewish State or Hitler aiming to make Germany a 'pure race' of white Christians, this mono-superiority complex was what ultimately led to war.

The fact that I had two nationalities amused them. Perhaps they could see the possibility of becoming Israeli Palestinians or Islamic Israelis, and the Jews could become Palestinian Jews like in Australia where everyone had dual allegiance stemming from our ancestors. It really was enriching to have dual nationalities.

"Why don't you talk to Jewish president Sharon or President Bush if you want to talk to terrorist? They are the terrorists, you know," a young, tall, skinny man asked me, and others seemed to laugh in amusement at the comedy of the truth to these people.

"Because those men don't listen to normal people; they only listen to their advisors," I replied, knowing their advisors often advised with hidden personal agendas and ulterior motives rather than for the greater good of the world at large.

"So why should we talk to you?" the elder of the men asked me with a serious tone, his hard face cold like a stone.

I didn't know how to reply. I was just a common person, a worker and a perpetual student, an unpublished writer, and just another pilgrim. My heart was now thumping with a growing fear that this was real. These people were not joking. They were here to pay tribute to one of their own children that had been shot dead by an Israeli soldier. It occurred to me that I may be taken as a hostage, tortured, or seen as a spy and killed for revenge for their now dead son.

"Because we do not have terrorists in Australia - yet our John Howard government is spending our money to fight terrorists, so this is the only way I will understand you're martyrs struggle; by talking with you. Learning from you why you would kill innocent men, women, and children in the name of Allah," I said, desperately serious and containing the fear.

It dawned on me that I called terrorists 'martyrs', and God 'Allah'. I realised the coalition would call their fallen soldiers 'heroes' or 'body bags'. The definitions were a bit like Ticker the Turk had taught me: it was all the same thing, only different languages, it all just depended on what language you were talking—or with whom. So much could be lost in translation that we had to make never-ending efforts in diplomacy as our key to resolving conflicts.

Now, surrounded by mostly Palestinian refugees who lived in outrageously poor conditions, I was using their language. I knew if I was in America, England, or Spain I would need to change the diction so that I may be understood. But the one common understanding was that the terrorists killed anyone at random. In that case, it was reasonable to argue that if the American or Israeli or coalition bombs killed innocent civilians at random, then they too were guilty of terrorist offences. Of that there was no doubt, I reasoned, without prejudice.

"Okay, so what do you want to know?" the man with a scar on his forehead asked me.

"I want to know, why do you do it? I mean why would you want to blow yourself up and kill innocent people?"

"Do you think we want to kill ourselves?" the elder man asked.

"I don't know, do you?" I answered like Sheikh Ali had taught me to do when I was seeking knowledge, wisdom, and enlightenment of my spiritual truth: with a question.

"Mr Al, you are intelligent man, you are smart and brave to come here with your friends. But tell me, what would you do if someone kills a family member or your children?" the elder man asked me.

"I would seek justice with the law in a court," I replied.

"But what if the law lets that murderer walk away free?" he added.

"Or if there is no court of justice because that court is corrupt or acts with prejudice?" a girl at the back asked.

"Then, you must appeal to a higher court or the international Court of Justice in The Hague," I answered.

"But we are poor people. We do not have money to eat properly or to have good education like you. Do you think we can afford to pay such expensive costs—" the girl replied but was cut off.

"Or to argue in a false court that can be manipulated and corrupt?" the man with a scar added.

"You think the international courts understand Islamic law? Or only English law?" the girl asked.

I was bombarded with legitimate questions by legitimate people who had themselves experienced an injustice on an international level. What we called legal may be illegal in other countries and vice versa. International law needed to be just, simple, and universal. Perhaps Sharia law was right—it was after all a simple, universal, and just law. However, it was impossible to argue in favour of any law that stoned women to death for a crime of love, desire, or need. This law was among other unjust Islamic laws.

The question of policing international law should be a global and unanimous international concern, not the whim of any one nation or a small group of nations.

"So is it okay for Israelis to kill Palestinians at random but a terrorist act if the Palestinians killed Israelis?" the girl challenged me. She seemed to be well-educated and spoke the best English of the group.

"I don't know," I lied. I knew instinctively, I would hunt down whoever killed my mother, in fact, I had hospitalised men for merely insulting me in public. In all honesty, there was no way of denying that we all would want justice if someone we loved died at the hands of a cold-blooded murderer or terrorist. But now I was learning about the truth that the Israeli military killed as relentlessly as any terrorist. I knew American bombs would kill thousands of civilians in Iraq. But above all, I knew that my natural instinct was to avenge the death of any of my family members with physical violence or in a court of law. But what if these people had no court to go to?

"If you truly want to stop terrorism, your government must stop killing or supporting Israel with the prejudice against Palestinians," the girl standing alone added.

"What would you do if someone killed your child?" the tall skinny man asked, screaming at me.

The horror, the sheer fear that these people must be living in as refugees in Syria in almost third world conditions, frightened the hell out of me. I no longer feared these people and I no longer feared the pain of the truth. In that instant, I understood the terrorist's predicament. Did that make me a terrorist? Or a terrorist sympathiser? Or a traitor to my country? God no, it made me an innocent man wanting to understand what we were never told in our Western media. But above all, it was making me a legitimate bipartisan eyewitness. *How would the FBI or other intelligence agencies respond to my inquisitive nature in search of the truth and justice?* I asked my conscience.

"Perhaps you should ask why we have what you call terrorists," the elder man asked rhetorically.

"Okay, then why do you resort to having terrorists?" I asked, happy to comply.

"Because they kill my wife and baby first!" the tall skinny man shouted at me with anger.

"And my brother!" the girl at the back followed.

"Mr, what would you do if you see your mother dying slowly because an Israeli bomb did not kill her fast?" the man with a scar on his forehead asked indifferently.

"Or if you have to clean your daughter's blood and pick up her head and scattered limbs after a bomb has cut her like that?" the elder man asked.

"Or if you don't know who is your baby from too many burnt bodies when you have to go to collect him?" a lady standing quietly near the door asked in broken English.

I could only sit in terrified silence as the rage began to intensify. My instinctive nature to defend my family and my country or all those who I loved was now making me understand these future terrorists. Was I crazy to understand these future terrorists? No, quite the contrary; by understanding that these people had their own personal reasons to avenge their loved ones, I also understood the Jewish need for a homeland. It was a vicious cycle that had to be broken if we wanted peace to reign. The solution to this conflict was in the air.

"What would you do?" they all seemed to cry out at once. The harmonious echo that followed as they broke into a series of questions that I could not answer made it clear that some of these people had lost a relative or a loved one to an Israeli helicopter gunship or a tank or bullet from an Israeli soldier.

Would the Americans create another state like Israel by invading Iraq? A state where terrorism was a way of life? Where violence and guns were the rule of law and the suppressed people had stones to throw at tanks? Was the invasion of Iraq the next stage in colonising the Middle East, having created the American-sponsored state of Israel?

The sad and painful answer was, yes. By illegally invading Iraq and killing innocent people in the process, we the coalition of the willing were taking international law into our own hands, and for every innocent man, woman, or child our coalition of the willing military killed, we would create another potential terrorist.

"We are not killers," the girl who lost her brother said with a more relaxed tone. "We are not allowed to kill anyone as Muslims. But if anyone kills one of our family members, then it is legal in all cultures for a murderer to face justice," she added. "But we must kill ourselves first if we are going to avenge the death of the one we lost. This why we have terrorist," she concluded.

"But two wrongs don't make a right." I parroted the echoes that we hear repeatedly from those that have never lost a relative to a heinous cold-blooded crime or a terrorist bomb blast.

"Yes, that is true. But you know that evil will triumph if good people don't fight evil," the elder man acknowledged with soft tone. "This is why we must fight back. We don't want to die, we don't want to kill anyone, but if we do not defend and fight the murderers then they kill more of us and enslave us to bad jobs and poor education like African Negro people or many Asian and South American people who live like animals because they do not have education or good jobs."

"You see mister—we are not criminals and we do not want to die or kill anyone, but if we do not have compensation from Israelis then we must avenge our family death," the man with the scar said.

"But terrorism is wrong!" I parroted, like anyone else would without understanding that terrorists simply don't have anything to lose.

"Yes. But the Jewish are terrorists first in Palestine ... now American military are terrorists to Iraqis," the girl added, frustrated. "If they did not start to kill Palestinians or invade Arab, Persian, and Muslim lands, then we would not have to fight with terrorism," she concluded.

I looked at Rema who gazed at me with a look of sorrow. The kind of look a mother gives her child when he loses a game.

"You see Mr Al. You in the West are told what your pro-Israeli media want you to know, but you know in Islam we are all one people, Jewish people are our brothers, but Jewish people say we are their enemy and terrorist. But I assure you, if Muslim man killed our brothers; we kill Muslim murderer like we kill any murderer. It doesn't matter what religion the killer is from. If there is no murderer then we don't need to kill anyone. This is why we fight Jewish soldiers because they murder too many Palestinian people and children!" the elder man added with a slightly angry tone, echoing what Rema had also said to me.

"I'm sorry," I uttered, clearing my throat as the hurt and fear made it difficult to talk.

They seemed to sense my genuine hurt inside and for the remainder of the night we drank tea and ate Lebanese sweets as we discussed the issue of terrorism and other issues that were subjects of my humanitarian interest, such as the meaningless death of the young boy they had all gathered to mourn. We discussed the countless Palestinian deaths, torture, and incarcerations that to this day continued in Israeli prisons. It was brought to my attention that over five million Palestinian refugees had been expelled from their homes at gunpoint by the Israeli army. We talked about the most recent town of Jennin massacre and the continuing need for Palestinian rights to return to their homes and their lands.

Yet the resonating words that struck fear were 'as Muslims we are not allowed to kill. So if we do kill someone, we must kill ourselves first. That is why if the West want to end terrorism, they must first stop killing our brothers and sisters'. Perhaps there was a peaceful solution to end terrorism after all.

It seemed to me that these future terrorists were as dignified as any military personnel in any army on Earth. They were resolute about their fate and did not fear death, but rather embraced it as martyrdom was assured to them. Perchance these Muslims who had taught the world so much about law, civilisation, order, religion, and spirituality, now had another lesson for the world. Perhaps Saddam Hussein had a lesson to teach the world about international terrorism, international law, the unjust economic sanctions, and faith in God. I pondered this.

As a street-fighter who had never started a fight in my life, I understood the instinct we had inside our genes that drove us to defend and fight savagely for our lives against the ignorance of an evil aggressor that threatened us. But what I could not understand was why the Israelis, with all their intelligence, did not agree to pay compensation to those whose houses they had destroyed or to civilian populations they had killed and maimed. This simple gesture would demonstrate to the world and the Palestinian people the naturally good intentions to create a just and legal nation of Israel, without prejudice.

It was thus that I decided to go to Israel.

Chapter 19
Jerusalem, the World's Capital

Creating a new middle East doesn't end with the creation of Israel and Palestine, it starts there.
Tony Blair
UK Prime Minister

Our stay in Damascus was short, but I had finally met what our Western leaders and the media called terrorists. On the third day, we drove back to Amman. For most of the journey, Rema sat quietly and I remained still, thinking pensively about the similarities between my father's lessons when I was a child to fight and defend my family, and what I was thinking about the Middle East. These future terrorists were no different to Big Brett who king-hit me after I broke his brother's nose. The fact was, any person who experienced a violent injustice was likely to become violent and act with rage. This was simply a natural, instinctive reaction that was completely understandable, making it a natural law.

The question in my thoughts now turned to the man-made complex laws and thus began the interest in raising awareness of the hypocrisies and injustices of any man-made law that benefit the law-makers more than the delivery of justice.

When we arrived at the Al Saraya Hotel, a group of mature-aged ladies were getting out of an Iraqi taxi. A second taxi carried others and one more mature and fragile man. They were all Human Shields that had sat through the worst of the bombing. These women were truly inspirational. It was clear they had just arrived from Baghdad as they appeared like they had been on a long, torturous journey of their own. They looked tired, dirty, and overwhelmed with the horrors they had endured during the bombing of Baghdad.

The saddest thing I remember was that they reminded me of my very own mother and grandmother as they walked with frail, tired muscles, needing my help to carry their bags up the hotel stairs.

Once inside, they became heroes to the few remaining Shields still waiting to go into Iraq. They told us of their experiences, the problems that continued to confront the Shields that remained protecting the destruction of property, the rising hunger, and the continuing bombing. What seemed to be the main problem was the total collapse of order and the hell resulting from the destroyed electricity supplies, opened sewers, contaminated water supplies, destroyed homes, and terrorised Iraqi populations who now lived in permanent trauma. It was clear that they had all witnessed horrendous crimes during their courageous attempts to make peace as peaceful warriors. What was obvious was that these were eyewitnesses to the crimes against both humanity and the natural environment committed by the George W. Bush administration-led coalition. Amongst this group were Tom Cahill, Faith Fippinger, and Judith Karpova, all of whom were from the United States of America. They were all equally determined to ensure their own commander and chief and his administrators be tried under international law for the crimes they witnessed. What resulted was simply an injustice.

These peaceful warriors acted in the interest of civilians, our natural environment, and world peace were charged, fined, and in some cases imprisoned for peacefully demonstrating when they returned to their homeland in North America. Their charge: conspiring or aiding the enemy.

The media did not cover these proceedings. It wouldn't look good to see grandparents being jailed for demonstrating peacefully against the most threatening regime on the planet.

The fact was that most Human Shields were highly educated individuals. Many understood the economic catastrophe that would result from the misappropriation of American dollars being spent on expensive bombs that destroyed rather than built things of human need. Some knew the impact a war would have on world oil prices and the knock-on effect on food, health, education, and other spheres. Many more understood about the irreparable damage to the environment; the animals caught in the crossfire like in the Baghdad Zoo; the thousands of years' contamination from nuclear depleting bombs; the carbon emitted from the burning explosions; subsequent fires; and the war machines—they understood the infinite human suffering resulting from war.

The following day, I travelled to Jerusalem via the King Al Faisal Bridge. At the border crossing I was made to wait for three hours as the

Israeli border guards scrutinised my passport that now had an Iraqi visa stamped. This nuisance was doubled as I missed the last bus into Jerusalem and had to pay almost ten times more for a taxi. Perhaps this was a plot to extract money from unsuspecting tourists as I was clearly the only foreigner on the bus from Amman.

When I arrived in Jerusalem it was late in the afternoon and I found a cheap hostel near the Gates of Damascus called the Al Faisal Hostel. The host was a young Palestinian man who seemed pleased to see another Western guest visit his humble business. He advised me of places to visit and things to do whilst in Israel and pointed me toward the old city of Jerusalem. There was so much world history that originated from this city that it truly was holy and internationally sacred.

I was anxious to roam the streets and was soon walking alone like any hobo, saving my few dollars by eating cheap Lebanese bread rolls with Swiss cheese, Hungarian salami, Spanish tuna, and fresh Palestinian green peppers that I bought from an Israeli grocer. The international flavours of Jerusalem were edible everywhere I walked. It was like the world had sprouted from this very city.

While walking around the narrow alleys of the old city, a small group of Orthodox Jews was walking toward the Wailing Wall. They were holding what looked like small beads and a Torah, which was the Israeli holy book not much different to the holy Christian Bible or the Islamic Qur'an. So it was comforting to understand their spiritual pilgrimage and I could not help but respect the devotion of these Israelites to God.

What I was learning was that these devotees were part of the vast majority of Jews, both Orthodox and non-Orthodox, who travelled to Jerusalem on their own pilgrimages. They were no different to Christians, Buddhists, Muslims, or agnostics and atheists all wanting to feel the ever-present aura of this uniting historically spiritual city.

There was no doubt that Jerusalem was a standout city of global significance with historical lessons for all mankind. As I walked in the footsteps taken by millions of pilgrims that included the prophets, popes, rabbis, imams, and the infinite number of civilians, I could not help but remember my first introduction to Jerusalem when I was thirteen years old selling newspapers outside the main entrance to a factory in Alexandria, South of Sydney.

After dragging my trolley laden with newspapers and magazines for over a kilometre from the shop, I would spread my merchandise out on the footpath using stones to weigh them down from flying away every time a heavy truck or a breeze blew by. So by 5:30 every morning before school I had already done my morning exercise, then I would sit and read my weekly literature while waiting for my regular clients to buy and hopefully tip me as well as buy a newspaper or magazine. During the waiting, I would read from my library, which included the magazines *Women's Weekly*; *Cosmopolitan; Cleo; Dolly; Time; National Geographic; The Bulletin*; and the newspapers *The Sydney Morning Herald, The Daily Telegraph*; and the *Financial Review*. So it was often frustrating to go to school and learn basic subjects that bored me to tears while I craved to be travelling and seeing all the places I was reading about. It was at that time when I realised the world was a big ball of wonders.

It was 1977, when *Star Wars* showed us a future between good, poor desert dwellers and evil, masked robotic military droids; when The King, Elvis Presley died; the Panama Canal was returned to the people of Panama; New York City had a blackout while construction on the Twin Towers of the World Trade Centre was completed; and I was reading about an Egyptian man who recognised that a country called Israel existed—he said this from a holy city called Jerusalem.

At thirteen years of age, most children were sleeping or just waking up when I had already learned that such holy chaotic places existed. *National Geographic* and *Time* were the favourite magazines because of the striking colour photos showing exotic people; human tragedies; the animal kingdom; the rich and the famous; and above all, our global geographic boundaries that united humankind. But the most memorable story was the Easter story of a man called Jesus Christ who died nailed to a wooden cross on a hill in Jerusalem. It was perhaps the most harrowing story of our human history; a story that had united and divided the world.

So it was truly magical to be walking among the inhabited old city upon cobblestones that only God knew how many foreign feet had taken pilgrimage upon.

Only now, as I walked through Jerusalem, I could not help but notice the strategically-placed security surveillance cameras and the heavily armed military police to remind me that Big Brother was watching my every move. There was no doubt about it. I was in the world's biggest jail and perhaps the most ruthless legal system on Earth.

To get away from the invasion of my privacy, I walked to the highest point I could find of the old city and found myself overlooking the Al-Aqsa Mosque or the Golden Dome Mosque that had been built with the Wailing Wall as its foundations. It was late afternoon as I sat down, watching the sun slowly sinking to the West as a large full moon ascended from the East almost simultaneously. It was like I sat in the very centre of the universe and I stretched my hands out so that in one hand I could hold the sun and in the other I held the full moon.

Here in the very centre, I had an epiphany. On the 20th of May, 1948, the United Nations Security Council endorsed the appointment of Count Folke Bernadotte of Sweden to act as a mediator between the Jews and Muslims in Palestine. On the 16th of September of that year he proposed to the United Nations a perfect, realistic, and above all a fair plan to make Jerusalem an international city under the control of the United Nations[8]. This ingenious proposal would have secured peace and made the historical city of Jerusalem the capital of the world where the United Nations headquarters could have been built and a global army of United Nations security forces employed as a neutral or impartial security.

It also would have given every nation on Earth a small stake, a diplomatic residence, and above all, a legal right for all the citizens on Earth to visit this historical, spiritual, and archaeological city without the existing prejudices that were physically visible as one walked around the city and more so if one tried to enter the Al-Aqsa mosque and was denied entry by groups of Israeli police strategically placed at the entrances.

However, the following day, on the 17th September, this innocent man of peace who was President of the Swedish International Red Cross was gunned down and shot by the Jewish terrorist group called 'The Stern Gang'[9]. The United Nations recorded the following to ensure justice may one day prevail against the Israeli terrorists who were never punished.

---

8 See Proposal to United Nations by Count Folke Bernadotte 16 September 1948
9 p136 <u>The Arab Israeli Wars</u> by Ritchie Ovendale

UNITED NATIONS
Department of Public Information
Press and Publications Bureau
Lake Success, New York

Press Release PAL/292
18 September 1948

CHIEF OF UN PALESTINE MISSION HOLD ISRAELRESPONSIBLE FOR ATTACK ON UN MEDIATOR AND OBSERVER

(The following has been received today at UN Headquarters from the Press Officer with the UN Mediation Staff in Jerusalem)

Dr Ralphe Bunche, Chief of the UN Mission in Palestine has sentthe following message to the Israeli Foreign Minister Moshe Shertok.

"The murder in cold blood of Count Bernadotte United Nations Mediator in Palestine and of Colonel Serot in the Katamon quarter of Jerusalem today (17 September) by Jewish assailants is an outrage against the international community and an unspeakable violation of elementary morality.

This tragic act occurred when Count Bernadotte, acting under the authority of the United Nations was on an official tour of duty in Jerusalem and in the presence of the Liaison Officer assigned to him by the Jewish authorities.

His safety, therefore, and that of his Lieutenants under the ordinary rules of law and order was a responsibility of the Provisional Government of Israel whose armed forces and representatives control and administer the area.

The act constitutes a breach of the truce of the utmost gravity for which the Provisional Government of Israel must assume full responsibility.

In this connection, I feel obliged to record the view that the prejudicial and unfounded statements concerning truce supervision attributed to you and to Colonel Yadin as having been made at your press conference in Tel Aviv on Thursday, 16 September and as reported in the Palestine Post of September 17, are not the kind of statements which would be calculated to discourage reprehensible acts of this kind."

Needless to say, this was only one of many more acts of Israeli terrorism to come. Yet such was the power of a few Zionist dynasties that terrorist acts could be obscured from the particulars of justice under the idiom 'he who owns the gold makes the law', and thus has been the case in Jerusalem for decades that followed to the present day.

Failure by the Israeli government to punish those responsible would have made them guilty as an accomplice to the crime; to this date, the Israeli governments had never punished nor paid compensation to the United Nations or Count Bernadotte's family. Justice may be yet to prevail. Nor had the Israeli governments paid compensation to the many displaced Palestinian refugees that were forced at gunpoint to leave their houses and their farmlands.

Notwithstanding these crimes, the successor to the post as mediator to the Palestinian-Israeli conflict was an American, Dr Ralph Bunche. He too endorsed the establishment of this great holy city as an internationally governed city: in other words, as the home for the United Nations and all other international bodies like the International Red Cross, UNICEF, Amnesty International, the World Bank, the World Health Organisation, The International Olympic Committee, FIFA and so on.

However, shortly after his endorsement, the Israelis under the leadership of Ben-Gurion illegally launched further attacks against Palestinians and thus acted against the United Nations Security Council and stopped by 'duress' the one true assessment that recognised Jerusalem as the one city on Earth that could unite all nations in peace: a city that truly could become our world's capital without further prejudices. With this revelation, I began to fear the Israeli authorities and more so, the Israeli police who I saw hitting an elderly man for selling sandals at the steps of the Damascus gate.

So while I walked around the old city, I began to notice the Asians from China and Japan; Indonesians; Buddhist monks from Thailand or Burma; African and Arab Muslims; Indian Hindus; European Christians; Greek or Russian Orthodox priests; South American Catholic pilgrims; and Jewish rabbis, amongst many others. Jerusalem truly was the capital city of our world. Sadly, I later confirmed that there were a handful of Zionist dynasties that benefited from selling weapons if Israel was in constant war.

The simple solution to peace in the Middle East was for Jerusalem to become the capital city of our world.

Under every scenario it was fair, just, and equitable on all grounds for the United Nations headquarters to not belong in a Western city like Geneva, or New York, or in any Eastern city like Beijing, Moscow, or Tehran. But there was no doubt that Jerusalem belonged to all the people on Earth and was the natural home for the international governing bodies.

The feasibility of this concept was daunting, especially as we knew the costs of the Iraq war and the costs of the Israeli and Palestinian conflicts equated to the Gross Domestic Product (GDP) of entire countries around the world.

To surrender Jerusalem as payment in compensation to the United Nations would be justifiably the minimal that both American and Israeli governments could pay.

All be it, in the name of who was perhaps the first third world warrior to die for peace, the honourable Swedish Count Bernadotte, we had to stand fast against those who would terrorise us. Be they Israeli Jews or Muslim extremists, Spanish Basques or Irish Republicans, etc.

For three days I walked around Jerusalem eating Russian salads; German kransky sausages; Japanese sushi; Jewish kosher herring; Chinese stir-fry; American burgers; French pastries; and drinking Italian café latte; Palestinian fruit cocktails; and Mexican Coronas.

At a time when I knew American bombs were destroying Babylon and the Jewish military presence was everywhere around me, I could not feel comfortable. It was just like a new system of apartheid between the wealthy, well-armed Israelis and the poor unarmed Palestinians had emerged. More to the point, I would later learn that Zionists had the financial means to employ entire military personnel with the world's third largest air force and were in possession of nuclear and other weapons of mass destruction. The manipulation of the media would guarantee people with stories such as this story you are reading, were censored or ridiculed for the masses that didn't read but believed what they were told from TV.

Even if the Palestinians were to kidnap one Israeli soldier it would be sufficient for the Israelis to kill a thousand Palestinians whist destroying civilian infrastructures like electricity power plants, government administration buildings, schools, service stations, and more civilian homes. There lay the crime[10]... It was a gross abuse of power and we were all guilty of not taking action to prevent such a crime.

Justice would be to find those few terrorists and jail them for life, or have them face a court then be executed if proven to be guilty. But to destroy entire towns or nations was simply a gross abuse of power, and violations against civilian populations were thus simply unjust.

On the third day, I caught a minibus to Tel Aviv where I had a haunting trepidation. Immediately after stepping off the minibus, I walked along a street that was filled with Western girls prostituting their bodies in public, men sprawled drunk and drugged along the streets, others screaming drunken abuse, and two others fighting on the street, but no one stepped in to stop the fighting. Yes, freedom was relative, as these people were no freer than any others in the Muslim or communist nations. Indeed, I suddenly felt like I had stepped into the most uncivilised city on Earth.

Tel Aviv was a stark contrast between the Muslim and Jewish nations. There, in Tel Aviv, I was able to differentiate clearly for the first time between the Jewish and the Muslim way of life and approach to humanity. Tel Aviv was and is the capital city of Israel. God bless its inhabitants who live in their very own perception of freedom.

What was interesting was that further away from the commercial centre of the city, there were manicured, clean streets, cosmopolitan restaurants and cafes, boutique fashion shops, and modern technologies to be offered. The wealth was in abundance as the shops displayed the latest fashions, electronic accessories, gadgets, computers, mobile phones, and every conceivable toy for big children to play. There were bars, bottle shops, and adult shops next to five star restaurants, cosmopolitan cafes, and European delicatessens.

After a long walk, I found a quaint café ideal to rest and read the newspaper in over a coffee. I was disappointed to read that the Israeli

---

10   In 2006 Gilad Shalit an Israeli soldier was taken prisoner by the Palestinian extremist called Hammas which resulted in a disastrous war with thousands of civilians killed, necessary infrastructure demolished and the environment further polluted with no outcome.

government had just signed a deal with Turkey offering over 800 jobs to Turkish labourers in the building industry. I figured it must be common practice for the Israeli government to offer remedial hard labour jobs to anyone but their real neighbours and original hosts; the Palestinian people. This prejudice was simply wrong and the Israelis had to stop impoverishing and enslaving the Palestinians to third world existences.

As I looked around, the Israeli youth seemed to be well-behaved, disciplined, and vigilant. To their credit, it was as if an entire nation of secret police made up the population of Israel as they protected and guarded the Promised Land from the phantoms of terrorists and the ignorance of the tourist.

Chapter 20
Third World War-riors

We will in fact be greeted as liberators.
Dick Cheney
USA Vice-President

As Iraqis defended their nation from colonisation, the Western media continued to propagate their victory over what was deemed to be the evil regime of Saddam Hussein. Yet, the images of the human suffering and the atrocities of the America-waged war were censored in the Western press. The people of the world were convinced that a handful of terrorists were threatening life on Earth more than global warming, overpopulation, and the encroaching natural environment. However, I had already been exposed to the truths not been told to the Western populations. My new mission now was to learn more about the Palestinian people with the aim of learning how their plight for survival may teach the rest of us how to survive our unstable future.

So the following day I went to the Palestinian city of Ramallah with the intention of visiting their leader Mr Yasser Arafat. As I crossed the border checkpoint, I noted groups of Palestinian men told to wait under the exhausting midday sun. They looked tired, dehydrated, and humiliated as their Jewish military guards laughed, joked, and drank cool drinks whilst under shaded tents and shelters.

This humiliation of the mostly young Palestinian men at the border reminded me of an incident shortly after turning fourteen. I was attending a public high school in South Sydney called J. J. Cahil Memorial High. A good friend named Peter Power asked me to go with him to a nearby suburb called Maroubra where there was a school dance that I knew my childhood sweetheart was going to be at.

Nelda Weissen was an exotically beautiful Argentinean girl with Jewish German ancestry that made her stand out a class above the rest. At fourteen, her athletically strong body was firm and her curves allowed her to pass for a much older girl, with well-developed breasts and a slim waist, and a sexy walk that turned heads wherever she went. On this night, Nelda dominated attention as she stood out from the other girls with her tanned, coffee-coloured, smooth skin shining beneath a semi-transparent dress.

At some point later into the dance, Nelda and I remained embraced, kissing in the shadows of the hall, holding each other as I attempted to explore her soft brown skin and taste her lips. Her long, dark, straight hair resembled strands of finely combed black silk, and her perfect smile glowed under the ultraviolet lights. Perhaps she was not aware that the lilac rays of the ultraviolet lights made her white undergarments glow through the thin material of her dress. She was undoubtedly the most attractive girl at the dance and I was both proud and overwhelmed to be with her.

"What are you doing here?" I suddenly heard a male voice asking me abruptly, with a hand on my shoulder, making me turn and break away from Nelda's sweet mouth.

When I looked at the boy asking the question it was one of the Maroubra beach boys that I played rugby against. Like most surfboard riders who developed solid muscular frames, this fellow stood strong alone but was flanked by two other taller but skinnier allies that made him look even more menacing.

"None of your business," I replied, wanting to continue tasting Nelda's warm breath.

I recognised this guy as I had met him before, and seen him start fights and then let the others do the fighting for him. He was a smooth-talking sharp-mouthed boy full of unsolicited wisdom and clever wit. He knew when to puff his chest out at the start of a confrontation and when to deflate it and run. Surrounded by his friends he would nag at anyone, but when he was alone, he would befriend anyone.

"What are you doing smooching with the Spanish fly? Ha, ha-ha ..." he asked Nelda, and laughed along with his two off-siders.

"Go away will you," she said to him, looking over her shoulder.

"Don't worry about him," I said to her, holding her chin and turning it back to my mouth, wanting to continue our moment.

"I never thought cats could kiss," he said, wanting to humiliate and discredit me to impress the world that revolved around Nelda's oil-black hair.

"Didn't you hear? We don't want you here," I advised him, thinking that could be the first warning, and continued in my heavenly world of romantic bliss.

"Ooh did you boys hear that? The cat talks," he said to his blindly following allies. I could sense he was getting jealous at my prized catch and it was becoming obvious that his troops were hanging around to impress this vastly more impressive girl.

"You're kissing a cat," he said to her as we kissed, and I knew he was going to do what I had seen him do before. He would pick out his victim and humiliate them or discredit them. He would fabricate lies, insults, and devise an excuse to demonstrate to his weak-minded followers that he was a good leader or a good catch for any girl. Like a true megalomaniac, he would always be in control and remained the leader of the pack. But deep down, he was like George W. Bush, the spoiled brat of a successful father.

I broke away from the kiss and led Nelda away to sit down so that we could get away from this mad man and his military advisors that urged him on to continue, but they followed us and gathered chairs to sit uninvited in our company.

"You don't mind if we sit down," he said, sitting between Nelda and I.

"No," I said, feeling agitated that this clown was interrupting one of the highlights of my life.

"Look, he's got new Adidas shoes," he said, pointing at my new shoes that I had bought specially for this special night. Like Nelda's white underwear, they glowed under the ultraviolet rays and I blushed.

"That's the best he's ever going to look," one of the clones decided to join in the humiliation.

"I didn't know Zitland hobos could afford Adidas," the other aide added.

"He must have stolen them," the chief-of-staff concluded.

I could feel the shame start to redden my face and thanked God it was dark so that Nelda would not see my glowing red shame. I felt the nerves start to agitate me with a fear that I would need to put an end to his verbal assaults. But I felt threatened by his two accompanying weapons of mass destruction. How did a Palestinian man live with dignity when it was the Israeli police that humiliated him?

"Look, I don't want any trouble with you boys but can't you see that we don't want you around here?" I asked him nicely, thinking this was the second warning, and looked for Nelda's approving smile.

"Don't worry about them Al, they're just jealous," she said, and I knew that it was true that I had something these boys wanted. The prized jewel! Like the world's second oil reserves, her hair was long, sleek black. It teased as she snapped her head back and gave me a quick kiss on the lips.

"Jealous of what, you?" the coward admitted; a Freudian slip.

"Look mate, I'm not going to tell you again. I don't want to have to fight you, now go away and leave us alone," I advised him genuinely and peacefully, thinking this could be my third and final warning.

"Oh. You boys hear that? He's threatening me now?" He had a cunning way of turning the truth around to make him sound righteous and others like wrongdoers. He was a little like many politicians, such as George W. Bush in his State of the Nation speeches.

"No I'm not," I said, wanting to correct the misunderstanding.

"Maybe we should ruin those new shoes," he said as he poured some of the contents in his soft drink can over my new glowing Adidas shoes.

Instinctively I quickly pulled my feet back and stood up. That was a mistake, as all the three aggressors stood up with me.

"What are you going to do about it?" he asked, challenging me in the shadow of his strongest ally.

"Nothing," I said, thinking that maybe Ticker the Turk forgot to tell me about fourth warnings and then looked down at my stained new shoe. I turned, embarrassed, to Nelda, who was now standing and reaching for my arm, wanting to take me away. However, my pride and foolish ego needed to have the final say on the matter. So with the pre-emptive knowledge that megalomaniacs like this spoiled brat who inherited his power rather than earned it, I let him know I was not scared simply by not wanting to play his game; like Saddam Hussein did not want a war or further confrontation with the Americans, and I stood firm on my ground before walking away.

"But I'm not going to tell you again. Now, if you boys don't go away then we will go away," I said, turning and realising that Nelda was far more beautiful than any superstar I had ever seen on television.

"See boys, he's a coward, and she's a fucking slut," he jeered his followers who also stood gawking at Nelda's beautiful body—or was it her white-laced undergarments that glowed, teasing anyone who appreciated the feminine appeals of a girl blossoming into womanhood? In any case, I had given him and his allies three stern warnings and a pardon; I knew like others they would not go away and they would continue to haunt, pick on, and discredit me until something was done about it. So I snapped with a half-body turn and a right-handed uppercut that connected squarely with his big-mouthed jaw. This sent the president reeling straight back to knock himself fully out when his head bounced on the hard timber dancefloor. His two friends, Nelda, and I froze temporarily with the shock of a head bouncing on hard wood.

As we remained mesmerised, I knew they would be ready to strike, and I spontaneously let loose, with a left hook to the ape on my right that sent him sprawling across the chairs. I followed with a right hit on the nose of the guy to my left. He went down holding his nose, but the ape on my right was getting up, and I knew if he got a hold of me I would get hurt. So I finished him off with a kick to his teeth. We would never see his teeth again. As I turned I saw the one holding his nose looking up at me, and as he started to rise, I ruthlessly kicked him on the side of his head, knowing that was all you needed to defend yourself from a coalition of foolish, spoiled brats.

For those who had never been in a street or pub brawl, it was a frightening and terrorising experience and survival instincts took over all logic and reason. Unlike arranged boxing fights, there was no referee to break up an unjust act. Fear and the instinct to survive was what made me psychotic to these boys. If I could, I would have killed them on the spot. Not because of a rational decision made to get rid of these evil characters and their menace, but because of my own instinct to survive and defend.

As I stood waiting to see who would be the next foolish follower to join that coalition of willing stupid brats, the United Nations in the shape of a large Chinese bouncer and an even bigger Kiwi Maori stepped in to drag me away screaming, abusing the three floored boys.

It was this dreadful experience that made me understand why terrorists exist, and above all, why bombarding and punishing the civilian populations of Iraq, Palestine or any nation is wrong. The only thing the Americans in Iraq or the Israelis now in Palestine would achieve was to aggravate and create more terrorists. There was nothing secret about the fact that all humans had a wild animalistic instinct to defend ourselves or our lovers or our families from any aggression or humiliation. So why were we, the mighty, all-powerful Western nations, now going to be the aggressors and invade Iraq or continue the humiliation of these poor Palestinian youths in broad daylight?

I was thrown out onto the street where my friend Peter Power waited in case of a reprisal. Nelda soon appeared and we caught a bus to Sydney's Circular Quay where we held hands and walked romantically under the Sydney Harbour Bridge. It was on that cool summer night on the steps of the giant pillars that supported the mammoth steel coat hanger, the Sydney Harbour Bridge, that I lost my virginity to Nelda. Sadly, I learned that Nelda was not a virgin. She had been having sex with older boys since she was thirteen.

The significance of this experience was two-fold. First, it made me respect those Palestinian youth that peacefully sat under the scorching sun awaiting permission to enter Israeli territories. As I knew instinctively, I would have been violent toward anyone who humiliated or threatened me in public. Secondly, it made me question the significance of man-made English laws that restricted natural liberties like sexual intercourse until a specific birth date.

It made me question if it was possible that laws were being created and invented to protect the interests of a minority few rather than to protect the freedoms and liberties of us, the majority. The truth was yet to come.

Once I arrived in Ramalah I visited the PLO headquarters where Mr Yasser Arafat's bomb damaged compound remained protected by two poorly-armed guards. If the Israelis wanted to kill Yasser Arafat they could do it with ease. However, he was of more value for the Israelis alive than dead. It was easy to depict the PLO as a terrorist organisation with an ugly image of an old stubborn man than a beautiful, educated, and sensitive girl like Rema or Dr Huda. Especially in a modern society now obsessed with image, material wealth, and brain-numbing entertainment or alcohol.

When I attempted to meet and speak to Mr Arafat I made light conversation with two young and scared PLO guards. I noted a difference between the Israeli army, police, and civilians who were well-armed with new age weapons, and the PLO guards who had old AK47s and even older revolvers. I realised there was an elite military that suppressed the inferior, poorer subjects. This military was also employed to uphold the apartheid system in Israel.

After a short while, a distinguished looking man appeared and explained that Mr Arafat was too busy at this stage and I would have to wait a week before he could see me. I explained that I was on a pilgrimage and wanted to speak to Mr Arafat about the Western people's misunderstanding of the Palestinian troubles and he agreed and thanked me for my interest in wanting to learn about the truth. Then he offered me accommodation and food. My money was running short so I gratefully accepted the offer.

I was taken to a nearby apartment block and told that this was where Rachel Corrie had also stayed. Rachel was the first of the Human Shields to be killed in cold blood for standing peacefully and unarmed to protect a stranger's home from destruction. The Israeli bulldozer driver simply ran over Rachel, killing her, and then destroying the Palestinian home. In any other country Rachel would be a martyr or a saint for dying innocently to protect a stranger. In Israel, she was blamed as the culprit and the Israeli bulldozer driver paid money for doing his job and he remained free to continue destroying Palestinian homes.

I was led to my room as a guest and told that Rachel had also slept on that same bed. I didn't think about it at first and was happy to find a resting place. However, later that night I became overwhelmed when I felt as if Rachel's spirit came to haunt me. Thinking about Rachel as she lay slowly dying with crushed organs, suffocating under the weight of the bulldozer, her screams muted by the Earth she had swallowed, I wept myself to sleep like a child. I vowed a promise to ensure her death was never forgotten. With this book, I honour my vow as I write with her courage.

Did the Western media label the Jewish bulldozer driver as a terrorist? I wondered during the temporary quiet peace of the Ramalah nights. "No, he was a murderer," Rachel seemed to whisper. Yet, our Western media were quick to dismiss her death as a radical peace activist, which was now almost as bad as being a terrorist. No peaceful group or environmentalist group could ever be accused of terrorism. Only a true terrorist would point the finger at peace groups, naming them as terrorists, I postulated.

Neither Rachel's family nor the people she protected peacefully had ever been compensated by Israelis. After three days sleeping in her bed I was inspired by her bravery and the courage she demonstrated as a true third world warrior. I knew that my money would soon run out and felt it was imperative to spend the last dollars going to Baghdad. So I hastily returned to Amman and made final preparations to enter Iraq.

***

On the 1st of May, 2003, George W. Bush declared the war over and the Human Shields that remained in Amman began to return to their homes defeated.

We had accepted that Saddam's was a brutal regime, but not a stupid one. They would not kill anyone without hard evidence and would only punish crimes according to Islamic law. If anyone else was placed in power, they too would need to be as harsh as Saddam in controlling a nation surrounded with enemies all too willing to invade, to disrupt, or to harm the Iraqi people for the untold treasures they possessed in oil, archaeology, art, history, and culture.

As I waited in the hotel, a Scottish man named Cory and the Spanish Basque Beatrice introduced me to a man called Majde. He was a Palestinian who lived in Iraq. His story was incredible yet real as he had the physical scars to prove what he was telling us. In 2002 his mother was in ill health, dying, so he went back to Jerusalem to visit her. The Israeli secret police arrested him and asked him to work for them in Iraq but he refused. On his return he was arrested and held for three-and-a-half months. His toenails were pulled out, electric shocks were applied to various parts of his body, and his face was still pockmarked with cigarette burns.

His wife remained in Iraq. His torturers told him she would be arrested and gang-raped in front of him by the fifteen Israeli men who worked undercover in Iraq. I found out later—from Beatrice—that he had been deported penniless, which is usual. Philip, a French Human Shield that had arrived and learned of Majde's fate had paid his fare into Amman and given him enough to keep him in a hotel for a while. Phillip and Beatrice took Majde to Amnesty International and the International Red Cross, but as he was no longer a political prisoner they could not help. I learned also that this was not an isolated event. This was one of thousands.

Mossad was the Israeli secret police that had become one of the most feared institutions in the world. However, very few people would ever understand the terrorising facts of Mossad. They had repeatedly violated human rights and continued to kill at random anyone they deem a threat to a Jewish-only state, with Palestinians as the poorer and lesser paid 'citizens' or modern slaves. Mossad continued to exist as an intelligence agency of little humanitarian value for the world at large, operating with the motto from the bible (Proverbs 24:6): "For by wise guidance you can wage your war" also translated to 'defeat by deception'. With this insight, I began to fear the Mossad agents more than Saddam Hussein's notorious secret police.

For the next few days, some of the shields tried increasingly mad schemes and pestered the Iraqi embassy for ways back into Iraq. But we were confronted with the same Iraqi consulate staff that now seemed defeated and tired of us. Uzma Bashir from the UK, Waratah from Australia, and Yakiko from Japan were the principal representatives of the shields that remained in Baghdad. Many others were not accounted for.

It was around this time that we received the news about Thomas Hurndall. He was the tall and handsome English peace activist I had met on the first day I arrived in Amman. He was a Human Shield in Baghdad shielding the Taije food silo and later the South Baghdad power station before returning to Amman. From here he went on to Palestine to shield more homes. It was there that he was shot in the head by an Israeli sniper as he went to shield two boys caught in the crossfire. The irony was significant and symbolic. As the American war machine pounded the Iraqis with hundreds of tonnes of ordinance, they never killed or targeted a single site where the Human Shields were. Yet the Israelis managed to kill two Human Shields within a two-week period.

This was yet another war crime committed by Israeli forces that again was never punished. Tom did not have a weapon when he was shot. He was wearing a high visibility orange vest to distinguish his humanitarian involvement, yet he was shot by a sniper. The Israeli army seemed unstoppable and untouchable. They simply could get away with murder, torture, and war crimes, and no country on Earth could stop them.

More Shields were now coming out of Baghdad. Most needed desperately to see their loved ones; others seemed traumatised and battle-weary. But all seemed to visit the Al Saraya Hotel for regrouping in Amman. All the Human Shields had financed their own journey and expenses to prevent a man-made and above all an avoidable human catastrophe: the creation of a third world nation in what should be one of the wealthiest nations on Earth.

It was a saddening experience to see well-educated people, sensitive to the future needs of humanity and caring for the livelihood of complete strangers, to be arriving so defeated.

Fortunately, the Human Shields proved to be effective peace angels. All the sites shielded had remained intact and functional. The power and water started as soon as the Americans allowed it. The Durham electrical power plant, the Taije food silo, the Jaizer water treatment plant, the South Baghdad power station, the Daura oil refinery: all these sites were shielded by peaceful people of the world and now remained as testimony to the human spirit and the bravery of these peaceful warriors. This could be seen as a victory for peace activists from around the world.

Fewer people would die in Baghdad compared to Basra, where children were again shitting themselves to death because there was no clean water. There was no electricity to power the refrigerators, and food supplies resembled the third world in this country that had traded its oil for food under duress of economic sanctions.

These were victories that third world warriors around the world claimed even if they did not become Human Shields or go to Baghdad to stop the war. What was encouraging was the number of third world warriors demonstrating in every country to oppose their governments. As I sat watching peaceful demonstrations taking place across the world, I was encouraged and motivated, making the promise to tell their story of untold bravery, heroism, and honourable intentions so they may be forever remembered by many generations in the four corners of the world.

The Human Shields and those who marched and demonstrated peacefully all over the world raised the awareness of those others who had not had the same advantaged education to understand the damaging consequences of a modern war or the consequences of remaining apathetic in ignorance.

Unfortunately these third world warriors were few. The majority of our world populations continued to live in a kind of modern slavery doomed to a lifetime of hard labour as ignorant workers, unemployed, or simply as media brainwashed people unable to understand the consequences of our actions against human greed, the environment, or the freedoms that all individuals on Earth had a right to enjoy.

Like the freedom of speech and the freedom to travel and reside in any country that may offer employment or a better life, the freedom for Palestinians to return to their homes was just as necessary as the freedom for the Jews to live in Palestine. These and many freedoms were what made us humans civilised and educated. These were basic human rights we all had to stand for and fight peacefully to uphold.

Amongst the many third world warriors that I met, one more deserved a special mention as he was fighting the problems of rape, torture, and murder in American jails. Tom Cahill was one of the few male Human Shields that remained in Baghdad. When he did come out of Iraq, he explained to me that he was an active representative of an American group who was silenced to avoid them from telling their stories.

Tom told me about his experiences in an American prison; the rape, the torture, and the abuse he and thousands of inmates experience whilst being locked in American prisons. He explained that he was one of the lucky ones as others were murdered in cold blood and their stories went untold. He wanted the world to know that crimes against humanity were not only an Iraqi or Chinese or Saudi problem, but more, they were part of an American epidemic that was not being reported anywhere in the world.

"There are more people living in American jails in proportion to the population than any other country on Earth," he said as we talked over a sweet cup of tea.

He told me his own story, retelling how he had been tortured with regular beatings, how they fed him an all-white diet of white rice, white bread, milk, white mashed potatoes, white fish, the white of eggs, and even white chocolate. He told of the thousands of people locked in isolation and how some had been in isolation for years as they didn't have families or friends and remained unaccounted for. Any attempt to tell his story was simply censored. Tom Cahill's mission in life was to tell the world and Amnesty International to look in American prisons for victims of abuse and crimes against humanity.

I recalled these memories knowing that this story would be criticised and censored by those who regulated the information allowed to be told. It saddened me with the painful truth that these third world warriors who fought and continued to fight without killing a single person or destroying a single home, had been discredited, silenced, and ostracised rather than hailed as the true heroes they were.

Tom Hurndall was shot for shielding children; he died nine comatose tortured months later. Rachel Corrie was crushed to death defending and shielding peacefully a Palestinian home and Julian Assange was discredited for telling us, the people of Earth, the truths that hurt us. There were many other great people that had been jailed, fined, defamed, or had their lives destroyed from a system designed to protect the elite few. We did not want or need any more martyrs, but these deaths and injustices deepened the commitment for all humanity to rise and demonstrate peacefully against any aggressive or unjust regime and any justification to act on war; in particular when the third world war would be our united war against the natural threats of global warming.

The fact was clear. We were all struggling to survive and it was becoming increasingly more difficult to pay bills and educate our children.

Yet there were third world warriors who had the foresight vision and educated understanding of the future and had sacrificed their time or their lives for all our benefits—even if we were strangers.

Mahatma Gandhi, Nelson Mandela, Martin Luther King, Mother Teresa, and Che Guevara were household names across the world. These were warriors who had fought selflessly for humanity rather than for a monarch or a dictatorship.

God bless the third world warriors …

Rachel Corrie 1979–2003

Thomas Hurndall 1981–2004

Chapter 21
The Balance of Power

Those who make peaceful revolution impossible will make violent revolution inevitable.

John F. Kennedy

"Allah … Oohhh ac-bar …" The Morning Prayer call to Muslims in Amman woke me up as it echoed through the streets. Whilst my limbs lay in the comfort of the hotel bed the symbolic gesture of 'the prayer' amused my thoughts to the point that it was inspiring me to go and pray. This common phenomenon shared by all religions was what united the vast majority of mankind. Muslims called it Salah, Buddhists called it meditation, Jews called it Telifah, and Catholics called it the prayer to God. It was all the same thing, just different languages and cultural traditions, just as Ticker the Turk had told me many years before. This was a humble act where we submitted ourselves for a short moment to pay our respect, appreciation, and humbleness to the greatness of our universal God.

"Allaaaaahhhhh Oh ac-bar …"

The incantation to pray again broke the morning silence in a beautiful sounding hymn that resonated through the valley. This was such a relaxing way to wake up in contrast to my old alarm clock. Why didn't the West see the beauty in waking up with a morning song or a call to prayer? I had already learned that some Muslims prayed as much as five times each day whilst the vast majority of Muslims prayed whenever they could, and many others had stopped praying altogether as they believed their absolute faith in God was sufficient for them to pray in silence at their own will.

"Allah … Oh ac-bar," the man sang a third time as the third world warriors in the Al Saraya Hotel and many more around the first, second, and third worlds of this third millennium continued their peaceful battles against the complex system that controlled their very lives in ignorant bliss.

As these thoughts of gloom and doom distorted my consciousness, I decided to join in the Morning Prayer, so I washed, dressed, and walked downstairs where only the hotel staff were awake, busily preparing the breakfast tables and attending to their chores.

"Salaam Alecum," they greeted me as I walked past.

"Peace upon you too…" I replied, holding the peace fingers at them whilst the young men giggled. I corrected myself. "Alecum salaam."

Walking out of the Al Saraya Hotel I could see the ruins of the Al Cazar with the old Roman columns silhouetted against the rising twilight sun. So I made my way slowly up the mountain, thinking all along how true it was that angels whispered to a person that walked, as divine thoughts filled my mind in the crisp morning air.

By the time I reached the top, the sun seemed ready to rise over the horizon and I stood facing the valley and the Roman amphitheatre only to realise that these were the lands where Buddha; King David; Hercules; Alexander the Great; Julius Caesar; Al Saladin; Genghis Khan; Abraham; Jesus; and Mohamed had roamed. Sacred lands to all humankind that inspired many other academics, poets, historians, politicians and normal folk to visit and walk in search of their own angelic wisdom; in particular for those wanting to contribute in making our world a better, safer and fairer world.

Only now, camels, mules, Oxen, horses and donkeys had been replaced by trucks, cars and busses that slowly contributed to the need for oil and the cancerous depletion of our greenhouse environment.

A single cloud floated west toward America from the direction of Baghdad as a single stream of light suddenly illuminated the cloud with a streak of silver lining that seemed to push the cloud further west. Standing on a clean, solid rock, I kneeled down and faced Mecca, bowing my head low so that my forehead touched this sacred land of the Middle East. And I prayed.

I prayed for justice to prevail and for the war to end.

I prayed for the day that we would unite to declare war against the polluting and damaging of our natural environments.

I prayed for a world with an advanced conscience where human compassion, understanding, and education were our government's priorities rather than the invention of man-made laws that restricted and inhibited our full potential to live enriched lives and keep us enslaved with mortgages, perpetual labour, and the ignorance of modern-day slaves.

However, when I rose from my prayer, reality sank into my consciousness. It was always nice to pray and unload responsibilities on God. It really was conveniently simple to let God fix all our problems and make this world a better place for all humanity. But the painful truth was that God had already made everything possible.

It was God that had given us life, land, water, animals, and everything we had. But it was unto us to do the right thing. It was thus right to learn, to imagine, and to take the necessary actions that would contribute to improving our lives both collectively as the human race and as individuals.

I sat upright and rested on my folded legs in total submission to the wonderful powers of the universe and recalled the Buddhist monk's words about the 'universal law of polarities'. There was no doubt, all good people on Earth wanted peace, the educated people who cared for our environment wanted a healthy climate forever, and our honourable world leaders were entrusted to endorse the actions needed to make life on Earth a comfortable reality for all. But why couldn't we stop the war? Were the negative forces of an evil empire so great? What evil reined among us in this fragile third millennium?

As the morning light now consumed the stars above, one bright morning star remained visible, and I smiled as it reminded me of Rema's 'Moaning Star' news tabloid.

This loan morning star glittering like a polished diamond held up against a beam of light sparked a realisation that it was not a star, but an American satellite that now floated inconspicuously above Earth, broadcasting to the world anything but the truths we needed to be told.

I stood up and faced the descending moon to the west and thanked God for my health. I turned and faced the ascending sun and recalled my promise to the third world children I had seen dying in Sudan. Standing on the ruins, I remembered the NASYO conference and all the perpetual students seeking further knowledge and addicted to discovering truths rather than accepting the lies told by a biased Western media with hidden agendas. I thought of Rema peacefully writing her articles, attempting to educate her readers about Palestinian history, culture, and injustices. I also thought about Ghassan and his family and wondered how they might be surviving. And I wondered about Shaima and Ammar and all the students from Baghdad University I had met. I also reflected on Dr Huda and Dr Zorba and those around the world like Prince Godwill from Nigeria, George Galloway from the United Kingdom, and Yakiko from Japan, who was still inside Iraq with Waratah from Australia.

Finally, with Rachel Corrie and Tom Hurndall's courageous deaths, I felt empowered to enter Baghdad oblivious to the horror that may lie before me.

I ran down to the Al Saraya Hotel where the hotel cleaners were now scrubbing and hosing down the marble floors.

"Good morning," Fayez greeted me with his warm tone. As always, he was impeccably dressed when he saw me marching past the hotel lobby, still sweating from my run.

"Yes it is, and Salaam Alecum to you Fayez," I replied hastily as I marched to my room and sat down to do a repetition of sit-ups, then push-ups, and the three three-minute bouts of shadowboxing. I felt my greatest fight was yet to come and it was imperative that I now got myself back into shape for what I believed was going to become the fight of my life.

It was the 1st of March 2003 and the prophecy that warned 'beware the ides of March' was all that came to my mind. I had used virtually all my savings and had helped the Human Shields any way I could. Some of the Shields were still in Baghdad and the last I heard of Waratah was that she was walking barefoot and begging in Baghdad, determined to stop this crime against humanity to the very end.

Judith Karpova had given me US$1,000.00 to buy a symbolic sculpture she had seen in Baghdad. And Mike, the Australian, dug deep in his pocket to give me $100.00 to give to Waratah on his behalf. I still had this money set aside and my last $400.00 credit with the return ticket to Sydney of my own. I felt that none of this money would mean anything after I was dead. I would be a prime target for the insurgents, terrorists, or American forces who may arrest me and allege that I was an enemy combatant like the fellow Australian, David Hicks. I remember reading a published poem by David Hicks and knew he was better educated and more informed about global injustices than most Australians. Yet, our media never credited his spiritual sensitivity to fight for justice. Instead, he was discredited, and later when he was released, silenced from telling the truth to the world as part of his agreement to be free. Such was the power of the English law regime.

So, I went shopping around Amman and bought 400 dollars' worth of bandages, disinfectants, pain-killing pills, cold and flu pills, band aids, and a large carry bag to carry it with. I would say to the Americans or border guards that I was delivering urgent medical supplies. *Why didn't I think of this before?* I kicked myself.

A taxi to Baghdad now cost over $1,000.00, but the $1,000 I had was not mine, and besides I may have needed it inside Iraq later. Clearly I couldn't afford the taxi. But a man told me about a desperate bus driver who would take anyone willing to pay $20. I found the old time-beaten bus with an elderly Iraqi driver. I explained to him that I needed to enter Baghdad and he was happy and pleased to see my bag of medicines and a crisp American twenty dollar note. So he happily accepted my bus fee. Now we just had to wait for other mad men or desperate people wanting to go into the war zone. All that anyone could do at this time was to retreat to the end of the old bus and try to rest in preparation for the journey ahead. The hot afternoon sun slowly hypnotised me into a conscious sleep.

In the back of this vintage bus complete with missing windows, dusty moth-eaten curtains flapped in the warm breeze. I could hear a constant tapping: TAP, TAP, TAP as the metal wire that held the curtains connected with the metal of the window frame.

I remembered Ticker the Turk's Islamic wisdom that was the basis of the golden street-fighter's rule. "Never start the fight," he had said, pointing at my heart.

TAP, TAP, TAP. The sound continued and I sank deeper into the memory of the millionth combination I would deliver from that unsuspecting old army-green kit bag. I recalled Pako (Frank), the South American Peruvian Indian elucidation of a warrior, when he said, "Warriors don't fight … they defend!"

TAT, TAP. And I understood the good sense of the little Sri Lankan Buddhist monk's philosophy about the Universal law of opposites that complemented the law of justice, fairness, and differentiated right from wrong. Only I could not understand why the world had not yet united to fight against the ever-threatening war with the depleting natural environment. Or worse, in this modern world of prosperity, how could we be so naïve and so apathetic to believe anyone who justified a war against our own: a war against the goodness of people as opposed to a war against the evil of ignorance? Or the looming war against natural disasters … Hurricane Katrina and the Boxing Day tsunamis were yet to come, and the many more unknown environmental catastrophes remained the source of a greater fear than my going into Baghdad.

TAP, TAP, TAP. My mind sank deeper into the terror of depression.

Only once before in my life did I feel the sense of destitution and utter defeat that I was now feeling. That was back in the early nineties when I found myself homeless, walking the streets of London during my first ever white Christmas. It was a night when it seemed that suicide could be justified, as the emotional pain of a tragic existence taught me the real pains of the truth: poverty was humiliating—nay, soul-crushing.

I had gone to London to try to get an extension to the copyright license for *The Wall* by Pink Floyd. This had been my first theatrical production as an aspiring writer/director/producer during my university studies. It had been a surprising success, and I was encouraged by everyone that approached me after the show telling me to take the show on tour. So I went to London to meet with Roger Waters and his manager, Mark Fenwick, to discuss my need for an extension that would allow my production team to take the show on a world tour. However, it was ultimately up to Roger Waters, who later spent over four million dollars on a one-night show in Berlin to celebrate the union between East and West Germany. After many efforts to take the show on a tour, even offering to donate proceeds to various charity organisations, his manager Mark Fenwick was succinct when he alleged that I was 'a nutter' to think Roger would allow me to stage *The Wall* again. The dream of staging the show in opera houses worldwide, as I believed it deserved to be staged, fizzled with an awakening reality that tore me apart.

When I returned to the empty apartment with a sense of loss and worthlessness, I realised that my last dollars had been spent only to learn that I had become delusional. The sense of failure was compounded as I found myself broke, hungry, and cold, in abandoned isolation, staying in a cheap attic studio. But above all was the deep-rooted depression that gripped my very soul as I could see through other rear windows facing the courtyard some family gatherings of people laughing and eating together while some children played in the snow in what was my first white Christmas. With the sound of 'The Little Drummer Boy, which had been my favourite Christmas Carol as a child, I switched on the gas and locked the door and windows, thinking, *Suicide is a justifiable option to end the heart wrenching pain of depression.*

With the gas hissing louder than the distant music and the laughter of families, the voice within my conscience echoed words my father had used repeatedly:

"When things go from bad to worse and you end up buried in shit, then it's time to start cleaning the handles," he would say, referring to the reality of life that we all faced. Which meant, when we made a mistake we needed to work harder and start again, and again and again. There was no better place to start than from where we gripped reality, the handles of our own destiny; our health.

"Make your job a daily exercise routine rather than work," he would often teach, which was similar to the Jewish proverb, "The best kind of play is hard work." In other words, get up off the couch or the bed and start living.

After all, lying alone waiting to die was an experience we were all destined to experience at some point in life; so why make a silly decision to cut our lives short when there are so many adventures, risks, highs, and lows awaiting all of us? Just the same as death is guaranteed to us all! With this awakening, fear subsided. These words of wisdom from a father to his son or daughter were perhaps the most significant ingredients in strengthening one's character that I could think of. While a mother offered emotional support, empathetic understanding, and the unconditional love for the child, it was my father who repeatedly encouraged me to get up, to fight for what was right and to never quit until God alone would defeat me with death.

As such, it was sad to know that the family law courts were profiting from separating children from their fathers or mothers rather than educating parents on the importance of speaking calmly to our children. By all means we needed to express our anger when we were angry, with raised voices or screams or even a painful smack, but we always calmly explained later the reasons for our anger. Even after my dad would beat me for my disobedience, he would always sit with me after and calmly explain why he hit me or why he was angry or why I should have done as he instructed me to do ... besides, it had been a parent's prerogative to educate the child accordingly since the very beginning of human time. Yet family lawyers would argue abuse, neglect, parental divorce, or anything but the truth in the name of profit-making justice.

What parents and children needed was education. Not only academic education, but the type of spiritual education one finds in Holy Scriptures, or is passed down with the unconditional love that our parents and grandparents have taught us.

Even my father's occasional aggression seemed to serve a purpose in my education, as I could count his beatings over my life span on one hand, and he would always explain and teach me after the beating why I was wrong or what I needed to learn from a beating. This was not an abusive parent, as modern law-makers who earn incomes from manufactured laws will argue. This was simply an ancient tradition that has worked for thousands of years and will continue to function irrespective of what profit-driven law-makers will argue.

Having said that, one does distinguish between abuse and correctional behaviour, as there are clear differences. In this case, common sense should prevail over man-made laws. This is because the universal law of polarities can be applied as if it were a God-made law rather than a law invented by profit-earning individuals. The fact is, there is a clear balance of power.

This balance of power, shared by two parents, could also be provided by peers, relatives, and good friends. It is a balance that could be applied to many matters, including international diplomacy and between warring factions. The wisdom of Buddha and our prophets remains eternal. Yet modern law-makers create new laws and then make absurd wealth from the ignorance of their subjects and their victims. Such was what I learned while studying, what I would call, the English Law regime at Sydney University, and working as the caretaker for a well-known female Judge who would placate every argument with her superior grasp of the man-made laws.

So why were we not teaching our youth to deal with the natural highs and lows of living rather than resorting to suicide? Or perhaps educating our children on social behaviours, the importance of family unity, or the excitement of perpetual learning?

This should be taught because there are so many children tortured by hunger until they die, so many people suffering unnecessarily with curable illnesses, and so much work in the humanities to do to make things right. That, for me, to die from suicide, alone and without a fight, would have been the ultimate act of selfishness. Perhaps there were lessons to be taught and learned by those in need of psychological help and an army of teachers, mentors, nurses, doctors, peers, and health care workers was what we needed more than military invasions and weapons of mass destruction. Particularly as global warming temperatures were creeping ever so close to the dangerous levels that would affect each and every one of us and all other life forms on Earth. This made war between humans the ultimate crime.

I rushed to open the window and let the gas escape the confines of the room while inviting the frost to bite me back to the reality that life was a hell to everyone at some stage of their lives. We all experienced the sensation of worthlessness, the pain of truths we hated to accept, the shame of imperfection, and the horror of a reality that we never expected to find ourselves living. In fact, we needed these sad, tragic, depressing experiences to find the courage to do the insane and crazy things we did that made our lives exciting: thus courage blossomed.

TAP, TAP, TAP, TAP. The wire sparred with the old time-beaten bus and again I was brought back to reality. I was going to Iraq amidst a war. But better to face my demons and enter the theatre of war than to live regretting my cowardice, to not stand and fight for what was right. Overcoming the tragedies we experienced in our lives was what made life worth living, I reasoned.

By late in the afternoon the bus had almost filled with mostly elderly men and women. A couple of mothers and their children sat up front but I was the only Western man and they all looked at me with resentment, or sorrow—as if I were going to be killed soon. By the evening twilight we left Amman destined for Baghdad. It was near midnight when we reached the border and we had to sleep the night in no man's land before being allowed to enter Iraq. Early the next morning, we entered Iraq and were greeted unceremoniously by an American border guard.

"Welcome to the United Next State of America," an American marine joked with a strong Texan accent as I showed him my Australian passport.

"Where are the Iraqis that you liberated?" I asked him with a more serious tone. But this shook him, and he immediately realised that I was not in the mood to joke around.

"They went home, Sir," he now replied, changing the tone to serious.

"Is it safe to travel inside?" I asked him.

"Yes Sir, we are giving this bus and your convoy a clear passage. You won't be shot down by us but I can't speak for the Iraqis," he advised.

The American border guards approved our entry into Iraq only after they had searched the bus. But I wondered what had happened to those Iraqi border guards I had met in my first visit. Would they still be alive? What about their families? If not for the undeniable fascination of the American marines who performed their duties like mechanical, well-programmed robots with body armour and armed with space-age telescopic rifles, guns and hand grenades, I probably would have collapsed and wept like a child as I recalled those fathers that had previously welcomed me to Iraq.

Along the first part of the journey I counted three civilian cars and a bus that had been bombed and completely destroyed. Their occupants were nowhere to be seen! But the damage to these civilian vehicles left no doubt that no one had survived. They were all civilian vehicles and burnt to bare metal.

Almost three hours later we stopped at a crossroads where an aging petrol station accommodated other civilian cars and a minibus. However, there was no fuel to refill and our driver refilled from jerry cans we carried in our luggage compartments. All the passengers seemed to be as scared and apprehensive as I was. Nobody had talked for the entire journey. Even as the bus slowed for all to see the burnt out civilian cars and the other burnt bus, we all looked in silence, wondering what may have become of their inhabitants in this remote lunar landscape.

In that abandoned roadside diner somewhere in the middle of the flat Arabian Desert, we all stood or sat in deep thought of our own. There was an eerie silence, as nobody spoke, and even the babies were silent. The wind at times whistled a soothing tune and carried away the foul diesel vapours that seemed to evaporate from the scorching midday heat.

Then, unexpectedly, we saw movement from the southern road that led to the Arabian Sea. As the speeding vehicle approached we could see it was an American military hummer jeep. It looked surreal as half-a-man protruded from the roof wearing big skiing goggles and his gloved hands gripped at a large machine gun that swivelled as the gunner turned his attention towards us. He looked like a Star Wars character with his mouth covered with what looked like a gas mask. It truly was like the dark forces of the empire had arrived in this barren, isolated setting. Or as if George Lucas, the director of the Star Wars films, had prophesised this very moment but forgot to show the enemy as elderly women, mothers with babies, grandfathers, and one stupidly crazy redneck man that now stood alone holding a pen and a notebook.

The jeep left behind in its wake a descending volume of engine noise. Then, the engine noise increased in volume again but this time from the south, and we all turned to look down the road again as about a mile away we saw the source of the increasingly thunderous roar that followed.

This was an American military convoy; a long slithering snake of vehicles that glided toward us from the south and headed north without slowing down or stopping. As they passed we could see the expressionless faces of the droids that turned to look at us. I could only imagine what they could see as a handful of civilian cars and one old broken down bus was surrounded by elderly men, women, babies, and a lunatic that posed no threat.

This convoy was an impressive show of military force. It seemed complete with tanks, trucks, jeeps, and prime movers towing cannons, cranes, other tanks, containers, generators, foods, and tankers carrying fuel and water supplies. Some prime movers hauled bulldozers, tractors, and machines I had never seen before. They drove past us without a hint of slowing down, in a convoy that lasted well over half-an-hour.

During this thunderous roaring time over a hundred million American dollars' worth of depreciating assets built with the sole purpose of destroying a country and our environment, drove past our small group. I was a dumbstruck eyewitness who understood clearly how far one hundred dollars could be stretched in a third world country, let alone how many schools, universities, and hospitals could be built in the third world with the money spent on these polluting and depreciating weapons of mass destruction.

Nevertheless, as the last vehicle drove past, I witnessed the terror in the eyes of all these women who stared in shock at the gall of the world's greatest superpower to invade and destroy a nation that was in desperate need of help. Perhaps they understood that the leader of those soldiers was drinking fine wine and eating fat beef steaks with crisp, fresh vegetables and sweet French pastries from the safety of a fortified white house some 20,000 kilometres away from the danger. *Is the chief-of-staff breathing heavily with excitement at the carnage?* I mused.

We did not leave the safety of this abandoned diner until that last vehicle, a Red Cross ambulance, had faded into the horizon. The silence that exploded was haunting and memorably eerie and a minute's silence was observed as if a tribute for the dead casualties who would fall to the murderous weapons that had just driven by.

We mounted the bus and continued en route to Baghdad, slowing down to a crawl every time we passed a bombed civilian bus, car, or house. As we got closer to Baghdad we began to see bombed tanks, trucks, personnel carriers, more civilian cars, and another burnt bus that had been targeted and hit. All were Iraqi vehicles.

On the out skirts of Baghdad we now began to see more bombed buildings, displaced individuals, and desperate people rummaging through waste or cueing for the limited fuel supplies around petrol tankers. In stark contrast to the Baghdad that I had first seen only weeks earlier under

Saddam Hussein's rule, this was now a destroyed city about to join the third world existence, or worse: with no police, no government officials, no order, and the city in ruins, the Americans had succeeded in creating a state in anarchy. The birthplace of civilisation, the city of peace, and the epicentre between the East and the West, was now a city in chaos where survival of the fittest and strongest was the only law.

When the bus finally stopped I stepped out and realised my exposure and vulnerability to the insurgents. I was the only white-skinned, blue-eyed man amidst the crowd of Arab Iraqis. Fear gripped me as I was suddenly grabbed from the arms and others grabbed for my bags, pulling and tugging at me from all sides.

"Mister—Mister I drive you—"

"Mister you want taxi?"

"Mister you have buck-shis—"

"Mister you buy bread?"

"Mister, water!"

It was the nightmare that had become a reality. I had now entered another third world nation. Iraq had been one amongst the wealthiest nations on Earth with one Iraqi Dinar buying three American dollars. Now, I could buy a thousand dinars for one dollar. The economic gains for those who could buy or invest in Iraq would be astronomical. It was beginning to make sense why invading Iraq would mean absurd profits to a few, as these people now fought for my few dollars in their newfound third world existence.

When I finally did choose a taxi driver who offered air conditioning, I became suspicious and petrified that perhaps he was an insurgent as we drove around back streets to avoid traffic congestion or delayed military checkpoints. We slowly meandered through a city now clearly destroyed. A city polluted and infected with open sewers, rotting garbage, and smouldering ruins. The sadness was overwhelming but the fear of being kidnapped by insurgents was too real to dwell in sadness.

What was daunting was the pinpoint accuracy of the American military weapons. Tanks were hit squarely as were all other Iraqi military and civilian vehicles. Some buildings had crumbled as if expert demolition teams had been sent to demolish them—shopping centres; administrative buildings; military compounds; police stations; industrial sites; and even some residential houses had been completely made redundant as piles of meaningless bricks and mortar. It was clear that the military strategy was to destroy infrastructure and the ability to self-govern, thus creating a third world nation.

The carnage was obvious.

The damage and pollution to our natural environment was criminal.

This was the truth from inside Iraq during the first three months of the 2003 war, as was shown to me by my taxi driver. But this truth would never be told in our Western media—perhaps soon they would re-introduce sedition laws to ensure the truth could remain hidden from the Western taxpayers who ultimately paid the literal price for this war, only to continue working as the modern day slaves that we were. Oblivious to the fact that we went to war on the premise of a lie, in effect, to protect Saudi Sultan and Western petroleum dynasties, we would all be working longer hours for less money value and our perpetual enslavement was imminent.

We, the people of the world, had squandered a unique opportunity to buy Iraqi oil at a fraction of the price, which may have prevented the financial collapse that shattered millions of lives in the 2008 economic crisis. But above all, it was our uniting global environment that would be severely attacked, as the plumes of black smoke, the exhausts of the military machine, and the destruction of a nation that I witnessed, were beyond measure.

When I arrived at Ghassan's family home they greeted me with open arms and offered food and drink, but I had bought them some sweet biscuits and cakes in Amman, which they were happy to receive. I also gave them some fresh bottled water and the bag with medical contents so they could do as they pleased with it. They smiled and laughed and thanked me time and time again.

After a short twenty minutes, Ghassan showed up, and the joy and relief to see him was overwhelming and we embraced like two men that now understood the horrific tragedy of war as tears ran down our faces.

Ghassan's mother soon made the sweet tea and we shared information about the circumstances that had brought us here thus far. He explained the horror during the first days of the bombardment, when missile after missile terrorised the Iraqi civilians, killing, maiming, destroying, and further impoverishing millions of innocent souls. Was this not terrorism on a grand scale perpetrated by the lies of the G. W. Bush regime? Absolutely, it was! Iraqis, and now I, were witnesses to the military terrorism led by the G. W. Bush administration, and the North American people were kept oblivious of the facts with meaningless entertainment on their television screens. Only the academics, the foot soldiers, the journalists, and the victims would ever know the truth to this crime.

Shortly after tea, I explained to Ghassan that I needed to find Waratah and any of the remaining Human Shields. He was quick to understand, and we quickly went searching for the remaining Shields.

As we walked back toward the city centre a group of young men approached us and asked us where we were going. Ghassan responded and they talked for about five minutes in Arabic and I could not understand them. But I did understand when one produced a handgun and gave it to Ghassan, which he in turn passed to me.

"This is for you Al. God willing, you never need to use it," Ghassan said, handing me the gun. It seemed perfectly hopeless because I had never used a handgun in my life. If I ever did need to use it, I would be doomed whilst I worked out safety switches or how to fire it in anger. But I felt some protection was better than none, and I took it.

"Who were they?" I asked Ghassan.

"They are my friends," he said.

"But they look like teenagers, are they Shiite or Sunni?" I asked him.

"Both!" he replied in stark contrast to all the media allegations I had heard that Iraqis were a divided people.

If there was anything in the Western media reporting about the problems in Iraq, it was always negative and never positive. This was becoming more and more obvious to me as I saw not a civil war between Shiite and Sunni, but a chaotic state with a deposed government. I wondered what an American city would be like if it were destroyed either by an invasion or a natural disaster like an earthquake, hurricane, or tsunami. Would they loot, rape, pillage, and plunder their own? Hurricanes Katrina and Sandy would later show how the American people were in adversity. Or more to the point, how climate change had declared war against all life on Earth, and the third world war was humanity against global warming. Yet our leadership invested in military weapons of mass destruction and ensured we kept working like the ignorant employees that we had become. The destruction of our environment was assured. We would all pay the ultimate price at some stage.

For the rest of the day we walked around the Baghdad suburbs, as Ghassan showed me some destroyed residential dwellings, an abandoned American personnel carrier, and the ever-present American military that now patrolled the streets. After a long day walking and talking where he explained his movements since the bombing and the loss of some of his neighbours that had been killed in the fighting, we ate some dinner in a nearby café that offered kebabs, and retired back to his home. It was encouraging to see Iraqis continue to live as normally as they could irrespective of the patrolling military machines that surrounded them. Many small businesses continued to trade, and the markets were still opened for business, as the population merely embraced the chaos and continued to live within the peaceful spaces and the human gaps of war.

That night I slept on the floor of Ghassan's small apartment and his wife went to her parents' house as a gesture to my privacy. What was it about these Muslim people that made them so hospitable and genuinely humane even in a war? Perhaps we should have taught the Muslims how to drink copious amounts of alcohol, how to worship a cricket team or a sport club like they worshipped God, or to have sex with anyone that lacked the self-respect required to be a Muslim. That night, I lay awake and unable to sleep.

It was impossible to sleep as sporadic gunfire could be heard throughout the night. First I would hear the single shot of an Iraqi sniper followed by the peppered retaliation of machine-gun fire returned by the Americans. That melodic rhapsody seemed to keep me awake all night and as the sun rose, I sat looking out the window at the empty streets and thinking how absurd Baghdad had become. I did not sleep that night, as my tired consciousness slowly entered the weary zones of the Dreamtime.

Chapter 22
Military Diplomacy

The first casualty of war is the truth.

Aeschylus 456BC

The following morning Ghassan took me to the Palestine Hotel in search of Waratah. When we arrived at the Palestine Hotel, I learned the meaning of 'chaos' in the real sense of the word. People were everywhere, as men, women, and children ran to and fro aimlessly in search of loved ones; for jobs; for food; for water; for medicines; for help. Any help would do, as they all seemed to be in severe need of something.

I asked Ghassan to wait for me outside the cordoned off area away from the hotel, and began heaving through a large crowd that now swarmed around the entrance to the hotel. As I got closer to the entrance, I could hear some of them chanting, "We need work! We want work!"

I made eye contact with the US soldiers and begun waving my Australian passport like an entry ticket to the now military-run hotel. "Australian," I said aloud so he would hear me over the chanting desperate Iraqis, and he motioned me to approach him then gave me a rite of passage to enter the fortified hotel parking area.

My first instinct was to look for Waratah who I last saw here in this very hotel. I still had Mike's $100.00 for Waratah, but I could not see her. I went to the small art gallery that Judith Karpova had asked me to visit to rescue her art with the $1,000 she gave me. But all I found was an empty shell of a building that barely resembled the gallery of artists I remembered. Returning to the hotel, I looked around for any of the Human Shields, but all I could see were American soldiers, well-dressed foreign media, and those Iraqis fortunate enough to have a job working inside the hotel, while chaos screamed and chanted from outside.

Walking around the Palestine Hotel in Baghdad, armed with a handgun, the memory of my last street-fight reminded me of this self-imposed mission.

Two weeks after I was shot, I was dismissed from hospital and stayed in my elder sister's apartment, which was freshly painted, homely, and meticulously sterile. She was the wisest and the most intellectual in our family. With her pool of knowledge, she soon graduated from Macquarie University as a lawyer, and after, was able to keep work at a minimum while she made herself ridiculously wealthy as a family lawyer, mostly divorcing and breaking up families.

Not long after opening her business as one of the few female lawyers in Australia, and among the first Spanish speaking lawyers, she quickly set herself up amongst Sydney's wealthiest in the exclusive Bellevue Hills in the eastern suburbs. She was blessed with an uncanny ability to win scholarships into Universities or entries into any place that she wanted. Her small frame and elegant dress sense seemed to be powerful tools to get whatever she wanted from the socially inept men that would wine and dine her not only around Sydney's elite social scenes but around the world's best resorts. So, as she was traveling around another fantastic location in Fiji with her friend, I was invited to stay in the comfort of her luxurious apartment. There I recuperated from that bullet wound with daily visits from a heaven-sent nurse.

After another two weeks in a bed, my mate Elk, the fearless Lebanese legend who tolerated pain like a black Texan slave tolerated the ignorance of a redneck cowboy, came to my rescue.

"C'mon mate, I'm going to take you out of here," he said, realising I was sinking into post-traumatic depression.

"Where are we going to go?" I asked lethargically.

"Anywhere that is not as sad as this place," he suggested, and I agreed.

We jumped into his car and as he pulled out of the driveway causing a speeding car to swerve, we heard some men scream racial abuse at the Lebanese Elk. What they didn't know was the Lebanese Elk's masochistic streak or his sharp wit, as he retaliated with an even sharper and more accurate string of abuse. So the speeding, abusive car stopped about fifty metres in front of us. Elk, as the masochistic driver, decided to pull up behind the offending vehicle.

When I saw a giant man step out of the other car's driver's side and a short, balding, fat man step from the passenger side, I asked the obvious question.

"Elk, what are you doing?"

"I'm gonna teach them some manners," he replied, suddenly becoming a teacher.

"Okay. But—" I managed to say too late as he hastily jumped out of our car.

As I looked at him walking away I realised Anthony El-Chah wasn't the captain of our rugby team for his handsome looks or his suicidal approach to tackling men like the giant coming at us. Instead, God blessed him with the mysterious ability of selling sand to the Arabs, ice to the Eskimos, or wisdom to the Jews. So I knew if anyone could talk sense into the Neanderthal man that came marching toward us like an Anglo-Saxon terrorist, it was going to be the great Lebanese Elk. It was imperative that I slowly step out of the car, cautiously observant that my mending sternum was still sensitive to Dr Newman's wiring.

"What's your problem?" I heard Elk ask Neanderthal.

"You bloody wogs, what do you think you're doing pulling out in front of us like that and not watching where you're going?"

I was instantly impressed to see that this Neanderthal giant man could speak clearly. Elk replied, and by the time I arrived at the scene there was an exchange of abuse that caused me to intercept.

"Hey, you can't say it was our fault if you—" I managed to say before he shut me up by grabbing my throat with his right hand and literally lifting me up to the tips of my toes.

"Mate, put him down, he's just been—" I heard Elk say before the giant grabbed Elk by the throat with his left hand to shut him up as well, and I heard the word 'shot' escape Elk's mouth like from a deflating balloon.

As the giant Neanderthal continued to talk and force his democratic principles down our throats, he now concentrated his energies on the trapped Lebanese Elk. This was his mistake, I noted, as he had slowly let me down a fraction where I was able to get my footing on Earth again.

The golden street-fighting rule was applicable, as we certainly didn't start anything. I wanted to give him his warning before sending him to hospital but he had shut me up with a terrifying grip to my throat. It was reasonable to assume that Elk was about to give him his second warning, but he too had been forced to keep quiet and was deprived of his freedom to speech. I was going to have to break the silver rule as the fear of death at the hands of this great man entered my mind. So carefully positioning my feet firmly on the ground, I targeted the giant's snout and with all the strength I could push behind my full roundhouse swing followed by my right shoulder, I delivered this giant beast of a man a blow that he would never forget.

The shock to his system released the death trap strangle that he had around my neck, but he held onto poor Elk who collapsed under the weight of Goliath. The smaller man quickly came toward us and I shaped up to this rounded, overweight, middle-aged man who suddenly ran back to the protection and safety behind the car for cover. I quickly realised that these men did not want to fight any more than perhaps have a good argument.

Thus, dismissing him quickly and seeing Elk on his back wrestling with the great ape in what looked like an obscene sexual position, I knew it was my mistake, and it was essential for me to rectify and apologise. However, the look on my mate's face was almost comical. I wanted to laugh out loud but I knew without help Elk would never be the same man again. He looked desperate. My captain was about to be murdered by a great white demon that talked. I turned to see that little fat man with both hands in the air, surrendering and pleading for us to stop the crime we were about to witness.

I nodded agreement to him and we dragged both men up, separating their entangled bodies. Elk fleetly got up, still wanting to fight on his own, and now I had to restrain Elk from the suicidal mission. As the now wounded giant stood holding his bloody nose, Elk stood his ground, ready to finish him off alone like a terrorist who would kill himself first before his enemy. But miraculously, the dictator raised his hands in defeated submission and continued to talk.

"Bate ... Dat wahs a blady booty," he said with his nose truly sunken into his face and a dripping stream of blood pouring from his nose that caused him to splatter his blood all over me as he spoke. My mind quickly translated what he had said as, "Mate, that was a bloody beauty," which was just as well as I was about to release another quick combination this time with his jaw lined up, for spitting his blood at me while he spoke; but that was not justifiable.

"We didn't want to fight you," Elk said, like the true diplomat he should have been. "But I was going to tell you my mate's just been shot and to let him go ... we could have argued and found a peaceful solution you know," he said, flashing his cheeky, mad Lebanese grin.

The reason for remembering that fight was symbolic under the circumstances. I did not give that man a third warning. I permanently disfigured his face and caused him excruciating pain unjustly, according to Ticker the Turk's Islamic rules. I vowed that was going to be my last street-fight. But above all, I recalled that perhaps we could have argued all day and later had a drink as the giant and his off-sider shook our hands and we talked for a while like old friends before wishing each other the best and sending our warm regards to the nurses that would treat his broken nose. But as time passed with an agonising fear of the unknown horrors that awaited me, it was that memory that inspired me to take action and now do what was right.

It was the memory of our history that taught us to make good and advantageous decisions. I always remembered Elk's words: "It doesn't matter how bad our problems are, there is always going to be someone with bigger problem than us."

I committed to memory the hundreds of millions that made up the third world, or the many more millions that lived below the poverty line in developed or developing worlds, or the many more that lived tortured in silence with physical abnormalities or mental illness: all be it, the abandoned poor and the disadvantaged. They suffered a suffering that many of us with educated lives never knew. A suffering not exclusive to the third or developing world, but to many in the modern world whose fates had been sealed with remedial jobs, repetitive and mundane existences, or poor health. Indeed, it was a suffering that could be eased with the silent joy of an education and our governments investing in our health, dental, and socio-spiritual development, not misappropriating our taxes in another meaningless war!

Religion did have a purpose after all: to make us spiritually content with who we were as was "the will of Allah, the same God as Jehovah and any other name in any language that describes our destiny." It was exactly as that Muslim Turkish boy had taught me so many years ago. God truly is a wonder worthy of individual study and global recognition, as the Jews, Christians, and Muslims agreed.

But now in Iraq, I felt the same sense of despair in a country that was not mine, watching the media frenzy eating from the scraps left behind by the American military. I felt for the first time the absolute anguish and the sheer desperation that terrorists must surely have felt to go on suicidal missions. I wanted to go and blow myself up and kill anyone that supported or justified this crime, the creation of another third world nation.

I had the Berretta handgun still in the back of my jeans and there were some American high-ranking officers congregating in a meeting with their backs to me. My instinctive nature to defend the weak stirred the killer instinct we men had within our genes. My thoughts were one-dimensional. I wanted to shoot those murderers who had created this crime against humanity, against the environment, and against the animal kingdom.

I reached for the gun and took hold of the handle. The hotel lobby was buzzing with excitement as coalition soldiers, hotel staff, international visitors, and Western media reporters everywhere moved to and fro with independent interests of survival. My eyes were fixed on the target; a medium-built white-haired male who wore three-star epaulettes and I guessed was a colonel. I began walking towards my target, feeling a sense of both excitement and fear. It was the same feeling as the experience before any fight. My nerves trembled, heart pounded, mouth dried and eyes watered while my fists remained firmly clenched as the focus of the target remained clear.

I was within three meters of taking the handgun out and shooting a high-ranking American military officer. Three more seconds, then I suddenly heard—

"Al!"

A familiar feminine voice called my name and unexpectedly, amidst the chaotic confusion and tainted image of army greens and desert dust, I saw a smiling Asian angel waving at me. Yakiko, the Japanese dancer, seemed to be gliding through the air and sidestepping those that crossed her path as she came to my rescue. Yakiko was a Japanese princess, physically petite and tastefully sweet. Her dress sense seemed surreal in this theatre of war. Wearing a short cream-coloured lace dress, a sexy, girly look, she invited everyone to gaze and stare at her beauty.

"Al!" she yelled from across the foyer. "Al, I am here," she seemed to say as she approached me. "Al, where have you been?" she asked, happy to see me yet demanding an explanation for my absence. She had remained in Baghdad after the NASYO convention and endured the full brunt of the coalition's bombardment. Her selfless courage and her sincere desire to do good made me believe that angels existed. She truly was a beautiful angel.

"I've been in Amman. It's a long story. Where is Waratah, have you seen Waratah?" I asked, suddenly forgetting my anger toward the military that simply did what they were told to do without any idea or knowledge of why they were paid to kill, destroy, and maim. I remembered my aim was to find Waratah. "Have you seen Waratah?" I asked again.

"No," she said, disappointed.

"Who are you with, Yakiko? Have you seen any other Human Shields? Where are you staying?" I asked her a volley of quick questions. But she seemed to be saddened as I asked her too many questions at one time. When I noted her disappointment I imagined her like the angel she was, cleverly dancing around the falling bombs and missiles. But more importantly, I realised she was still traumatised by her ordeal in this man-made hell. The expression on her face spoke volumes as she remained speechless, unable to answer me. I grabbed her hand and led her outside where Ghassan was anxiously waiting.

"Yakiko, wait here with Ghassan, I want to look ten more minutes for Waratah," I said to Ghassan, waving and running back into the amounting chaos at the steps of the Palestine Hotel.

When I returned there were several hundred Iraqi men and some boys chanting and pushing and demonstrating that they needed food, money, and above all were willing to work for the new American administrators. These were a patriotic people. However the hunger pains were clearly expressed on their faces and the well-fed American soldiers could only look and stop the mass from entering the hotel.

"We want jobs," they chanted. "We want jobs." It was heart-wrenching to see these proud people in one of the wealthiest nations on Earth so impoverished and reduced to a third world existence.

As I waited for the chanting to stop I saw four distinguished Iraqi men speaking to an American sergeant. Curiously, my attention shifted.

"We are Iraqi military," I heard one man say in broken English. "We must see your generals," he demanded.

"I'm sorry Sir I can't help you," The three-star American marine sergeant replied, intelligently waving these men of.

"Maybe I can help you," I said to the disheartened group of men.

"Who are you?" The most eminent looking man asked me.

"I'm Al from Spain and Australia," I replied, noting their confused looks, and asked them, "who are you?"

"I am General Abdul Kadhim Madhi Al Khouzaie from the Iraqi Army," he said, extending his handshake in friendship. "This is Lieutenant Ahjmed from the Iraqi Special Forces and Commander Mustafa from the Iraqi Air Force and Captain Mohamed from our navy," he introduced.

"What are you doing here?" I asked, wondering what these high-ranking officers must be doing confronting the American military at the base of the Palestine Hotel.

"We have come to get money," he said with a strong Arabic-English accent.

"Money? From the Americans?" I asked, stupefied.

"Yes, the banks are still closed and now under American protection but we wait too long for our money now we must have some money like American say," he demanded of me with a strong Arabic-English accent.

My mind went into an overdrive, as I tried to fathom what was being said, and thought it odd that these men should be here in the first place. So I did what any sensible person would do.

"Come with me," I invited them to follow me. We approached the wall of American soldiers that guarded the entrance to the Palestine Hotel. They were mostly teenagers with big guns who I knew had seen too many war and James Bond movies. So I explained that I was an Australian Spaniard double, secret, and private agent, showing them my passports. They looked at me in awe as I told them who the four men behind me were.

"This is General Abdul, Lieutenant Ahjmed, Commander Mustafa, and Captain Mohammed," I said, introducing them to the American corporal that greeted me.

"Come with me Sir. Jimmy, Mick, Bobby, Harry, let this gentlemen through!" he ordered his soldiers to step aside as he escorted us to his captain.

"Captain Madden, this is Special Private Agent Al and these …" He paused, forgetting the names of the men I was with. But they were quick to his rescue.

"General Abdul Kadhim," the Iraqi general quickly interrupted, extending his hand in friendship.

"Lieutenant Ahjmed, Iraqi Special Forces Commander!" The lieutenant followed rank in military customs.

"Commander Mustafa, Iraqi Airforce," he said on cue.

"Captain Mohamed. Iraqi navy." He saluted military style.

"Oh please don't salute, please!" Alarmed, the American captain quickly pushed his fellow captain's hand down. "We don't need to show rank here," he added, looking over his shoulder, hinting paranoia. "Please sit down," he gestured to a low-sitting coffee table and comfortable leather sofas.

We all sat and thus began the discussion of various details about payments that the American administration had promised some forty-odd high-ranking Iraqi military officials to surrender their weapons, and that now needed to be made. The captain realised the seriousness of these men and the details of the discussion, and pointed us in the right direction.

"This is beyond me," he said, facing me. "You had better go and see Major Naels." He then advised writing a note and address on a piece of paper that would later serve as a ticket to higher ranks.

We all stood and walked away like good friends, smiling and happy to have met on good terms. Just as the Iraqis walked ahead of me I asked the American captain, "Do you feel right about what you are doing here?"

He looked at me with a tired look on his face and admitted, "Sir. To be real honest with you, I would much rather be at home back in the states with my wife and family."

"I understand," I said, sympathetic to his predicament. "It must be hard to do what we don't want to do."

We shook hands firmly, accepting that we were just the pawns in this deadly game of chess and our kings, queens, and statesmen were those that ordered us to our early graves.

"Ghassan!" I suddenly remembered, thinking we had been in this meeting for almost an hour. I took the Iraqis to an angry and cursing Ghassan and a patiently quiet Yakiko.

"That was the longest ten minutes in the history of time!" Ghassan cursed, and Yakiko smiled, looking at the men that were with me. I made the necessary introductions and Ghassan suddenly changed his tune.

"Salam Alecum!" he said to the men, shaking hands with an apologetic tone.

I quickly explained to him what we had discussed in the meeting and he immediately realised the serious nature of the mission we had now been thrust into by what I was now understanding as the will of God. Soon we were on our way to the next meeting.

When we approached a well-fortified and protected compound to see Major Naels, I knew this was now getting more serious. This compound was more like a fortress with two Abraham tanks and heavily armed soldiers all around.

One thing the American military had learned from their cowboys as they slowly exterminated the red Indians was the need to have strong, impenetrable forts when colonising lands. This base was exactly like a ring of caravans, but now they were heavy steel military vehicles surrounding the Baghdad Olympic sporting stadium.

There we passed the note to the guarding soldiers who read it and then conducted routine searches while a black American female soldier searched Yakiko. I declared the gun that I had and explained the need for my security. They understood but took it from me anyway and we were escorted to see Major Naels.

After a short wait, we were led to a makeshift office and a distinguished looking man introduced himself as Captain Farlow. He was a dignified American captain who provided inspiring leadership to his men and the Iraqi-English translator who happened to be a young, beautiful Iraqi girl clearly in need of work to support her family.

Captain Farlow explained that Major Naels was now much older and 'a bit forgetful'. "If you know what I mean," he added, pointing with his index finger to the temple of his head in a circular motion, and completed the sentence by saying, "senile."

"Oh." I was speechless and hoped the Iraqis didn't understand the meaning of that word. But Ghassan looked at me with the same expression as a shocked academic. I reasoned that perhaps this military campaign needed senile mad old men who were easily led to become the leaders of an intellectually disadvantaged battalion, in order to aimlessly destroy homes, lives and our natural environment.

We all sat down and explained to Captain Farlow the Iraqi officer's reason for being here. After a brief discussion he said this was above Major Nael's capabilities to deal with and sent us to another secret location. It was becoming increasingly clear that the American military had the same complicated bureaucratic system that was designed to filter the wealthy and powerful from the poor and hopeless. At the same time, they created more jobs for common people that had attained the most basic level of education, e.g. as military personnel, police officers, or, as I would learn later, federal agents who were too busy spying on our privacy rather than reading books that could teach and reform even the most disadvantaged person.

"You need to talk to Colonel King and Major Gerald." He wrote some details and handed them to me. It was another introductory letter and a pass to enter our next location.

"Where is this?" I asked Ghassan as I passed him the note with an Arabic-inscribed photocopied note on the back of the note.

"Ah," he smiled. "That is Saddam Central Palace in Baghdad." The smile was one of pride rather than joy.

We parted from this fort, waving goodbye and leaving the young American soldiers with the sense that they had done a good job. But after they returned the gun, I asked them, "How do you feel being here?"

"Man, this place sucks," was a young American's response.

"There's no booze or bars or women here like they had in 'Nam!" another joked, with a sense of truth to his disappointment.

"The pussy here are all covered up!" another joked to his army friends who laughed in amusement.

We parted with high fives and well wishes, to the astonishment of the Iraqi military gentlemen, and went to the next location. This was Saddam's house: his palace in downtown Baghdad.

When we arrived at Saddam's Palace, it dawned on me the enormous wealth that must exist in Iraq. I had seen many other mansions around Baghdad and other palaces throughout my travels. Whilst Saddam's Palace was not as spectacular as Windsor Castle, Camp David, or Buckingham Palace, it was nonetheless an impressive building with spacious, landscaped gardens and other administrative buildings surrounding the main palace. Now, an American leopard tank safely guarded the main drive and barbed wire created a no man's land between the main road and the first check point, where more young American soldiers waited in the existing guardhouse and well-protected bunkers.

By now I was enjoying this small chore I had been asked to do, and enjoyed even more talking with the young American soldiers placed as mobile targets for any Iraqi insurgent drive-by shootings. So as we approached the check point entry I introduced myself.

"Private Secret Agent Triple Three," I said, holding up three fingers, "but you boys can call me Al." Then I introduced the men I was with and they were beside themselves as I handed them the gun. I could sense their awe as they asked me some intelligent, interrogating questions.

"Hey man, are you CIA?" one asked, excited.

"No."

"You with the FBI?" the other followed.

"No."

"You're with the UN, aren't you?"

"No."

"Who are you with?" they seemed to ask at the same time.

"I'm with the third world," I replied, not realising the truth to my reply until much later when I thought about that brief encounter. Nevertheless, this reply confused my interrogators and gave them something to talk about as I could hear their juvenile arguing well after we had passed the first checkpoint.

We walked to the instructed designated spot, and shortly after an almost-new air-conditioned Toyota minibus arrived to pick us up and take us to the palace where some Iraqi girls worked alongside American female soldiers as front-of-house receptionists. It was clear that they were still in the training stages and it was as if they were preparing for the future American-led administration of their newly acquired state called Iraq.

I passed them the note and shortly after, we were asked to enter and were seated in a large hall that contained romantic gold-trimmed furnishings over a white, polished marble floor. I knew from my days demolishing bathrooms and as a construction labourer that this floor was not cheap and I estimated over $50,000 worth of marble alone. However as I had never been in Camp David, The White House, or Buckingham Palace, I couldn't compare interiors, just exteriors.

The obvious observation is that some of our leaders have missed the point if they think that grandeur is what We the People want to see in our leadership. What the world needed in the prelude to our war against the natural environment was common sense and simplicity. To value the simple things in life was becoming the contemporary virtue of this third millennium, while materialism and the hoarding of wealth beyond need, such as that of the Sultans of Saudi Arabia, were now seen as a mental illness.

The people of Earth were in desperate need of a fair distribution of incomes, and like the "liberated" Iraqis, I saw chanting outside the Palestine Hotel, in desperate need of jobs. Jobs that would lift our spirits by giving our lives meaning and value; irrespective of what it was we had to do, as long as we were doing something, rather than the nothing of condemned criminals. Why the G. W. Bush administration and those leaders that misled us and lied to justify this evil act of war against the Iraqi civilians and our natural environment were not imprisoned, was beyond natural justice. The forces of evil truly were greater than the genuine kind spirit of humanity.

After a short moment, a well-built and stern looking African-American man approached us and introduced himself as Major Gerald. He sat down with us and I let the Iraqis explain their situation to him with Ghassan translating any misunderstandings. Major Gerald was not surprised by our visit and it seemed that he was expecting us. He was however, particularly interested in me and wanted to know who I was. I told him the painful truth.

"I'm just a slave," I said to him. He looked a bit surprised to see that a white-skinned blue-eyed redneck amidst this chaos would refer to himself as a slave. Perhaps he thought I was using some code language, because he smiled warmly and with a genuine tone of understanding said:

"I understand."

We both seemed to know that we were still the slaves of our lords, both doing the works that our masters needed us to do. A black and white bond, like the black ink on this white page, seemed to come from our mutual understanding. We both knew that neither of us wanted to be there in Baghdad. This was not our problem, but if we didn't attend to our master's wishes, we would soon become isolated, discredited, punished by costly legal proceedings to defend our good honour, defamed, fined, impoverished, and/or imprisoned.

Such was the power of the nepotistic inheritors of wealth and the megalomaniac leaders they appointed or employed as government officials, law-makers or judges. Later, Saddam Hussein would learn this as he faced the unjust Kangaroo court in a makeshift court room, rather than the natural justice allowed to sovereign leaders in the international courts of Justice in The Hague.

Many people had argued that the Americans terrorised the Vietnamese under the paradoxical front of 'liberalisation', 'democratisation' or 'capitalisation' for Vietnam. Now, as we sat talking briefly about our place in Iraq, we both sensed the insensible nature of this war, which was clearly visible everywhere around us. Only the dense rainforests of Vietnam seemed to have disappeared, and the surrounding dry desert forewarned us of the catastrophic future the world faced as global warming continued to claim our fertile lands.

When I looked at the Iraqi military men staring at me with amusement, I knew that these men of war needed to discuss issues I didn't want to know about. Ignorance would become my saving strength, and I was simply happy to confirm that in war, money buys the military, the navy, and the air force, while the king, queen, sultan, banker, or most crazed megalomaniac with the most money, will be able to employ assassins like Adolf Hitler employed an army to exterminate humanity.

"Anyway, you men need to talk, and I don't need to know the details or the amounts," I said, standing. "The less I know the safer I will be," I reasoned, knowing the truth.

Ignorance was the key to our freedom from persecution and too much knowledge could be the chains to our regime's watchdogs and intelligence-gathering agencies; as WikiLeaks founder Mr Julian Assange was to learn. What I would forever fail to understand is how any government or people could call Edward Snowden a criminal for exposing the truth? Did we not understand the importance of knowing that some government officials wanted to spy on us, the normal people? Were we becoming so dim that we would forget everything our ancestors have gone to war for and to defend our natural freedoms?

It simply did not make any sense that either Edward Snowden or Julian Assange could be classified as criminals simply for blowing a whistle; for raising our awareness and for teaching us something sinister, immoral, and unjust about our very own leadership.

The thought that it was us, the good, normal, and common people who were spied on by our very own government spy agencies was haunting. It would be just a matter of time for these spy agencies to catch up with any one of us as perpetual students of our world experiencing, looking, studying, or simply living among the dark side of humanity, to be locked up by a regime threatened by the fact that we are all humans sharing this one restricted planet Earth, and surviving peacefully with the ever diminishing natural resources.

The question was, why were our governments justifying the destruction of lives, property, resources, and our environment with meaningless war that benefited only nepotistic inheritors of power and wealth?

In Australia, some members of the government believed that our invasion of foreign lands with our bombs and military was not a terrorist act or a crime against the natural environment, simply because the natives of those lands terrorised us with their ruthless defence and use of terrorism as the only weapon they have to fight against our superior military machines.

The Islamic State fighter (ISIL) were exactly what the Iraqi general and the Special Forces commander had told me would result from the wrong and illegal invasion of Iraq. It was the Iraqi military strategy to defend their sovereignty and the natural legal reaction of self-defence. This fact was the hard, painful, and bitter truth we had to face.

However, our governments blindly and stupidly followed the mantra of modern war. Were we not the terrorists by invading and attacking foreign natives in their lands?

The tragedy of the truth was simple. We were wasting our wealth in destroying our environment and sacrificing civilians wrongfully.

We had entered the third millennium future where We the People are kept uneducated, ignorant of the facts that would empower us to live freely, or travel the world peacefully like the Muslim pilgrims that go to Mecca, irrespective of the Sultans that govern the holy lands of Medina, Mecca, Baghdad, or Jerusalem with well-armed and uneducated or senile military diplomacy. As Saddam Hussein learned when he was escorted to the gallows, the truth was irrelevant to those few megalomaniacs who governed our destiny.

Chapter 23
Economic Hitman

Economic hit men should be illegal but they're not.

John Perkins

As I walked away, I saw another American officer who seemed to be waiting for instructions or orders or maybe his lunch, so I introduced myself casually with a warm Australian greeting.

"G'day mate! What brings you to Saddam's Palace?" I asked, with a half-smile.

He gazed at me with a pitiful look and then smiled back, "You must be Australian." He recognised the native Australian greeting immediately as we shook hands.

"Yeah, and you must be American," I joked. He smiled again and nodded as if to say, obviously.

We talked briefly and when I asked him why he was here in Saddam's Palace he explained that he was a captain in the civil regiment burdened with the task of recruiting Iraqis to work for the American administration.

"What do you mean?" I asked him to clarify my ignorance.

"We have to rebuild Iraq so I have to employ Iraqis and get them to do work for our contractors," he answered.

"You mean private companies?" I quizzed.

"Yes, the army will oversee that American contractors are protected as they rebuild Iraq," he added.

"That makes sense," I said, knowing the Iraqi insurgents would be furious if an occupying nation dictated who could work and get paid to rebuild after the damage caused by the terrorising bombs that killed their children in their own backyards.

Or in other words, the large private corporation executives did the deals in boardrooms and got back to the business of playing golf, while letting the workers rebuild in a hostile environment as the military and the insurgents killed or maimed each other. The painful truth could not be any clearer. Everything was now making sense.

We talked for a while about the American plans to rebuild Iraq and how his job was focused on the infrastructure such as roads and bridges using Iraqi labourers, before changing topic to the differences between American and Australian cultures, only to realise we had more in common than one might have expected—only the American people went to war to oust British monarchs in the war of independence while Australians, Canadians and the Commonwealth states continued to be ruled by the Queen of England from the other end of the world. The brilliance of her regime lay in the invention of laws, and the capacity to manipulate the truths with the editorial control of the media. This book would be destined to censorship from publicity, and my good repute would surely be tainted like Snowden and Assange, simply for telling the facts as they are.

By daring to travel and explore our world as free agents and speaking with the terrorists rather than killing their families, I had discovered the truths that many megalomaniacs would want silenced. The Sultans of Saudi Arabia, like any nepotistic leaders, such as G. W. Bush or Uday Hussein and many others worldwide, would be threatened by the fact that We the People of Earth do not want to buy their absurd decadence that comes at the cost of our natural environment.

We had entered the third millennium with an unjust war, and as such, the third world warriors that marched and chanted against those leaders now begun to make sense. In Australia, Canada, and throughout the Commonwealth, the well-groomed propaganda machine glorified the Royal family. It seemed they could do no wrong, and the murder of Lady Diana Spencer could be disguised and brushed under the carpet. Yet the people's princess' death would not be forgotten by those who understood the power and natural hatred that jealous husbands are capable of exerting, especially if one had his own highly trained assassins who vowed to devote their life to serve the Royalty and be paid to honour their secrecy.

J. F. Kennedy could be shot dead by highly trained and paid assassins, and We the People would believe the manipulated media. This was not conspiracy talk. This was a practice employed by Mafia and powerful megalomaniacs since the origin of humanity.

The twin towers of New York could be destroyed and we would believe what the media reported without question.

Gang warfare was no different to the first, second, and any other world or civil war; where some megalomaniac with money would pay a war monger to do a mindless job like killing without thought or conscience, in the same manner that Hitler, G. W. Bush, or the Saudi Sultans could employ their military machines to destroy humanity.

Yet, the majority of Australians I spoke to considered England a foreign country and Australia firmly standing on her own as a sovereign state, some arguing that the real king or queen of Australia would have to be an Aboriginal elder with a sound mind rather than a foreign queen. This was the natural truth: that the English regime made laws that could manipulate or placate the facts in the interests of "The Crown." Yet how does one demonstrate this prejudice and absurd power that nepotistic powers are capable of exerting? The answer was yet to come.

When Ghassan showed up and introduced himself I mentioned to the officer that Ghassan would make an ideal translator and the captain was quick to note that Ghassan's command of the English language was more than competent.

"If you want a translator, I can work for you." Ghassan jumped at the opportunity to get a job.

"Well if you come and work for us, we pay $5 per day," the captain offered.

Ghassan, who was desperate to work, was quick to accept the offer, not knowing that American private security contractors were earning as much as thirteen hundred US dollars (US$1,300) per day, an amount that would be paid from the Iraqi oil exports and overpriced contracts. This was a 'legal' way of importing Iraqi dollars into the American economy. Much the same way the developed world continued to charge the third world nations whose minerals and plantations they owned.

I remained silent so as not to dampen Ghassan's hopes for a job, but the injustice was obvious.

Were we, the people of the world, aware of the effect this war would have on oil prices? Or how the increased fuel costs would be passed down to our food, which, among other things, would become more expensive for us, the paying consumers? I wondered what would happen to inflation, interest, and the future of the world economy if we allowed the American contractors to dictate their terms and charge as they pleased to rebuild Iraq. Or worse, if a trillion American dollars was squandered by a handful of family dynasties that controlled our banks, media and the quality of our lives.

The truth was horrific and painfully sad to accept. It was better to live in the bliss of ignorance, cheering my football team with cheap beer and my mates, than to take the action like the third world warriors were doing around the world.

Later as ambassador to Iraq and the 'supreme authority'—under duress—over the Iraqi people, an American man named Paul Bremer dictated various orders designed to make the Islamic 'Shura' the main system of Iraqi governance. It basically meant that Saddam Hussein had been right to govern his nation under Islamic laws. These were an older system of laws than the man-made laws of the English law regime. But above all, this was simply a diplomatic step to suit the American administration, with Order 39 claiming that up to 100% of Iraqi assets could be owned by the Americans and the coalition of the willing. Other orders ensured that all profits earned in Iraq by foreigners could be 100% repatriated. In other words, the door was now opened for Iraq to suffer the same fate as every other colonised third world nation on Earth with the American superpower exercising her unrivalled power to own Iraqi assets. Only now, the Iraqi people would be the new third world survivors, fending on their own and struggling just to survive like in Africa and South America, and the many indigenous people that made up the third world countries.

"What is the truth behind this war?" I finally asked this captain before parting.

"The truth?" He paused to think and looked around the grandeur of Saddam's central palace, and replied bluntly, "Oil!"

It was common knowledge that with the second largest oil reserves in the world, Iraq and the Iraqi people had an annual earning capacity of about USA$38,500,000,000 per year!

The Iranians were not far behind, making this region one of the wealthiest regions per capita on Earth. Hence the piracy, the pillaging, and the destruction, by highly paid soldiers who served their masters with blind faith so they too may earn the income to feed their families, irrespective of the truth to their crimes.

The agony of the truth was that our need and greed for oil was also the cancer that would kill us. Our health was compromised for brief encounters of happiness until the carbons we breathed and ate poisoned our bodies, supplying painfully slow deaths. We would all eventually suffer the ill health from our dirty deeds.

Oil was also why it took just seven years for Saddam to repay in full the compensation to Kuwait, America, and the United Nations after the illegal invasion of Kuwait in the 1990 war.

"But what if the basis for this war is proven to be false and the Americans fail to find weapons of mass destruction?" I asked the captain naively.

"We will find them," this officer in the intelligence core replied confidently.

"But if you don't, will you then need to pay Iraq compensation for this illegal invasion or pay the coalition of British, Spanish, and Australians compensation for misleading us into a war that should never have taken place?" I asked, but the answer was not of military or national security concern.

The officer shrugged his shoulders and replied, "That is not of our concern."

He affirmed this was not a war to defend the West from imminent danger of invasion but a war to rob Iraqis of their oil. Thus we could rightfully label this greater threat to world peace and humanity as economic terrorism. That was to say, if we allowed our need for oil to drive us into a war, then we lived in the terror of economic indicators that one day would cause our jobs to be lost as we used our money to destroy our world with manufactured bombs rather than build or restore the world we inherited from our fathers.

Job creation was the essence of good governance—why were our governments not spending the hundreds of billions of dollars in restoring and improving our world rather than on weapons of mass destruction and using them against civilians like Iraqis? This was the question we all should have been asking.

Iraqis had spent thirteen years suffering the economic sanctions imposed on them by an American administration and blindly supported by a world relying on American trade or aid. Indeed, any nation that did not trade with America like Cuba, Iran, Venezuela, North Korea, or Syria may have found itself victimised and terrorised by future American administrations. This was the economic terrorism that was unspoken of in the West but was felt by civilian populations in countries whose governments opposed American economic practices.

Under the policy of 'divide and conquer', the Americans had sent in special agents called 'economic hitmen[11]' to start the war between Iraq and Iran. Only when John Perkins, an American, spoke out of his role as an 'economic hitman' for the American government, did this truth surface[12].

Major Gerald was an honourable man like the majority of American soldiers that I would meet. He didn't believe there was any real reason for him to be there other than to do his job and not think about the consequences.

Now, in the hands of American administration, the oil reserves would be exported to foreign countries to pay the Americans to rebuild Iraq in any manner and at any cost desired. Naturally the vast bulk of the wealth would go to American contractors and the rest of the world could feed on the scraps and leftovers. This was business by stealth and the worst kind of terrorism. Millions of civilians were affected by the most inhumane torture imaginable as it starved them of food and deprived them of a fair job's pay and basic medicines. Here was the source that created third world nations. Here was the seed that would sprout the Arab spring as desperate people united with arms to fight and war for survival. Here was the evil of our greed and above all, the impetus that would unite an army of crazed people under the banner of an Islamic State (ISIL).

As I learned, some of the Iraqi high-ranking officers were offered large amounts of money and amnesty by the Americans if they surrendered peacefully. Others were offered rewards in excess of twenty million

---

11   Read book *Confessions of an Economic Hitman* by John Perkins
12   From radio interview with John Perkins by Amy Goodman

American dollars if they changed sides and disclosed locations of the Iraqi most wanted list. In legal terms, this was the equivalent of bribery or blackmail. The tragedy lay in the fact that Australian, American, and British taxpayers worked like donkeys to pay the taxes that would pay such ransoms and military invasions without ever knowing the truth to their lifetime's work. We were all being hoodwinked by the well paid, groomed, and prejudicial bias of our nepotistic leaders.

The corrupt nature of this war seemed so obvious and clear, that the masses would never believe the truth even if it bit them. There was no doubt about it; this was the greatest crime against humanity since Hitler's Holocaust and We the People were delighted to see funny television shows, sad melodramas, and mindless sports rather than take the action required so that our children would not suffer the foreseeable injustices of the future third world of the third millennium.

As we walked away from that meeting somewhat relieved, I was not interested in knowing the details of the costs involved in buying victory. However, I did ask the Iraqi Special Forces commander what he would do now that Iraq was in the hands of the American military.

"So what will you do now that you have your money from the Americans?" I asked him as we sat in the car, driving through the embattled city. He looked at the others and then he looked into my eyes deeply and replied.

"We are Iraqis. We are Muslims and we live in Iraq. This is our holy land and we are the most attacked, most invaded, and most occupied nation on Earth. We know war better than the Americans and we are not in a hurry to die. But you will see that until the Americans are gone from here they will face the same fate that all our enemies have faced and every day one American soldier will die and others will hurt forever," he replied with a serious, assertive tone.

His answer sent a chill down my spine and I needed to break away from the dark thoughts he stirred. "But what will you do now?" I asked him, alarmed.

"Now we wait for orders," he replied.

"Orders from the Americans?" I asked stupidly, like any intelligent soldier would have asked.

"No, from our president. Because we do not take orders from anyone that is not our true president. And our president is Saddam Hussein," he answered.

"But where is he?" I continued my interrogation.

"I don't know," he replied with a genuine frown. "But wherever he is, he will emerge to teach the world some of the lessons he has to teach as a truly wise man of Allah."

I felt the chill down my spine tingle at the haunting thought of what would happen if Saddam was to be given a true opportunity to argue his case before the international court of justice. Under any law, be it English, civil, or Islamic law, Saddam was not a common criminal. Whether we liked him or not, it was absolutely true to say that Saddam Hussein was a sovereign leader that had successfully governed the most hostile nation on Earth for over thirty years. This alone entitled him to a fair trial in The Hague as a sovereign leader.

The truth that Saddam Hussein was the president of Iraq and as the sovereign leader of the nation was protected under the Geneva Convention and international law was never told of by Western media outlets. It was essential to censor and silence his trial. Lest the truth be told and We the People demand that those responsible for this illegal war face the wrath of justice and serve prison sentences.

"But what if they capture or kill him?" I asked.

"We are a democratic state Al," the general pointed out. "If our president is killed, we, the people of Iraq will choose our next leader. But we will never accept anyone that is appointed by non-Iraqis," he added.

It seemed so logical to me at that moment that I could not for the life of me understand the total ignorance of the coalition of the willing to stay and fight rather than to pack their bags and go home to their families. Were we so dim?

"Now, you must go Al. It is not safe for you to be here. Go look in your own country and see what you need to do there to help your own people before you can help my people. God willing, we may meet again when the Americans are gone," he advised me.

"But what if they don't go?" I challenged him.

"Al, the Romans, the Greeks, the Phoenicians, even the British have learned it is better to trade with our people than to fight against us," he concluded.

"History really repeats itself," Ghassan interjected.

There was a short silence as all the men stared at me for a reaction. But all I could say was, "Insha Allah justice will prevail."

They seemed to like that as they smiled and nodded approval of my learnings. But we remained silent as we approached the drop-off destination back at the Palestine Hotel.

Watching these men enter their own cars and drive away, a distant gunshot broke the silence. I recalled what it was like to be shot in Sydney and I realised that in our own country we had our own wars to fight. We had gangs shooting each other; street criminals robbing, raping, and pillaging; drug addiction; alcoholism; domestic violence; child abductions and child abuse; homelessness; fraud; corruption; and an array of social and mental health problems. Yet we let our leaders convince us of the need for this grisly war.

Applying the laws of relativity, terrorists are an absolute minimal problem when domestic violence alone is killing two women every week in Australia, children are being abused in the privacy of their homes, and corruption is robbing every one of us from the freedom to learn, to educate, and to make our lives more rewarding.

With this awareness I accepted the new challenge; the question on my mind was where to begin and how to raise the necessary public awareness so that we could change the current self-destructive course we were all steering.

The answer was 'ingenuity', and inspired not by these military men but by the people who I learned to call the third world warriors.

Chapter 24
Man-made Hell

Everyone thinks of changing the world, but no one thinks of changing himself.

Leo Tolstoy

With thoughts of problems we faced in our own country, I returned to Ghassan's apartment exhausted and now immune to the sporadic gunfire that was slowly killing Americans, English, Spanish, Australians, French, Germans, other Europeans, and Iraqis. I fell asleep with all my clothes on. It would be late in the following morning when Ghassan woke me up with a nudge.

"You sleep like a new-born baby," he said as I sat up on the makeshift bed on the floor. It was my first sleep in days and the war seemed distant.

"Now I understand what it's like to be a born again," I replied, sleepy-eyed, but I didn't think he understood my meaning.

I desperately needed a shower and as the main water supplies had been destroyed by the American bombs, I showered like the rest of the Iraqis: using bottled water and my hand to minimise the water waste.

The electricity remained off as the power plants had been destroyed by coalition bombs to punish the civilian populations. There was no fresh milk or basic fresh foods as the fridge remained off and empty. So we had to go to a nearby café that used a generator for its constant supply of electricity. There was not much on the menu. We had a cup of sweet tea, some Lebanese sweets, and a French omelette with Turkish bread for breakfast. Ghassan had things to do and I went back to the Palestine Hotel in search of my Japanese angel Yakiko, as promised.

On my way to the Palestine Hotel, it dawned on me that now I was the unwelcomed visitor to this land. In stark contrast to my previous visit to Baghdad during Saddam's government, the people now seemed frightened, sceptical, and highly paranoid.

Without a government or police and with no order, our governments had created a chaotic socio-political environment where danger loomed around every corner and old rivals could hunt each other down.

Nevertheless, the Iraqi people seemed to continue with their normal lives as best they could. Rubbish littered the streets in stockpiles and smouldering ruins continued to cast smoke into the atmosphere, punishing our sense of smell with the constant scent of polluted smoke. I remembered thinking, *This is what hell must smell like*, as the burning carbons were scented with diesel vapours, melting plastics, and charred excrement.

Ghassan had things to do for his wife. But he got me a trusted civilian taxi to the Palestine Hotel and my driver seemed distressed that petrol queues were growing longer and fuel was now more expensive.

Refined petrol cost five cents a litre (or approx. twenty cents per gallon) while Saddam Hussein was in power. To think: we could have had petrol cheaper than water if we had invested in green renewable energies or negotiated a treaty with the Iraqi government rather than destroying a country and creating the terrorising animosity between violent criminal nations. Why on Earth the perpetrators of this obvious crime were not facing the courts of justice was beyond me. But my resolve was yet to come.

Now I had to pay three times more for the taxi ride and I knew things would only get worse for as long as the Americans remained in Iraq.

It was just after midday when I met with Yakiko at the Palestine Hotel. The heat was punishing. But she needed to find a cheaper alternative as her intention was to stay in Iraq with the Human Shields to help Iraqi orphans that seemed to roam the streets looking for their fathers or dead relatives. The fate of the many children without parents was haunting. She told us about an abandoned prison on the outskirts of Baghdad where some children and other people needed urgent medical attention. She was particularly concerned about Fatima, a young orphaned girl who had tuberculosis.

I told her we should wait for Ghassan, but after a short while we agreed to walk down to the nearby hotel that Ghassan had told us to visit. The owners were at first reluctant to take our American dollars, claiming they were full and could not risk having us stay in their hotel. But when they learned we were Human Shields, they changed their minds and welcomed us with open arms and at a discounted rate.

Shortly after settling in the hotel, Ghassan arrived with a friend who was to become our taxi driver and we all went to the abandoned prison that Yakiko had told us about on the outskirts of Baghdad. Along the taxi ride to the jail, we could see that even in the more remote outskirts of the city, Iraqis were living on the edge. There was a commotion of desperation and helplessness as people picked up the pieces of their shattered lives amongst the ruins and polluted streets. With the now familiar garbage-lined streets it was impossible to adjust my sense of smell. Smouldering piles of garbage set alight cast a constant smell of smoking maggots, burning plastics, and raw fuel that made it hard to breathe, let alone smell ... we were clearly in a man-made hell.

When we arrived at the abandoned prison, we saw that about five families and a dozen young children had moved in and shared the compound. I was still shocked at the magnitude of damage, waste, loss, and human suffering caused by modern warfare. An abandoned Iraqi army truck almost fully loaded with mortars and live ammunition was parked where children played games near the entrance to the prison. The military waste was criminal to say the least. Yet tax-paying workers continued to work to pay for this crime.

We entered the prison through the main gates that hung loosely opened like ornate rusted steel and I remembered thinking that perhaps I was having a nightmare and these were the gates of hell. The noon sun welted every blade of grass to a rusted, crispy, dry leaf. The air was heavy to breathe and our sweaty unwashed odours intensified our sense of smell. This experience reminded me of my first visit to hell back in 1986 when Sudan endured the satanic wrath of a devastating drought and in a town called Kassala I walked among those destined to die painfully slowly from hunger, thirst, and curable illness.

Now, as we entered this abandoned building, Satan surely rejoiced. There were more snotty-nosed children all orphaned from the loss of their fathers or families, watching us and extending their hands for donations. Some played barefoot amongst burnt remains and raw, infectious sewerage that flooded the ground floor corridors. Others appeared too weak to stand and simply remained sitting.

The overpowering smell of stale urine and disposed rotting garbage at times caused us to dry retch and heave. It seemed important to contain ourselves to not embarrass these destitute humans that lived worse than my dog. These were the new inhabitants of the George W. Bush-manufactured 'Iraqi freedom' in one of the most oil-rich countries on Earth.

I have already been to hell, I thought again. Until, Yakiko took us deeper inside Satan's lair where amongst others was the young girl who we learned was Fatima. We were in an old prison kitchen which had been converted into a shared dormitory for the children and families that slept here. It was dark without any electricity and chosen as the dormitory for its cooler breeze. There was no gas or running water. It smelled of burnt wood as they used an old fireplace for cooking and warming the room during the cold nights.

The criminal human suffering created by the invasion was beyond belief. Yet the crowds cheered as the home team scored another goal and the beer flowed cheaply to stunt the rebellious nature of the masses. Let there be slaves – a few chanted as the working classes continued to work for the rest of their lives in pursuit of owning their own home free from the invisible chains of a mortgage.

Meanwhile, behind a torn blanket draped down from the top of a double bunk bed, Fatima smiled when she saw the ray of hope in the shape of a Japanese angel named Yakiko, accompanied by Ghassan and myself.

"We have come to help you," Yakiko said softly to Fatima in a broken Japanese-English accent. "You are going to be okay. We are going to take you to the hospital now," she whispered again to Fatima in a warm and comforting tone.

Fatima, like many other Iraqis, knew some English and understood. But she was far too weak to dress herself. So we left the women to dress her and prepare her as Ghassan and I were shown around the prison by some of its new occupants: the orphaned children that followed us like shadows and an elderly man that spoke with Ghassan as we walked.

The empty shell of this building remained as it had been left, with the bedding piled and burnt in a large bonfire to kill the bed bugs, flees, and the vermin that had infested the prison mattresses. Only a rusty clump of metal bed frames remained scattered over the dusty courtyard.

As we entered the corridors we could only imagine the human suffering of the inmates as the cells defied imagination as to the severity of human torture we humans could impose on our very own fellows.

I remembered thinking how it was the maliciousness of self-righteousness that created the prejudices and hatreds that crucified Jesus Christ. Had we not learned anything as a human race?

The horror that our media incited hatred and fear in the same way that Adolf Hitler used the medium of film as propaganda to rally the Germans into killing Jews, gays, mentally challenged people, and poor vagrants, was magnified.

An evil force had taken the new lease of this prison and ensured that these people, mostly children, would die as slowly and painfully as inhumanly possible! Only this time it had been the coalition of willing Western nations that had created these third world prisons.

When Fatima was dressed in a loose-fitting, dirt-stained dress, I carried and placed her in the waiting taxi, then we all drove to Saddam's Children's Hospital. The chaos seemed to have multiplied from our first visit to the hospitals before the war.

Now the screams came from every ward and every room and the waiting rooms were filled and overflowing onto the streets with mostly mothers and grandparents with their sick or dying children. The most horrific sight was the single children who sat or slept on the floor awaiting a miracle to save them as they lay abandoned.

Diseases from the open sewers were now infecting more children than every terrorist's bomb would ever kill in a century of terrorism. Yet the Western media censored this fact and smiling news broadcasters told us of how heroic their soldiers were in the face of a war George W. Bush had started.

As I looked around Saddam's Children's Hospital I saw the families that my mate El-Chah had prophesised when his daughter Maddie lay in a coma-induced sleep. A collection of mostly mothers embracing their children as if their hugs and gentle rocking would save them from the pain, the hunger, and the injustice of modern warfare.

I felt guilty not for a crime I had committed, but for witnessing this shockingly outrageous crime against humanity and not doing anything to prevent this from happening. By now, I had run out of tears and could no longer cry. My face had become the mirror of the faces that stared back at me with blank expressions as they awaited, at worst, the fateful, slow death of the children they nursed, or at best, saving their children so they may grow up traumatised and bearing the scars that the G. W. Bush regime had self-righteously and undoubtedly been responsible for inflicting.

Eventually, a young student volunteer doctor diagnosed Fatima with contagious tuberculosis and told us she could not be treated here as she may infect other children. Then he sent us to another hospital. Saddam's Children's Hospital was over-stretched and there was simply nothing they could do for Fatima.

On our way to the next hospital, we witnessed the same destruction of property, the same damage to Iraqi government buildings, and the same military presence by an army that held little if any regard for the human suffering around them. The American military were more focused on staying alive and avoiding the rampant Iraqi snipers that we were now calling terrorists than caring for the Iraqi population. War was ruthless: dog ate dog, men tortured each other to death, women wept openly in public, and children suffered for the rest of their lives ... and from there terrorism was understandably born.

In the next hospital, the scene was repeated and by now it seemed we were all immune to the screams and the pleading for mercy. Again, the volunteer skeleton staff of overworked unpaid doctors and nurses told us to go to a specialist hospital that may be able to treat Fatima. But that was the only hospital that may be able to help. It was amazing to see the human spirit of the Iraqi people as they worked in the hospitals without getting paid but rather for the love of their fellows. The most inspiring vision was the civilians, mostly women cleaning the foul mess of spilled blood, vomit, mucus, dust, and excrements with rags a bucket of water, kneeling and wiping in the absence of a simple mop.

I remembered looking at Fatima as her eyes drifted to and from the colourful lights of reality, her eyelids shutting and opening like mine had done when I was shot at Sydney's Coogee Bay Hotel.

I knew what she was doing: desperately trying to see the very last spectrum of the light that gave us the meaning of life, for all it was worth.

Fatima was not alone, the hospitals were now all overcrowded with innocent victims spilling out onto the streets, whilst in some executive board room a handful of mentally challenged nepotistic megalomaniacs gained some perverse pleasure, as the value in their shares boomed so their children could snort cocaine up their noses, or their enriched wives could buy another ten thousand dollar dress. It was simply astonishing. I would never aspire to be wealthy beyond my means and never respect the absurdly wealthy beyond sympathy.

I spoke to Fatima and tried to act like the angelic nurse that once had saved my life, speaking to her with a calm, reassuring tone in my voice. But I wasn't an angel or a saint. I was a street-fighting thug, a deluded pilgrim and now a pathetically weak man as tears seeped from my eyes; the truth was hurtful, I was like the rest of the world population, just an eyewitness to this historical tragedy: an apathetic witness to a crime.

In this newly created third world hospital, Fatima was given one bag of precious drip, which seemed to invigorate and add a few extra hours, days, weeks, or months of life in hell: a deadly sentence of untold pain and humiliation as she lost control of her bladder, with urine flooding the floor beneath our feet.

From my shame, I could not stay with Fatima, and walked away leaving her in the hospital emergency bed awaiting her fate. I walked around the hospital observing the amazing efforts by a volunteer medical staff of mothers, nurses, doctors, and armed Iraqi soldiers wearing civilian clothing to defend or protect the hospitals. Some elderly ladies, no doubt mothers, attempted to clean the floors with rags along the hallways. But all they achieved was to smear the dry blood, the crusty vomit, and the filth around the granite tile floors.

At one point I noted a man screaming with excruciating pain as he was wheeled across on a stretcher, crying and pleading for mercy, with his young son following him closely, wiping his tear-stained face. It was like the child had also run out of tears but the dirty streaks on his face told the story of extreme anguish unlike any we may ever know.

As I walked along the hospital corridors, there were countless more victims of this unjust war who had suffered from the shell-shock. These were the many that were not killed instantly by an American missile and thus did not register in the American media as civilian deaths. Yet, they too would die over a long period of pain, isolation, shame, and an agonising death similar to Fatima's.

These shell-shocked victims haunted me the most for many years later. These were the civilians who simply stood too close to a terrorising military bomb, meaning the sound waves shattered their brains or fried their organs. Some of these fathers, elderly grandmothers, school children, and infants now sat on the floor motionless like living zombies. Their clothing and bodies were stained with dry blood, infected pus, excrement, and dirt. Some staggered, supported by the walls or with walking frames as they dribbled saliva, blood, and mucus—others like Fatima had lost control of their bowels and bladders and many others simply sat or lay where they fell. Some vomited blood and others the little food they got, due to shell-shocked stomach organs. The dead were taken to the rear end outside and laid on a pile for the flies to feast. The smell was indescribable.

The constant screaming; the pleads for mercy; the hands that grabbed my loose shirt or touched my legs; the horror of seeing adults crying as their children lay dying; the variety of open wounds that remained untreated; the smell of disinfectants mixed with infections; the look of despair on overworked volunteer doctors and nurses who were not paid to do this humanitarian work; all the destruction I had seen in such a short time; the knowledge that it was my Australian and Spanish countrymen; the knowledge that my American and European allies had created another third world nation—these things were driving me to breaking point.

I walked outside in search of fresh air, looking to be isolated, where I may cry on my own, but there was nowhere to hide from my shame. My legs finally refused to walk any further and dropped me on my knees near the entrance of the hospital. Here, with both hands covering the shame on my face in what we had done, I wept aloud as if my own mother had died. Time lapsed as the truth materialised.

Operation Iraqi Freedom was a lie paid for by our tax to protect the interests of a few oil and financial institutions, and we the working classes believed that lie of a 'national security concern'. Were we truly so powerless?

After an unknown number of minutes on my knees, with no more tears to shed, I composed myself and went back inside to join Ghassan, Yakiko, and Fatima, who were getting ready to leave the hospital as there was nothing more the doctors could do for Fatima. So she was released to die alone in an infected, abandoned, Iraqi prison with other orphaned children.

There was nothing more we could do for Fatima. Like the tens of thousands of victims of this war, she would die a painfully slow death as we in the modernised world lived oblivious to the facts of our unjust actions; we who worried about what we were going to wear to work today and believed everything our profit-making media told us to believe. We who boasted aloud of the car we had bought, the fashion labels we wore, or the drugs and alcohol we consumed; for us in the modern first world with a lot to learn, the truth was unforgiving.

Then I heard a familiar screaming and turned to see a man wheeled away, with his son following the man that pushed the rolling hospital bed out on the street. They had been left alone under the heat of the afternoon sun with no one capable of helping them. I walked over and pushed the wheeled hospital bed under the shade of a nearby tree, but every bump along the cracked road caused the man to squeal and cry for leniency and there was no way of easing his pain.

I handed the boy some American dollars, stupidly thinking that this paper may save his father, and walked away, holding back the tears that would result in the post-traumatic stress syndrome as an internal pain from the truth I was witnessing. Ghassan looked at me with a blank expression. We knew the worst was yet to come for this father and his son.

Modern war was beyond an atrocity. It was a man-made catastrophe where the civilians paid the price for not standing up and marching or demonstrating profusely against their governments. We walked away like everyone walked away from the wounded, however the look on that man's face would disturb me many sleepless nights later. Could I have done any more for Fatima or that unknown man? He was not an old man, but a father of maybe thirty or forty years of age. He had strikingly handsome features with short, curling black hair, a well-proportioned nose, perfectly white teeth, and a solid, muscular body. There was a resemblance to my mate Elk. But then I looked at the child and was reminded of what becomes of children who lose their parents or families in war. These were war orphans and the coalition of willing nations succeeded in creating tens of thousands of war orphans in the name of colonisation, oil fields, and dictated democracy under duress.

Meanwhile in North America, Europe, and Australia the football fans stood and cheered as their club kicked a goal, the women discussed fashion labels as if their lives were dependent on what some gay man had designed, and the American college cheer-girls jumped for joy whether their teams won or lost. The bliss of ignorance was euphoric, and the free modern world sat in comfortable lounges watching television commercials that told them what to buy, what to read, what to wear, which car to drive, or what to do to be 'normal': I had now become the mad man for venturing to learn the truth.

After a few days trying to find Waratah and walking around the devastation and anarchy, it was impossible to argue that this or any war could ever be justified. This humanitarian and environmental man-made disaster was, without a doubt, a gross violation against the interest of each and every one of us in the international community.

The only strength I had was the knowledge that my pen was busy taking notes of the crimes I was witnessing.

I wrote: *Hell is a man-made place where the human race is tortured with hunger, disease, thirst, and the painful truth that it is not God's will but the will of ignorant men who created the Hell we call the third world ...*

Chapter 25
Saddam's Message

It's not the job of the government to tell the people what they should or shouldn't say.
George Brandis,
Australian Attorney-General

On my last day in Baghdad Ghassan introduced a well-groomed man that claimed he had seen Saddam Hussein shortly after the coalition announced to have bombed his hiding spot. He spoke near-perfect English and his suit and tie suggested he belonged to the Iraqi elite. We made small talk for a few minutes and then he reached inside his jacket and withdrew an envelope.

"Mr Al, please take this letter to the world," he asked, handing me a handwritten note that I couldn't read as it was in Arabic. "Please help us to not become like our Palestinian brothers who live in fear of the Israeli terrorists that destroy Palestinian homes and kill our brothers. Please help us?" he pleaded to me.

I explained my mediocrity and powerlessness, but Ghassan told him that I was a writer, at which point this mature man turned to me and as we shook hands in peace he reassured my destiny, saying, "Ah, very good. A writer is a gifted person as the pen is mightier than the sword."

"But I am an unknown writer," I admitted.

"But you are educated like a king," Ghassan interjected.

"Yes but—" I stuttered.

"Get out now," the stranger advised me. "Come back when the Americans have gone, because soon we begin to fight, because for us, the war begins when Americans say war is finished."

This warning touched the very nerve of my consciousness. It was this military tactic that the Mujahidin used in Afghanistan against the Russians and that would later result in the Iraqi special forces and military creating ISIL (Islamic State of Iraq and the Levant), also known as ISIS (Islamic State of Iraq and Al-Sham). The truth was terrorising to our government and our leaders, who would continue to justify and argue in favour of absurd military spending to fight this terror, rather than succumb to the fact that peaceful dialogue, negotiations, and compassion are the ingredients to ensure we make our third millennium sustainable for all life on Earth, lest we forget that the third world war will be humanity versus the natural forces of global warming. This is a fact many individuals cannot accept with their heads in the sand and their hands in their pockets.

As this man spoke, I remembered Ticker the Turk's lesson of the warnings that one should give their enemies. The PLO repeatedly warned Israelis to end the system of apartheid or face the wrath of terrorism. Saddam Hussein warned the Americans of the dire consequences for American soldiers, expressing a repeat of Vietnam. It seemed to me that Saddam had given the Americans his third warning now and in my heart I understood the dangerous consequences after the third warning had been issued.

This man warned me. "You will see in Ramadan, you will see in one year from now and two years and forever," he said, deadly serious. "Every time they kill one of our leaders, another will rise to continue our tradition of self-rule. No one, not even the Americans, will ever tell Iraqis how we must live."

As he spoke, I didn't think of what he was saying as a threat but rather as the natural reaction any person or child would have when a bully starts a fight. That is, you would absorb the insults and the beating, perhaps retreat and cry aloud at the sting of the pain-filled truth that we were weaker than the bullies that hurt our spirits.

But our spirits were never broken while we were alive, and thus we prepared for the retaliation to amend the injustice imposed on us by that bully. Perhaps we sought justice by publically shaming the bully to our superiors like the United Nations or our teachers or the police. But if they failed to restore justice, then all hell was unleashed. As we said in the Western world: the gloves were off.

As a street-fighting thug, I understood that need to fight back, the need to stand up and hold your ground or forever live as a coward.

"Mr Ali," this noble man addressed me with undeserved respect, and concluded, "Saddam Hussein is not a bad man. He is our president. And

Iraq needs men like Saddam to protect our people from Kurds in the North, Israelis in the West, Iranians in the East, and now Americans that attack us from the Arabian Sea in the South."

"You see my friend," Ghassan suddenly interrupted the pregnant pause. "You already know this, but your people in the West don't understand we just want peace. We don't want your army to invade us ... to occupy our land and tell us how to be or how to live ..."

"Now you must go," the stranger demanded from me.

There was not much I could do or say as I simply listened to these educated men who were peacefully warning and teaching me. After a few comforting words where I found myself apologising for my ignorance, the distinguished man retreated, saying the now familiar phrase of peace and friendship used by the people that created civilisation.

"Salam Alecum," he said, shaking my hand in friendship, then walking away into the war-torn street.

Ghassan later explained that this man was an intelligence agent for the Iraqi military and the Ba'ath party. He was told of my presence and given this task of handing me the note directly. Ghassan also advised me to leave and to return after the Americans had left Iraq. Saying "Ali, you must leave now. Iraq is too dangerous for you to stay."

The following morning, I was happy to take his advice. However, leaving Ghassan and his family was more painful than I expected. His wife was pregnant and the economic sanctions had already given her one miscarriage. Did the Western women understand what it must be like to be pregnant and unemployed, with your country sanctioned from international trade by a superior military, and you expecting to give a natural birth, or were they simply too busy paying the bills and working so that their governments could justify the injustice of another modern war?

Ghassan and I shared an intimate moment walking along the Tigris River and then we sat with his father by the river's edge. We talked and discussed the future and we foresaw the creation of yet another Palestinian state where children and young men would ultimately be throwing rocks at American tanks. A state controlled with prejudice and biased racism against a majority of the population at gunpoint; a third world nation where the minority who controlled the power with absurd wealth employed family and friends rather than the most suitable person to do a job; a nation where survival depended on one's ability to evade corrupt policemen or criminal gangs that threatened with bribes, blackmail, or life-changing violence. Perhaps this was what the world faced as global warming continued to diminish our food supplies for the ever-increasing global populations. Perhaps this was our future and we were all responsible and guilty for our ignorance.

Were we that stupid to not understand how unsustainable the path we were on would be for our children?

Then both Ghassan and his father agreed that it would be best for me to leave Baghdad, as things would only escalate for the worst; a reminder that my life was in danger.

Yakiko had decided to stay with Fatima the day before. I last saw her as we drove away and she waved at me the entire time until the car lost sight of her. Ghassan organised an exclusive taxi ride out of Baghdad, which I paid with Judith Karpova's money.

This taxi ride was long and lonely. I sat alone in the rear as the driver attempted to comfort my distressed emotions but soon realised I had become a zombie of war. Like so many others who survived war and realised that Satan was a nepotistic megalomaniac; like so many kings, queens, sultans, emperors, and supreme leaders in our time whose evil deeds behind fortified walls would never be known. I fell asleep and awoke only to show my passport at the border and then in Amman.

The following day I visited Rema and we parted without a kiss, just a solid handshake like two good friends that understood and accepted that God's will was far stronger than anything we might want to predict. I thanked her family and wanted to kiss them all but refrained, thinking that it was not a Muslim gesture for a stranger to kiss women that were not his family or lover.

However, when I looked at Rema's grandmother, the fragile little Palestinian lady, I could feel the sorrow this lady must have experienced for most of her life as she had lost her husband, a son, and her lands to the Israelis yet remained dignified. I gave her a strong hug and kissed her cheeks, apologising from the depth of my heart for my sheer ignorance and apathy about the Palestinian suffering. But I don't think she understood me as she just smiled innocently. This amused Rema's sisters and her mothers who all laughed and heckled me like I had just told the world's funniest joke. But sadly I could sense they too were hurting.

Rema as always remained composed, dignified, and in control of her iron-clad emotions. It was embarrassing that the Australian Embassy had refused her visa application. This was my first experience with the Australian Immigration Department and the realisation that the Australian immigration laws discriminated against the poor, the uneducated, and those who most needed our help. Rema was poor and could not demonstrate sufficient funds and so even with me as her sponsor she was denied a visa. It was painful to admit that Australia did not accept poor people to share in the ridiculous wealth of the Australian nation. We wanted it all for ourselves, the embassy staff seemed to say with strong English accents and without so many words.

"But I will pay for all her expenses," I said to the Australian ambassador in Amman.

"But we don't want her kind," he replied like a true racist.

It was a sad thing to live under a regime that protected the dictatorship of its ruler or the monarchs who least needed help. People in Saudi Arabia work their entire lives to protect the interests of their sultans. In North Korea, the people worked for a man that inherited his power having never worked a day in his life, yet who had the capacity to kill on a personal whim. Around the world there were dictators who governed with personal interest rather than the interests of humanity or their people. Kings and queens were monarchs that already had the very best a life could offer—what more did they need other than the freedom to roam the streets or travel the world visiting wonders, climbing mountains, or eating exotic food with strangers and so much more?

In Australia, it was this unjust phenomenon that we were learning to stand against peacefully; we had learned to work so that we might live happy and rewarding lives and not be enslaved by a government, employer, or monarch. We learnt the advantages of an education over the lack of knowledge that apathy produced. We learnt to have the freedom of travel and to choose which countries we wanted to visit and work or holiday so we might distribute our wealth to poorer people in foreign lands. *So why can't we share the vast spaces and wealth we have without prejudices?* I wondered as the taxi carried me away from Rema's dignified family.

Leaving the Al Saraya Hotel staff as they waved goodbye was equally difficult. Fayez, who had become the mentor and guardian to so many Shields, looked me in the eyes and knew I was dying internally. He seemed to know that I was leaving my heart in Amman, my spirit in Palest-Israel, and my soul in Baghdad.

He gave me a warm, manly hug and said, "Al, the truth will always prevail."

I nodded with a half-forced smile, holding back the tears. But when the taxi drove off from the hotel, I was overcome by emotions and wept like a child all the way to the airport.

It was a long, lonely flight back home to Sydney. When I arrived my appreciation for the Vietnam War veterans was magnified. It was like they had returned home to find a society that turned its back on them. The Human Shields returned to prosecution, social isolation, and political prejudice. It didn't matter that these peaceful warriors of mostly women had made titanic sacrifices for complete strangers in the name of world peace and global justice. The media had won. They had managed to sway the painful truth and manufactured a big, warm, and comfortable lie while keeping the workers entertained and happy to be working for the rest of their lives to pay the taxes that may justify absurd military spending on weapons and the destruction of our natural environment and human lives

It was beyond me how peace activists could ever become threats to national security. But that is exactly what too many of the Human Shields and peace demonstrators across the world in various countries were accused of, while the media ensured it censored the stories of human tragedy, injustice, and the gross abuse of power by our very own regimes.

There were no family members or friends at the airport on my arrival. No fanfare to say, "Congratulations on fighting the war with peace! On standing up against your rights peacefully!" Nor was anyone interested in the criminal activities of the coalition military. It seemed like everyone was still interested in their sports teams, in their beer or drugs, or in their other meaningless, self-indulgent vices. How pretty the dress, how wonderful the day at the horse races, how precious the jewellery, and how important it was that some actor had sex with another actress behind his wife's back.

The subjects of economic sanctions, the history of Iraq war orphans, or the injustices endured by Palestinians were not to be discussed, let alone the scale of human suffering that would result from the creation of another third world nation.

Upon arrival, my credit card limit was overdrawn and with no money it was a long walk from the airport to my family home in Zetland. I arrived broke and hungry, daunted with the task of conveying to a mostly ignorant society the truths about our very own problems and narcissistic creed.

Over the months that followed I tried to contact our leaders, with a letter to John Howard and King Juan Carlos of Bon Bon, the International Courts of Justice, and the United Nations, to convey the message I had been entrusted to convey; all to no avail. Ghassan helped me translate the letter I was given by that Iraqi intelligence agent. This was what the message said:

In the name of God, the most compassionate, the most merciful

To the International Courts of Justice and the United Nations Security Council

Our sovereign nation of Iraq demands justice in the International courts of law with a fair trial in The Hague against the Coalition that now occupies illegally, has destroyed our homes, is killing and torturing our people. We want to summon the administration of George W. Bush, Tony Blair, Jose Maria Aznar and John Howard to the courts for the illegal invasion of Iraq and the crimes against humanity by their military against our people. Our leader President Saddam Hussein and our

> *people have endured thirteen years of economic sanctions we have paid in full all compensation due for damages to Kuwait, America and the United Nations. We have complied with all United Nations Security Council requests and adhered to our global concerns and need to disarm for peace. We have surrendered and destroyed our last line of defence, all our al-Masoud missiles and made peace with our brothers in Iran and Kuwait. We ask the Kurdish people to stop terrorizing us so that we may have peace with the Kurdish people. We seek everlasting peace and not war. We plead to world communities for the immediate and unconditional departure of the Coalition armies or we have the right to defend our nation until all foreign forces leave our lands. We have repeatedly made our claim that we have no evil Weapons of Mass Destruction as alleged by Mr Bush. We want the world to help us disarm America and the Israelis from such weapons of mass destruction as they make threaten the world peace for our future children and all mankind.*
>
> *Greetings to the people of Palestine, men and woman, living and martyrs. Greetings to our brothers in all Islamic nations and greetings to all peace loving nations around the world.*
>
> *God is great, God is great, God is great*
> *There is only one God, God is the greatest, Praise be to God*

With this letter in my hands, my fear was no longer of the Iraqis or Muslims or terrorists, but of our very own Western powers. However, the truth had to be told for justice to prevail and for those responsible for this crime against our world to face the wrath of justice.

History had taught us how the German Nazis used the mass media of film to persuade the German people of the prejudices shared by the Hitler government—now the media was successfully persuading the prejudiced elite ruling class to believe that Saddam had weapons of mass destruction, as a premise for invading and controlling Iraqi oil fields at any cost.

The reality I was witnessing was the facts that our leaders would not want to publicise, especially as my eyewitness account and testimony only endangered the regimes culpable for this catastrophic war with long term consequences against all of us.

I now began to fear our very own police and spy agencies.

The truth was already hurting some of us.

Chapter 26
Natural Laws

To speak his thoughts is every freeman's right, in peace and war, in council and in fight.

Homer
Father of Greek literature
Pre-700BC

From the day we were born, we learnt best from the mistakes we made. Each and every one of us would make mistakes that would cost us friends, money, material possessions, and above all, the time we had to do good on this heavenly Earth. What is significant is the difference between a genuine simple mistake and that of a criminal act.

As we travelled along our personal journeys of life, we carried with us the lessons learned from the mistakes of our childhood and our youth. Lessons we later felt responsible for sharing with our children, friends, lovers, or with the general public as we told our stories in written books.

Now I recalled personal memories with the aim of teaching those who wished to learn as I did, from the written works of others, that there were some mistakes we were best avoiding by learning quickly how to change ourselves, before becoming ill, jailed, or the victims of the foul, malicious actions seen by the less-educated and prejudiced as the victims of crime.

When I learned that cigarette smoking and alcohol-related disease and death were slowly and painfully killing more people than AIDS, domestic violence, terrorism, existing wars, and road traffic accidents worldwide combined, I quit smoking and stopped drinking alcohol and decided to change myself by caring for my health and the environment. I called this change my conversion to Islam, and was fascinated by the reactions of many people who I thought knew me.

The financial reward to my end of smoking and drinking was a bonus as I suddenly began to have extra money, and not long after, I enslaved myself with a mortgage and bought my house. The rising equity would later go towards making my dream come true. So in essence, by not drinking alcohol or smoking cigarettes, I could live my dream.

What I was not expecting was to realise how much our lives were restricted by government-approved drugs, propaganda, and the manufactured laws of what I now understood as the English law regime; a regime all Australians understood as harsh, prejudicial, and expensive, to favour mostly the law-makers and its keepers: as our forefathers the Australian Aboriginal and the convicts had learned. In brief, what I realised was that we were paying our hard-earned money to pollute the environment and damage our health with the English law regime's approval, while the elite few educated had the knowledge to prohibit their own children from smoking or drinking and yet encouraged the ignorant working class to buy their filthy products. This was a decisive moment to changing my life, many years before going to Iraq and my subsequent pursuits to understand the dark side of humanity and the immorality or prejudices of our man-made laws.

So when a new-age girlfriend challenged my masculinity, yelling at me shortly after I had quit drinking and smoking saying, "You're not man enough to hit me!" I instinctively slapped her with the back of my hand as I suddenly stopped the car I was driving.

The look on her face was haunting.

In that instance it was clear that I had become a madman to womankind and an ignorant fool living in the bliss of my nicotine and alcohol-filled ignorance.

Over the years that followed, I became semi-obsessed with my madness and began my personal, self-indulgent studies into the dark side of humanity, using my physical aggression and violent ways as the premise. As a humanities student, my studies would be covert and focused on the evil nature innate in us all; hence why I went to Iraq to speak with terrorists in the first place.

I was only to learn that I was far from being alone and that my thoughtless aggressive reaction to any form of threat was not unique. We are all capable of acting maliciously, dangerously, and with evil intent. Such is human nature and the need for religious and spiritual wisdom.

Whatever the case for my covert studies of our human world—my good fortune was the blessing of having a calm, loving, and educated mother who taught me the stupidity shown to us boys on television, while strength was taught to me by the ancient traditions passed down from father to son. A tradition shared by all cultures, races, and religions, and from as far back as the start of human memory where we were taught the importance to stand up and defend not only our lives but those around us.

Undeniably, the Hollywood film industry had a lot to answer for, producing films that promoted and encouraged illegal behaviour to our children, or films that glorified warfare, stupidity, and sexual perversion. But how does one take action against the very tool used to keep us tamed, passive, docile, and ignorantly entertained?

The best solution was to stop paying my money to see meaningless, violent films, or to switch television channels every time I saw the stupidity we were shown as mindless entertainment. It was also good to stop playing the time-wasting, violence-promoting video games. With more time to spare, I began to read more and it was thus that one realised it was empowering to be educated.

By reading, we broadened our vocabulary and analytical skills. We learned from the wisdom of others who shared with us their own stories in their own voices. We learned to express ourselves and above all, we learned to defend ourselves from any kind of intellectual, moral, ethical, or spiritual threats made against us.

This revelation was not new, but as I was about to learn, an important secret kept by the elite. The wisdom had been passed down from the very origins of ink and paper from the times of Egyptian Pharaohs, to Confucius, Socrates, Buddha, Abraham, the Apostles, and the countless many more who had shared what they learned with those able to continue to learn with literature. This was truly a privilege of the few of us that can find the time to read.

As university graduates we learnt the responsibility we inherited upon graduation to continue learning and sharing our knowledge as teachers, professors, professionals, or doctors, so that others less fortunate may benefit from our work, and thus we earned our livelihoods

The question now was to understand why we, the educated people of the great Western nations, were blindly marching into a modern war rather than investing the money it was going to cost to destroy a nation into people's lives, restoring the environment, and ensuring our children received free education. Why squander the wealth on destroying our world rather than improving it and creating jobs in every industry? It was simply absurd how the powerful could be so criminal and We the People of Earth so poor and powerless.

Needless to say, why were we mindlessly and stupidly blowing up money in the shape of terrorising military bombs rather than building a better world? Why not repair old roads, bridges, schools, housing, and health care facilities, or restore international relations with our enemies? Were our banking, petroleum, and political law-makers that powerful that we could not reclaim the natural wealth that belonged to all of us rather than a few nepotistic dynasties?

With a family tradition of legal practitioners and as a student of law, I had already learned that the tough thing to do was to remain above the law and not break the law so as not to give our money to those who relied on their elite education or the police with hefty fines.

It was already common knowledge that police officers are those who will do what they are told to do as long as you pay them or buy their service. The security of a weekly income truly was a sweet enticement to some, and it was not uncommon for these mindless servants to obey their political masters irrespective of the moral, ethical, or logical consequences to their actions. Time and time again, people were marching and demonstrating peacefully against the stupidity or criminal actions of their governments only to be stopped by a well-paid, uniformed and uncompromising police lines.

Did these police officers not understand their job was to protect the people not the governments? Perhaps we needed reminding that it is us, we are the people that pay the taxes to employ the police so we may be protected from crazed criminals. In particular, a criminal government that would send our families to war on the premise of a lie, or advocate the destruction of our world with military spending rather than maintaining educational facilities for our children.

Yet the maniac nepotistic inheritors of power like G. W. Bush and the monarchs like the Saudi Sultans could pay their police officers to protect their interests while those of us who worked tirelessly throughout our lives were now spied on by our very own paid police.

The tragedy, the horror, and the terror that our own police were spying on our freedoms was beyond words. We, the free people of the advanced modern world, were no more free than the North Korean people when secret undercover high tech police officers were watching our metadata and our activities in the guise of national security.

For our governments to label Edward Snowden or Julian Assange criminals simply for blowing the whistles and raising our public awareness was terrorising to any free thinking person. What will the critics have to say about the truths that may hurt them if they were to read this book, I mused. It would be interesting to see what absurd allegation would be made against my genuine academic interests in the dark side of humanities, or simply for understanding that terrorist are not the greatest threat we face, or that global warming truly is the greatest threat to all of us. Terrorists are an absurd minority, and above all, terrorists have a cause to defend their families if they are attacked by our military in their lands, or if our governments are mindlessly destroying our planet with modern warfare so that weapon manufacturers may profit. I refused to buy the lies told to us by our power thirsty politicians.

What some of us know is that if we didn't like the police, lawyers, or judges that make a living from criminals and then make absurd profits from the basic or common mistakes people make, the best way to let them know was by doing the right thing and not breaking the natural laws, yet challenging those laws that were simply manufactured for the creation of wealth by the legal industry workers.

Nevertheless in a split moment of stupidity I slapped the face of a woman I loved to prove her wrong and demonstrate that I was 'man enough to hit her'. The fact was, I had succumbed to her trap and committed the ultimate illegal act of stupid cowardice by physically hitting a woman. So I quickly went to her father as a matter of honour.

"I'm sorry I hit your daughter," were my sad, apologetic words of regret.

"You will regret that for the rest of your life," he replied, clearly biting back his anger like the true gentleman that he was. Ian Bloxom or

'Blockhead' as he liked to be known, demonstrated his greatness by not striking at me or abusing me for hitting his precious daughter. Instead, he invited me to sit with him and calmly recounted similar regrets he had with his wife and daughter. He explained how he found peace as a man by expressing his anger and directing his aggressive, masculine energies as a man toward his music. He found the bongos, the tambourine, the xylophone, the drums, and the triangle, and played with any percussion he could find rather than hit any man, woman, or child. With his newfound artistic passion he became the Sydney Symphony Orchestra's leading percussionist and played in numerous successful rock bands. But above all, he taught me the most valuable lesson any man can teach another man: aggression and violence were for the cowards who could not accept the torturous pain of the truth and acted impulsively with violent rage. Or worse, for those who declared wars and started fights only to send other men to do the fighting in the guise of 'national security'.

It was Blockhead's wisdom and willingness to teach me through dialogue rather than with a mindless beating that was among the most important lessons of my life. To discuss, argue, scream, teach, and shout rather than act with physical violence was the way of the future.

That was the last time in my life that I hit any person or animal. Perhaps the West could also learn from an artistic man like Ian Bloxom and understand there was no excuse for violence or war in the modern world.

Nonetheless, violence continued to dominate our criminal correction institutions. The torture of Iraqi prisoners by American military in Guantanamo Bay was irreprehensible. There was simply no excuse and no argument for torture in the modern world; needless to say less reason to wage modern warfare.

So when Saddam Hussein was killed by a group of masked men that cursed and rejoiced, the world witnessed yet another injustice; the killing of a natural-born leader that governed a sovereign nation. The difference between this execution and other martyrs was that Saddam Hussein had not been crucified to a cross, but hung on the noose of a regime that had been fabricated by military aid and paid for by our tax dollars.

The facts that we knew were that Iraq did not have the alleged weapons of mass destruction. Saddam's word was the painful truth. This made anyone who supported the Iraq war guilty of prejudice, ignorance, and above all, crimes against humanity, the animal kingdom, and our uniting natural environment.

What I was learning was the necessity of ignorance for evil to triumph and the truth that justice will always prevail with time. In a universe filled with irony, the surrounding sultans and their families dined in opulence beyond human necessity, and laws continued to be invented by English law-makers whose principle purpose was to protect the elite wealthy and powerful from the mediocrities that we, the people on Earth, were deemed to be. It was history repeating itself and we were kept happily entertained and enslaved, with lifelong debts and mortgages.

Perhaps we needed the ignorant to continue living in the bliss of mindless entertainment and a lifetime of work. But we had a responsibility to ensure life on Earth remained preserved for the benefit of all our children who would inherit our legacy.

In North America, the war of independence formed an amazing nation with a document written by the people for the people: *The American Constitution*. This constitution, after reading it, gave us hope for a fairer and more equitable world if the world were to embrace the good intentions drafted by the academic forefathers of the past. Its values were humane, fair, and above all, futuristic. However, it did not entitle the American governments to act on whims, with prejudices or illegally contravening international laws; hence the illegality of the George W. Bush administration to wage war against the people of Iraq. What the American people had the power to do was to punish their very own administration with crippling fines, jail sentences, or death sentences if proven to be like Hitler, a leader that dictated with personal rather than public interest.

In Australia and other Commonwealth nations, we continued to be the loyal servants to maintain the regime of our British sovereign 'the crown' and were better to remain in ignorant bliss and accept this regime than to rebel, as those in the Eureka Stockade[13] learned. In particular, the English law regime had the power to censor people, to jail whistle-

---

13   The **Eureka Rebellion** of year 1854 was an Australian historically significant revolution of gold miners of Ballarat, Victoria, Australia, who revolted against the colonial authority of the United Kingdom.

blowers like Julian Assange, or dispose of any person like a princess who slept with the enemy or a dictator that threatened the kingdom of monarchs such as Saddam Hussein, or the Iranian people who ousted their monarchs.

It seemed only logical to expect the Australian people to evolve conscientiously and realise that this great country, with less people than some of the mega-cities across the world in a land the size of continents, had the natural wealth and resources to give each man, woman, and child free education, free dental and health care, and a healthy life in the workplace with the capacity to travel the world in a wealth-distributing pilgrimage. Yet we were given the remedial jobs and fed breadcrumbs, in relative terms, while our noble lords earned grossly disproportionate incomes that only bought the curse of wealth; mental illness.

The tragedy of this arguably illegal war against Iraq was monumental, yet we were continuously entertained to keep our minds on anything but the truth.

When the American troops began leaving Iraq, the words of the Iraqi Special Forces commander echoed between my ears: "For us the war will begin when the Americans are gone." As well as the advice given to me by the Iraqi general: "Go back to your own home and look at the problems in your own country before you try to fix the problems in another country."

As I silently watched what the media called the 'Arab Spring', with revolutions taking place in Syria, Tunisia, Egypt, Algeria, Oman, and Yemen, there was nothing I could do. But I did take the advice and began looking at some of the many problems we faced in the West. What I learned would become the premise for my next book as I became the victim of the English law regime. However, with the truth on my side, this would be a battle I would cherish for the years that followed, knowing justice would prevail in the time to kingdom come.

I had witnessed a genocide perpetrated by the crown, the George W. Bush administration, the Saudi sultans as part of the 'coalition of the willing'—a coalition built on misinformation, lies, ignorance, and deceit.

Until now, it was this terrible genocide and crimes against our natural environment that the third world warriors foresaw when they marched and rallied against our governments before the wars. But many more saw further ahead as they argued against the decisions to misappropriate our tax dollars to destroy our fragile global ecology. This alone was simply a criminal decision that would affect millions of lives during a time when the world's greatest scientists were agreeing on the looming catastrophes that would result from the climate changes.

A handful of governments were telling us to go to war and to continue building orphan-creating weapons; orphans that would be the most vulnerable amongst the monsters that shared our neighbourhoods, war orphans who may one day become terrorists or monsters for not having received the same education, the same chances in living productive lives, or the same love that a parent shared with a child.

The Iraqi general was right to advise that we should look at our problems in our cities and suburbs before spending our tax dollars in a modern war. The Institute for Economics and Peace[14] had vast amounts of data to back the idea that war amongst us was a debilitating notion, in particular as we continued to present a global united front against the natural environment with diminishing resources. With an increasing global population demanding more or less, those that would suffer the greatest were the vulnerable children—at least until global warming left us no other option but to self-destruct from the absence of resources to be shared by an ever-growing global population.

The writing was on the walls for everyone to see, yet few could read or understand the word spelled out there:

---

14 The Institute for Economics and Peace is a non-government funded school that studies the opportunity costs of war against peace.

Chapter 27
David and Goliath

Ignorance is the curse of God; knowledge is the wing wherewith we fly to heaven.
                                                    William Shakespeare

As at 5 March 2013 there are:

4,488 dead American military in Iraq
32,000 more permanently wounded
Unknown tens of thousands Iraqis dead
Unknown hundreds of thousands of displaced Iraqis
Unknown number of mutilated civilians
Unknown number yet to die from war wounds
Unknown collateral damage to the environment
Unknown animals abandoned and slaughtered

Today, what we know is that we, the free people of Earth, each have different needs, wants, and desires. Yet we all have to survive. We have children and other family members we love and thus work to keep happy families. The financial crisis of American banks resulted after the invasion of Iraq, which made the few global dynasties untouchable while the global economic meltdown began the demise of our future.

The warrior instincts to fight for what is right and defend what we love or the values we believe in are innate, or instincts shared across the animal kingdom. That is to say, it is within each and every one of us: you, your family, including mothers and children, have the capacity to fight.

A generation has grown since I went to Baghdad and the future of life on Earth as we know it is increasingly threatened. The future looms with dark clouds of uncertainty for all of us, as populations grow and food resources diminish.

We have already seen the social unrest begin in many nations with the Arab Spring across Tunisia, Libya, Syria, Egypt, Oman, and the ongoing wars in Afghanistan and Iraq. The Ukraine and Russia crisis over Crimea may just be the tip of the iceberg as Europeans become hungrier for the natural gas reserves that make the Russians stronger. The rising tensions in the South China seas between Japan and China, or the tension between Koreans, are all simmering conflicts waiting to explode. It is not a matter of if, but when they explode, which is what we should all be trying to avoid. The economic collapse of Greece is just the tip of the iceberg we all face.

Add in global economic collapse and the increasing intensity of natural catastrophes, and we see that the depleting natural environment will have us all competing and fighting for our survival. A third world war amongst us is inevitable, unless we all begin to change and declare the third world war a war of all mankind against our depleting natural environment.

Why on Earth would we shoot the messengers, like Julian Assange who created WikiLeaks so that we may be privy to the important information we need to know about the people we vote for and entrust to lead us into the future?

Why would Edward Snowden become an exile from his own country simply for telling the hard-hitting and painful truth about the invasion of privacy perpetrated by the American government against their own people?

When I heard some of the Human Shields were being imprisoned or fined for trying to prevent the illegal invasion of Iraq by the coalition of the willing, it became evident that the powers that governed our lives had the capacity to keep us enslaved with our mortgages and lines of credit while they, the dynasties, continue to get away with genocide, murder, grand fraud, and gross violations of human rights in quests for power.

Saddam Hussein was not a common criminal; he was the elected sovereign leader of a country that threatened the sultans of Kuwait and Saudi Arabia. He helped and supported Palestinian people from the apartheid system in Israel. He was the envy of many dynasties as he successfully ruled for over thirty years the most invaded, most hostile, and one of the wealthiest countries on Earth. It took an illegal invasion by a coalition of misled nations to destroy his disarmed military that today continue to defend their lands united as ISIL.

Saddam's legal arguments were censored and We the People, who needed to know the truth about our world, were equally kept in the dark about the facts and the truths we needed to know.

The censorship of Saddam Hussein's trial should be of great concern for those in the intelligence-gathering communities who are seeking to make the world a better place. Yet we continue to drink cheap alcohol, smoke legal nicotine, and eat cancer-provoking processed foods while watching anything on our screens, rather than confront the painful truths, such as the admissions and testimonies made by creditable people like the North American Senator Luis "Scooter" Libby against the G. W. Bush administration, claiming the war had been manufactured. This resulted in the government taking costly legal action to discredit, silence and expel Mr. Libby.

Senator Paul H. O'Neil was fired for standing firm against the criminal actions he would not be a part of.

Mr. George Galloway MP in the United Kingdom, received little positive publicity about his very own realisations that Palestine and Saddam Hussein posed zero threat to the UK, the USA, or the world, as they were not only impoverished, but did not have any weapons of mass destruction such as the Israeli and North American arsenal.

Perhaps the eyewitness account by the human rights lawyer, Ms Waratah Rose Gillespie, who went on to write her own book to demand justice on behalf of those victims to the illegal war, was simply too much for some people to accept, and her sudden death would not be lost in vain.

The sociologist and human rights campaigner, Ms. Kathy Kelly, as a vocal peace warrior has been arrested and jailed simply for standing up against her government's creed for war. As a peace activist, her own government have criminalised her good ethical compass as her society champions mindless fashion designers and nepotistic leadership.

One need only understand the facts shared and taught to us by the self-confessed Economic Hit man, Mr John Perkins, to understand the truth of North American, British, and Israeli economic policies that protect corporations rather than our global environments. Least of all do they protect the extreme poor in third world nations, or the evidence that was produced by Dr Huda to showcase the inhumanity of economic sanctions on the people of a nation while the leadership lived in the decadence of power.

In Australia, the confessions of an intelligence officer named Jane Errey, who was fired for not writing propaganda that justified Australian's involvement in the war, was alarming, as we, the Australian people, were deprived of the truth as the lies continued to be manufactured. When the United States Secretary of State, Collin Powell, lied and deceived the United Nations assembly in his famous speech of mobile chemical labs, the people on Earth would believe this lie with blind faith over the media.

But above all is the former chief legal advisor to the UK foreign office, Sir Michael Wood, when he gave evidence to his own British government that the invasion of Iraq was illegal without a second United Nations resolution. This should have been broadcast to the world for the truth and justice to prevail against those powerful, untouchable people that control the media and the information We the People will believe. Hence, we must give all our journalists, writers, academics, and artists freedom and protection above our power hungry politicians.

What we all know is that the increasing number of civilian casualties, the never-ending circle of violence resulting from a foreign occupation in Iraq and Palestine, and now the rise of ISIL are all negative consequences resulting from the illegality of the invasion of Iraq. We cannot argue against the terrorists that now have multiplied as they defend their lands from the foreign invasion of our armies.

We need only learn from the historical facts over the death of Count Bernadotte of Sweden to understand the roots of terrorism, and pray to God that justice may one day prevail, and those responsible for his murder face the justice they deserve.

Perhaps we could learn from the criminal misappropriation of funds by a handful of banking dynasties that resulted in the sublime mortgage crisis. We need to change our consciousness before the environment threatens all life on Earth.

With these and many more witnesses, evidence both scientific and economic, with the basic human understanding between what is right from wrong, and as an eyewitness to a genocide, I could no longer remain silent.

There is so much to lose if we do not summon the administration of George W. Bush, Tony Blair, John Howard, and Jose Maria Aznar with their advisors and their partners to answer for their crimes against humanity and the global environment. We must not remain apathetic.

When I failed to get a response from the international courts in The Hague, or the United Nations Security Council, or a reply from the John Howard administration, my mediocrity was evident. The common phrases I heard repeatedly were in tune with the common understanding that:

"There is nothing we can do about it."

"We are powerless."

"Why bother?"

"You're nobody and nobody wants to know from a nobody!"

"You've been brainwashed."

"It's safer to keep quiet and obey."

"There are many innocent people in our jails."

"They will kill you."

"You will be framed and discredited…"

With these and other threats and odds stacked against me, I can only stand by the facts of the matter and wait for truth and justice to prevail.

The facts are clear: when Saddam Hussein was captured he told his captors, "I am the president of Iraq, and I want to negotiate." Later, when the judge asked Saddam who he was, Saddam replied, "I am the president of Iraq." He repeatedly asked for justice, asked for the world media to tell his story, to be given a fair trial in The Hague. However, the Western, American-appointed judge told his clerk, "Write down he was the former president of Iraq." Thus, the presiding judge breached his responsibility as a judge in any court of law as he performed his duties with clear prejudice.

Dr Huda Salih Mahdi Ammash, the American-educated Iraqi scientist wrongfully labelled Dr Anthrax, was jailed, silenced, and infected with cancer. Her research into the illnesses that were caused from the depleted uranium shells used by Americans in the 1991 war made her a target of the Americans, to censor her from disclosing her findings. Her published works on the consequences to a nation under economic sanctions have never been published in the Western world. She surrendered herself on 9th May 2003, and was released in December 2005 as there was no evidence or charges that could be filed against her. But the damage had been done, yet that crime went unpunished. As the deputy of the Ba'ath party, she would have become the first woman to govern a Muslim nation.

We saw how the Iraqi elections were manipulated to exclude the Ba'ath party, denying Iraq's democracy. We saw that when the votes in Palestine showed overwhelming support for the Hezbollah, some of our Western governments failed to accept the democratic will of the Lebanese or the Palestinians.

The world economy is on the brink of a global depression, yet the media tells us to keep spending our money on cheap plastic products, costly fuel-consuming cars, high end accessories, meaningless products like alcohol and cigarettes, and to keep paying our taxes to pay for the bombs and our overpaid and often corrupt politicians and law-makers.

When the new interim Iraqi government led by Iyad Allawi imposed martial law, it justified all death penalties imposed by Saddam Hussein against criminals or those who attempted to assassinate him. Whether we like to know the facts and truth or not, be it right or wrong, we as outsiders have no right to impose our beliefs and force our governance, as that contravenes international law and is a danger to every nation on Earth, as every nation has a right to self-governance.

As environmental catastrophes continue to kill, maim, and destroy lives and property, and as food supplies diminish against the increasing trends of population growth, we are told to build weapons and armies as if our fellow poorer people or a handful of terrorists are the greatest threats to our lives.

The truth is, the future of life on Earth is in our hands. Our generation is on the brink of tipping the environmental scales to the point of no return, to the level where we will all be terrorised by the absurd increases in the cost of food, healthcare, education, and life, which will make our world the third world in this third millennium.

While an elite handful of dynastic families determine our destinies from the safety of palaces, white houses, and fortified sanctuaries, we all stand to lose our disappearing forests, our jobs, our homes, our families, our freedoms—unless we take positive, peaceful action against the modern-day criminals like dictators, unjust law-makers, and the ignorance we are told to accept.

War amongst ourselves is no longer an option. Our war is against global warming. We need to invest in building our environment, not destroying it. We need to educate our children not to be selfish, materialistic, and violent with hatred. We need to learn, to understand, and to accept that we are all individuals on the same globe. We share the planet and we need to know how to take and how to give. God does not only bless America, and the Zionists are not 'God's only children'—we are all God's children and we are all responsible for making this world a better place.

We know a third world war could mean the end. Let us make it a peaceful overthrow of those who opt for violence or abuse power for personal gain. Let us remind our warriors and our police that their obligation is to protect us.

The looming third world war in this third millennium has the potential to be unlike any other war in our history. It is a war against our environment, against disease, hunger, and ignorance … it is the most significant war in the history of the world as it affects all life in perpetuity. The third world warriors are the new breed of warriors that every government and dictator should fear. We are all third world warriors if we are educated and truly free from the chains of slavery.

We, the free, the educated and wise men, women, and children who understand the importance of world peace as a way to combat the disastrous events of the future, *are* the future. It is up to us not to be afraid of imprisonment from the English law regime, not afraid to stand in the frontlines as Human Shields. It is up to us to be willing to learn, chant, bang drums of war, and demonstrate peacefully against armed paid thugs wearing bulletproof vests and hiding in armoured personnel carriers like cowards.

Mahatma Ghandi proved that to stand up and march, to rally, and to protest loudly yet peacefully, is the bravest action anyone could take against an army or police force or military paid not to think but to act on orders given to them from some madman that has inherited power.

The Human Shields; Voices in the Wilderness; Greenpeace; Doctors without Borders; Amnesty International; Friends of the earth, The International Solidarity Movement; Truth Peace and Justice; Dr Bernardo's; UNICEF; Save the Children Foundation; and the many more non-government organisations (NGOs) and anti-war groups; the environmentalists; and the anti-government groups that blow whistles and make noises if their government is not acting in the interest of the people: these are the true third world warriors of this third millennium.

To see our mothers and grandmothers, our sisters or brothers, friends or lovers becoming boisterous and loud when they learn of a wrongdoing by our governments, is not a shameful thing. We should be proud of them.

Women in particular have a sense of distinguishing right from wrong, and women are the highest and most important members in our families. It is the very reason that Muslim women and Orthodox Jewish women and Catholic Sisters cover their hair and dress without sex appeal. The hijab, the burka, the nun's habit, or the Jewish scarf are all a woman has as a weapon against a man's brutal sexual instincts. Why the mostly male French parliament made wearing hijabs in schools illegal was almost perverse ignorance. Whatever happened to women's freedom in France?

When the 2004 Boxing Day tsunami struck, killing over 250,000 and displacing millions, we all saw the graphic picture of a woman running into the giant waves to rescue her children, and it seemed to personify the maternal instinct inherent in women to protect with their lives those they love. My sister Nenni didn't need to be told by my father to protect her older sisters or me; she did so instinctively. Perhaps women are better placed to lead us into the third millennium.

I recall these third world international warriors, like Rachel Corrie who died protecting a stranger's home; Rema Albess who devotes her life to teaching others about the injustices taking place in Palestine; the Australians Waratah Gillespie and Donna Mulhearn; the English Muslim woman Uzma Bashir; Americans like Faith Fippinger, Judith Karpova, and Antoinette McCormick; Yukiko Muragishi from Japan; and that Spanish Basque, Beatrice. Yes, it is mostly women that are braver and tougher than any street-fighter, any American marine, and any man I have ever known.

These women are the real heroes of the third world war, fighting war with peace against the cowardly instincts of men like George W. Bush; Tony Blair; Jose Maria Aznar; Richard Perle; Dick Cheney; Donald Rumsfelt; and John Howard—men that now hide in absurdly comfortable and protected residencies, enjoying the benefits of their crimes.

When the Australian government announced the introduction of sedition laws[15], I realised my fight for what is right was yet to come. The freedom of speech, the right to education and knowledge, and access to truth is absolutely vital in all nations for all individuals. It is our only way to ensure that our governments are not corrupt, or worse, acting with criminal intent. If we, the people, need to comply with laws and learn to debate, to argue, and to resolve conflict with dialogue not with meaningless violence or war, then so must our governments.

On the 22nd of April 2003 the American warplanes manufacturing company recorded a 105% profit in the three months that the coalition forces destroyed Iraq. In money terms, hundreds of millions of tax dollars were misappropriated. This extortion was theft on a grand scale.

The theft of our taxes did not make front-page news. The powerful news and media allies knew how to censor or manipulate the news to arouse minimum attention and oppress public objection; after all, the Western masses were now drugged with nicotine, drunk with cheap alcohol, blinded with television propaganda, and ignorant of the crimes against humanity being committed with their taxes. Yet less than a handful of work-related deaths during attempts to insulate homes in Australia and make them more energy efficient caused a national inquiry, paying legal workers' exuberant fees with our tax dollars. No inquiry was ever launched for the many dead soldiers, civilians, and Iraqis from what was clearly a crime by the coalition of the willing.

In 1945 a gentleman of peace was assassinated by Jewish Zionist terrorists for finding a solution to the warring factions in Israel and Palestine; a realistic solution that would make Jerusalem the epicentre of international bodies like the United Nations, International Red Cross, UNICEF, religious institutions, scientific research, global media offices, international courts, etc. However, since then, scores of both Israelis and Palestinians have been killed or

---

15 **Australian sedition law** is the area of the criminal law of Australia relating to the crime of sedition. Effectively defunct for nearly half a century, these laws returned to public notice in 2005 when changes were included in an Anti-terrorism Bill announced by Prime Minister Howard prior to a "counter-terrorism summit" of the Council of Australian Governments on 27 September. The Bill was introduced on 3 November and passed into law on 6 December 2005

maimed. Schools, bridges, hospitals, the environment, and countless homes have been destroyed. The financial and environmental costs are unforgiving. Perhaps the time is near when we all must face the truth.

Peace starts with disarmament. Saddam Hussein disarmed the most-invaded nation on Earth, and no WMDs have ever been found. Perhaps now, it is the Israelis or the Americans, Chinese, Russians, or British who need to disarm. Perhaps making Jerusalem the capital city of our world is a positive step into the future.

It is aggravating to know that the third world is suffering with a death-rate of three million (3,000,000) children each year, along with all the evidence, witnesses, historical facts and ongoing injustices of the Iraq war. With my promise to the three Ethiopian children, the three-year-old girl Zainab, and Fatima, I vowed to stand up and fight the ignorance of racism, the arrogance of the spoiled rotten wealthy dynasties, and the sheer stupidity of the masses with the only weapon I had: knowledge.

If Sheik Ali in Suez was right with his idiom that the pen is mightier than the sword, then all I can now do is write my story as an eyewitness to a crime. A crime I can only compare to the Jewish Holocaust. Only this time, it is our governments and law-makers that have committed the crime on behalf of corporate giants.

On the first of April 2005, my mate Greg O'Shea was found dead in a cheap roadside hotel. On the night of his death, he had gone to see his son, but after a bitter divorce his witch of a wife played manipulating scenarios to prevent him from seeing his son. To my horror, I knew she would be emotionally raping Greg and his confessions and testimonies before his death confirmed it. The witch, who knew how to emotionally rape a man, had pushed him to the extreme of suicide.

The fact that suicide worldwide kills more men, women, and teenagers every year than the Vietnam, Korean, Iraq, Afghanistan, Syrian, Libyan and Israeli-Palestinian wars combined,[16] and tenfold more than terrorists,

---

16 The World Health Organisation (WHO) estimates that each year approximately one million people die from suicide, which represents a global mortality rate of 16 people per 100,000 or one death every 40 seconds. It is predicted that by 2020 the rate of death will increase to one every 20 seconds.

should concern each and every one of us. Yet our media tells us to declare war against a handful of terrorists and we stupidly believe and accept this misinformation.

With these thoughts in my mind I awoke on my small recycled sailboat ready to sail to Cuba and the Caribbean in the early morning with the sun yet to rise, aware and conscious of the fact that some people relied on criticising what they didn't know rather than embracing the truths supported by facts.

However, the dream remained fresh in my memory and in the dark silence of my solitude I sat up. The cabin was dark, like a black well of oil where wealth never ceased. I clicked the switch to my ecologically friendly low energy LED lights and sat up in my salvaged and now restored plastic boat as she gently rocked with the cleansing wind. My writing pad was at hand, and there was so much knowledge I had to share. I made a vow to tell the truth, the whole truth, and nothing but the truth, so help me God. I had witnessed a horrendous and cold-blooded crime: genocide, and the creation of another third world nation. I could no longer sit in silence and live with my guilt. I reached for my weapons as a new age peace warrior. With a pen as my sword and the writing pad as my shield, I peacefully began to write:

> *"I hate the truth!" my mate Greg screamed across the roof of a sports car. "You know why?" he asked, screaming, before answering his own revelation. "Because it's true ... the truth hurts!"*

Third World Warriors

Bibliography

The Origins of the Arab-Israeli Wars
by Ritchie Ovendale, London and New York: Longman, 1992. Second edition.

The price of loyalty: George W. Bush, the White House and the Education of Paul O'Neill
by Ron Siskind, Simon & Schuster 2004

Invasion of Iraq
by Waratah Rose Gillespie,
Mekamui publications 2004

Other Lands Have Dreams
by Kathy Kelly,
CounterPunch press 2005

The Great War of Civilisation: The Conquest of the Middle East
by Robert Fisk, Pub. Fourth Estate 2005

Squandered Victory
by Larry Diamond,
Macmillan 2005

The Islamic Paradox
by Rev. Marks Gerecht,
aei press November 2004

Dangerous Allies
By Malcom Fraser

Further Resources

The Sierra Times Feb 9, 2003 "The Real Reasons for the Upcoming War with Iraq" by William Clark
FEASTA Jan 2003, Oil, Currency and the War with Iraq" by Coilin Nunan
The Invisible War by W. H. Bohart and Richard Sutton
Brother Nathanael Kapner;
PO Box 1242; Frisco CO 80443

The Institute for Economics and Peace

www.realjewnews.com
www.wikileaks.org
www.worldtribunal.org
www.counterpunch.org
www.antiwar.com
www.voicesinthewilderness.org
www.iraqbodycount.net
www.greenpeace.com
www.jordantimes.com
www.spr.org
www.clw.org
www.soaw.org
www.commondreams.org
www.peacefulaction.org
www.humanrights.com
www.icj.org
www.pcbs.org
www.terrorism.com
www.zmag.org
www.casi.org.uk
www.thecostofwar.com

Other Third World Warrior Organisations Affiliated with the United Nations:

- Abolition 2000
- AFARM
- American Humanist Association
- Association for Progressive Communications
- Association "FOR SUSTAINABLE HUMAN DEVELOPMENT"
- Baha'i International Community
- Centre for International Cooperation
- Centre of Concern
- Earth Charter
- Education With Enterprise Trust
- Education International
- Experiment in International Living
- The Franklin and Eleanor Roosevelt Institute
- GCS (Global Cooperation Society) International
- Global Education Associates
- Global Policy Forum
- Good Neighbours International
- The Hague International Model United Nations
- Information Habitat: Where Information Lives
- INFG—International Network for Girls
- Institute for Development Research (IDR)
- Institute of World Affairs
- International Agency for Economic Development
- IACERHRG
  (The International Association "CAUCASUS: Ethnic Relations, Human Rights, Geopolitics")
- International Campaign To Ban Landmines
- International Union for Land Value Taxation
- IPPNW Hamburg
- The League of Women Voters
- Legacy International
- The Lifebridge Foundation

- National Council on Family Relations
- NAN (No to Alcoholism & Drug Addiction)
- Napredna omladinska alternativa Republike Srpske (Progressive Youth Organisation, Republic of Srpska)
- The National Group of Georgia of the International Society for Human Rights (ISHR-IGFM)
- NGO Committee on Disarmament
- Nuclear Age Peace Foundation
- Pathways To Peace
- Quaker United Nations Office
- Society for Conservation and Protection of Environment (SCOPE)
- The Society for the Psychological Study of Social Issues (SPSSI)
- Soroptimist International of the Americas
- State of the World Forum for Emerging Leaders
- Surgical Aid to Children of the World
- Together Foundation for Global Unity
- TRANS Youth Association
- UNA-USA—United Nations Association-United States of America
- United Nations Association of Puerto Rico (UNA-USA Division)
- Wainwright House
- We the Peoples (A Peace Messenger Initiative)
- WGG—The NGO Working Group on Girls—UNICEF
- The Wittenberg Centre for Alternative Resources
- Women's Action for New Directions (WAND)
- Women's Federation for World Peace
- World Council of Independent Christian Churches
- World Federation of United Nations Associations
- WIT—World Information Transfer
- The World Peace Prayer Society
- WSO—World Safety Organisation
- World Young Women's Christian Association
- The Wyndom Foundation
- Yachay Wasi
- The Secretariat of Youth for Habitat International Network

Documentary Films:

Fahrenheit 9/11, Michael Moore
Control Room, Jehane Noujaim
The Corporation, Mark Achbar
The President V's David Hicks, Curtis Levi
The Power of Nightmares, Cutting Edge SBS television
Iraq's Missing Millions, Foreign Correspondence ABC television
Weapons of Mass Deception, Danny Schechter
Truth Lies and Intelligence, Carmel Travers
The World According to Bush, William Karel
Zeitgeist, Peter Joseph

We are all witnesses of the history that the future generations will learn from.

We trust you to do the right thing and talk amongst friends and family and help get the message across that education is our basic right. It should be the responsibility of our governments, sultans, Kings or queens to ensure we all receive FREE education.

Supplementing military spending with free global education would guarantee we all understand the world can be our heaven or our terrorists' hell.

Welcome to the world, of the third world warriors ...

www.ingramcontent.com/pod-product-compliance
Lightning Source LLC
Chambersburg PA
CBHW070632160426
43194CB00009B/1439